ALVEDISTON

A HISTORY

IN MEMORY OF THREE ALVEDISTON
RESIDENTS WHO WELCOMED ME IN 1980
AND PROVED TO BE GOOD FRIENDS:

ANTHONY BULLEN,
JUDITH FERGUSSON
AND
TRISTRAM SYKES

ALVEDISTON

a history

Biddy Trahair

Biddy Trahair

First published in the United Kingdom in 2011
by The Hobnob Press, PO Box 1838, East Knoyle, Salisbury, SP3 6FA
www.hobnobpress.co.uk

British Library Cataloguing in Publication Data
A catalogue record for this book is available from the British Library

ISBN 978-1-906978-06-8
Typeset in Minion Pro 12/16pt. Typesetting and origination by John Chandler
Printed by Lightning Source

The cover incorporates a painting, 'View of Alvediston', owned by Rosalyn Barnes

Contents

Foreword

I WAS VERY pleased I could help Biddy with the history of Alvediston. As I was born here in 1926, I knew all the people in the village, and names of fields and lanes, and who worked for whom. I wish her all success as she has worked so hard on this.

Roy Marks

Biddy Trahair was born and brought up on the Isle of Wight, where her father's family had lived for many generations. Her love of social, local and family history began in childhood, and she was introduced to the area west of Salisbury on foot and ancient bicycle in the 1970s when she was working as an occupational therapist in Salisbury. Since 1980 she has lived in Alvediston, where she and her husband Richard, enjoy being part of the local church and community. They have two daughters.

Introduction

IN 2000 THERE were celebrations throughout the valley to mark the millennium. As I was interested in the history of Alvediston, I volunteered to put on an exhibition in St. Mary's church, and I began to research more seriously, using both written and verbal sources. The most exciting outcome of the exhibition was the reunion of many former inhabitants, some of whom had not seen each other since their schooldays. I also met more people who were researching their family histories and could provide both memories and photographs. The idea of a book to compile all this grew, but so did the volume of material, much of it conflicting or leading onto new paths of enquiry. As the years passed, my original sheets of information changed almost out of recognition, and my concern to ensure that what was finally published was fair to past and present inhabitants sometimes made completing the task seem impossible, so I apologise to all those who have been waiting patiently, and thank the many people who have contributed. I hope that this book will provide enough historical background to put the stories of Alvediston into context without getting bogged down in detail. The bibliography may help those who wish to pursue the various strands further, and doubtless there will be much to discuss and refute, but I hope nothing to cause offence.

Features and People of Alvediston

~ Origins of the name and parish of Alvediston ~ Research from maps ~ Roads, Tracks and Development ~ The Ebble ~ Coombes ~ Location and orientation of houses ~ Enterprise ~ Some of the inhabitants during the past 150 years ~

WHEN EDWARD HUTTON, in his *Highways and Byways of Wilts.* described Alvediston as 'charming in itself, a little lonely place half lost and wholly unafraid in the midst of the downs' one suspects that his impetus was more poetic than factual. However, there may be more to the description than first meets the eye. The origins of the village are elusive and early maps sometimes 'lose' the village altogether. Even today there are times when it feels lost to the view of those who should service it. The unusually heavy snowfalls in February 2009 and the freezing temperatures in 2010 highlighted its isolation, which is exacerbated by steep hills on each road or track accessing the village: to the north, south, east and west, while there are those who remember the winter of 1977, when the whole village was cut off by snow, and the pub served soup and sandwiches to beleaguered residents. Neighbouring villages still look on Alvediston with some puzzlement, as the sobriquet 'Elluvadistance, (used by those living only a mile or two away,) testifies. However, there is no doubt of its sense of identity, nor of the force of character of some of its more notable residents throughout its history.

~ *Origins of the name and parish of Alvediston* ~

ROM THE BEGINNING there is a wealth of controversy over the origins of the name Alvediston, and when and how it became established as a parish. Throughout this book, reference will be made to 'The Hundred of Chalke' written by Charles Bowles in 1830. He was well-known locally as the recorder of Shaftesbury, one of whose duties was to help solve boundary disputes, so an interest in local history was invaluable, but his statements are sometimes challenged and his digressions intemperate, which makes his record all the more entertaining. The volume of the *Victoria County History* of Wiltshire covering this area, (*V.C.H.*), was compiled in 1987, drawing on a wealth of sources, both original records and personal accounts, scrupulously annotated, often at odds with Bowles, but also open to challenge. Neighbouring Ebbesbourne Wake has had two local historians in less than a hundred years: William E.V.Young, M.B.E. (1890 – 1971), also known locally as an archaeologist, archivist and museum curator, whose manuscripts on his family and village sometimes refer to Alvediston, and Dr. Peter Meers, (1929 – 2008), who, after an eminent career in medicine and medical research, rekindled his lifelong interest in history in retirement, writing two editions of 'Ebbesbourne Wake Through the Ages' and some notes on a further revision, which have some interesting ideas about the origin of Alvediston.

Bowles' unique but now discredited view was that references in the Domesday Book to two hides of land within the area known as 'Chelche', held by a woman called Aileva, mean that: 'There can therefore, in my estimation, be no doubt but that the possessions of this Aileva, or Ailefe, not only constituted, but imparted the name of Aileva's Town, or Alvediston, to this place.' Would that it were that simple!

'Chelche' was another name for Chalke, the estate which King Edwy donated to Wilton Abbey in 955. Wilton's early history is also controversial. Its claims to be the 'ancient capital of Wessex' and even of England are disputed, but there was a royal palace there and a series of abbeys, monasteries and nunneries, probably beginning in the eighth century. In 890, Alfred the Great founded a religious house for an abbess and twelve nuns, drawn from the aristocracy, on the site of his former palace. Wilton Abbey maintained close links with royalty and aristocracy: kings endowed it with money and land while their daughters and sisters became nuns there without feeling too hampered by vows of chastity or poverty. The *V.C.H.* is rather airy about the extent of the Chalke estate. In the chapter on Broad Chalke we are told that it 'included most of what became Broad Chalke and Bower Chalke (sic) parishes and other land further west in the Ebble valley'; in that for Alvediston: 'Wilton abbey apparently held the whole of Alvediston in 1066 and all except the estate called Trow in 1086.'

In 1066, the Chalke estate covered an area in the region of a thousand acres: the imprecision arises because areas were measured in 'hides', which could vary between forty and a hundred and sixty acres, depending on the productivity of the land. Domesday Book records that before 1066, the estate paid tax for seventy-seven hides and had land for sixty-six ploughs, each requiring eight oxen. Inhabitants were classed under the feudal system vigorously introduced by King William I. All land was held under the king, so technically he owned the whole country. Tenants-in-chief, who might be individual 'barons' or church institutions such as Wilton Abbey, were directly responsible to the king for the land they held, and gave military and judicial service in return, but these duties were shared among the next layers down. Sub-tenants held land on a similar basis; beneath them came 'sokemen', smallholders who were responsible to both tenants and sub-tenants, villeins who farmed smaller acreages in return for work on their lord's land and 'bordars', whose acreages were tiny. Freemen and slaves had no land, few rights and worked for others. Another group, the 'burgesses' lived and worked in towns, but some of them held country estates, (cultivated by bordars, freemen and slaves), directly from the king. Finally, knights provided military service for the king via the tenants-in-chief. They, too, owned land but, wary of insurrection among powerful barons, the king ensured that their land was held as separate estates, dispersed around the country. Thus, when considering one of the estates in Alvediston, the layers of ownership can seem incredibly complicated, but clearly, at the time, they provided a strict hierarchy which brought order to a disparate land.

Alvediston does not appear in the Domesday Book, but Trow does. This manor on the western boundary was about one tenth of the whole Chalke estate, seven and a half hides, of which Aeleva held two. However, when William I redistributed his conquest he gave Richard Poynant (sometimes spelled Poingiant), presumably a Norman, the whole of Trow. What happened to Aeleva? It is tempting to mythologise her as a feisty Anglo-Saxon defending her land against Norman invaders and, when vanquished, riding disgruntled into the mists of time, unaware that her name was immortalised in a brave little township for over nine hundred years, while the wretched Richard Poynant is lost in obscurity. Even if Bowles' name theory is wrong, Aeleva deserves a place in the history of Alvediston.

What about the rest of the land between Trow and Ebbesbourne Wake? In 2004, Peter Meers meticulously researched the Domesday Book for the third revision of his 'Ebbesbourne Wake Through the Ages' and calculated that this area is equivalent to the second of two manors mentioned in the entry for Ebbesbourne Wake. Alfward and

Vitalis held these manors in 1066, and they were passed to Robert Fitzgerald. Peter Meers believed that Alvediston and Trow were combined into a new entity 'somewhat after 1165 when the name Alvediston first appeared' (as Alfweiteston). Did the name originate with Alfward? A complication arises because, while Ebbesbourne seems to have been part of the Chalke estate granted to Wilton Abbey in 955, it had been given away by 1066. Meanwhile, the *V.C.H.* quotes an obscure document of 1197 referring to 'Alfetheston'. With the vagaries of spellings it is possible to attribute the name to a variety of characters, but concrete proof is lacking.

~ *Research from maps* ~

TROW AND FIFIELD Bavant, (east of Ebbesbourne), have an interesting historical connection. Peter Meers drew maps from his research highlighting this. Until 1885, Fifield included a long 'tail' going southwest from the river Ebble to the Dorset boundary. This squeezed Ebbesbourne to the east, while Trow squeezed to the west. The Scudamore family held lands at both Fifield and Trow, so the former was known as Fifield Scudamore. When Peter Scudamore died in 1293, his widowed daughter, Alice Bavant, inherited his land, hence Fifield Bavant.

Maps from the sixteenth century are held in Salisbury Library: Saxton produced his in 1576, John Speed in 1611, Aldwell and Richard Hardinge in 1618. When the new Lord Salisbury was flexing his muscles over the boundaries of Cranborne Chase, Aldwell was commissioned by Lord Salisbury and Hardinge by the defendants. In 1677 Matthew Hardinge produced a simpler version of the latter. Andrews and Dury's was published in 1773 and the first Ordnance Survey map followed in 1811. The *V.C.H.* prints a map from 1842. The discrepancies between these are fascinating.

Details of Wiltshire maps by Christopher Saxton, 1576 (above), John Speed, 1610-11 (below) and Johan Blaeu, 1648 (opposite).

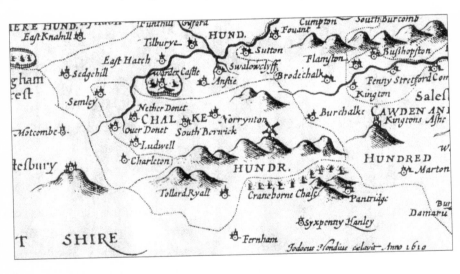

Saxton shows 'Norrynton', 'Alveston' and 'Fyfebuck' but no Ebbesbourne Wake. Speed has nothing between 'Norrynton' and 'Burchalke', (Bowerchalke). Aldwell has drawn his map with north pointing north-east with consequent alarming topography, and Norrington is at a substantial distance from 'Alverston'. Mathew

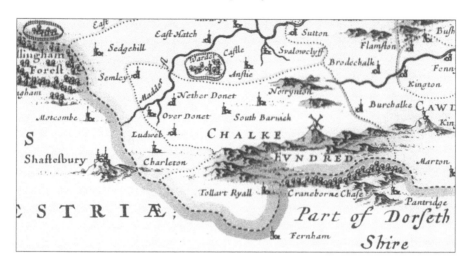

Hardinge has Norrington and 'Aston' close together, but the church is at Norrington. Andrews and Dury make a clear distinction between 'Norrington Farm or Norrynton' and 'Alvedestone or Aston' which is shown as a spreading village with its church to the north of the Ebble. To the east, the road meets the river Ebble, with buildings on either side of the road at 'Castle'. The hill which separates Ebbesbourne's West End from Alvediston is still called Castle Hill and Mike Longstaffe, a resident, has tried to find out what this castle was: possibly a sort of palisaded enclosure for drovers to keep their animals in overnight, safe in the valley before returning to the heights of the Ox Drove next morning. There is a track down from the Ox Drove nearby. The *V.C.H.* suggests that West End itself was called 'Castle' in the late eighteenth century, perhaps from the evidence of this map. Strangely, the two older, semidetached cottages on the hill come within the Alvediston parish boundary, while their neighbours are in Ebbesbourne, a so-far unexplained anomaly. There was once another cottage in the clearing on the bank opposite. Unnamed 'Barns' are marked at Trow and Elcombe, which are named for the first time on the early O.S.map, where Trow appears as 'Trough' and Norrington as 'Northumpton or Norington'.

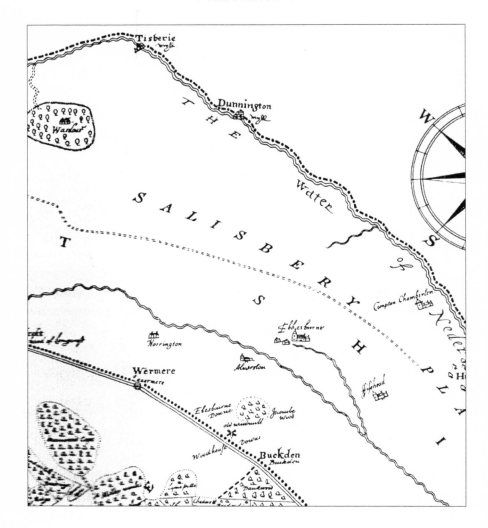

~ *Roads, Tracks and Development* ~

ARLY MAPS SHOW no road through the valley, but there were two ancient downland routes: the Ox Drove to the south and what became part of the London to Exeter coach road to the north. This is known variously as the Drove Road, the Old Coach Road, the Salisbury Way or the Herepath. The last name,

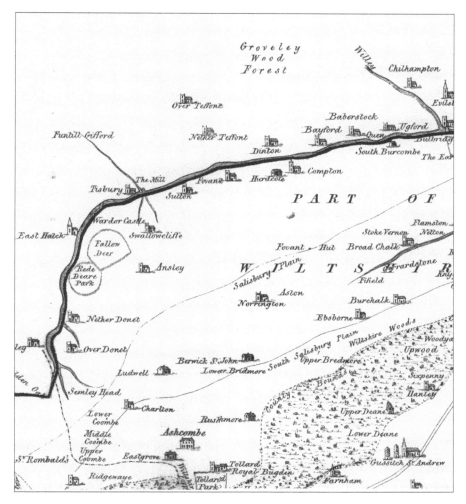

Details of maps of Cranborne Chase by Thomas Aldwell, 1618 (opposite), and Mathew Hardinge, 1677 (above).

which appears on the 1842 map, will be used for clarity, since both join Salisbury and Shaftesbury. 'Herepath' is the Saxon for a main road, deriving from 'here', which can refer to an army or formation of soldiers. When used by horse-drawn coaches it was an exposed and rough ride, so the driver, passengers and horses must have been relieved when they had scrambled down the steep slope of White

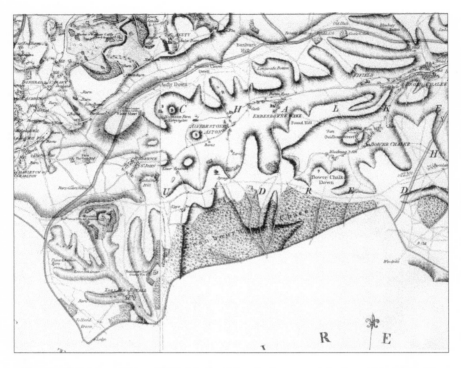

Details of the 1773 map of Wiltshire by John Andrews and Andrew Dury (above), and 1st edition Ordnance Survey map at 1-inch scale, 1811 (opposite).

Sheet Hill and were able to rest at the staging post called the Glove Inn. The Herepath was turnpiked in 1762, but in 1788 a new coach road was created in the valley to the north. It was a toll road, now the A30, which still links London with the West Country. The Glove Inn survived this change, but became obsolete about a hundred years later, when railways finally put paid to the stage coach, and in its new incarnation is known as Arundell Farm.

By 1773, a more complex web of tracks is clear. On the Andrews and Dury map the Ebble valley looks like bladderwrack seaweed with fronds creeping up the coombes, and hills resembling the little round bladders which children love to pop. The valley road, still in use, is like a vein running close to the Ebble. From the west, a track leads

to Norrington and on up to the Herepath, at Swallow Cleeve Down; another leads south to the Ox Drove at Trow Down. The barns at Trow are joined to Norrington by a track. Continuing eastwards, the cross road at the centre of the village is reached. One way leads south past the barns at Elcombe to the Ox Drove while another goes north down the street, turns right and meets what is now no more than a drive and footpath, but was then a lane from the valley road straight down to the river, past the church and north-west, petering out into a track up to the Herepath at Ansty Down. Cottages are marked up Elcombe Lane, including one in what is now a clearing on the west side, and they fill the west side of the street; more are on both sides of the valley road opposite Shortsmead, where the ruined forge and chapel now stand. Both Samways and the Manor are marked but not named.

By 1811, there appears to be development along all the lanes around the centre of the village, and to the east the now-ruined cottage in the field at West End is marked. Cottages continued up the street and into the lower end of Elcombe Lane. A new track past Samways went up the hill to join one leading to the Herepath.

In 1842, Trow and Elcombe are marked as Farms, and Church Farm is another entity to the north. The *V.C.H.* quotes an 1842 tithe award, listing Norrington,(which would include Trow,) Samways, Church and Elcombe farms each comprising about four hundred acres. A building at Twenty Acres appears for the first time, between the church and Norrington, while Samways and the Manor House are named. The track from Samways to the Herepath crosses that from the church like a pair of tongs, but the current road over the hill and zig-zagging down had not been built. Buildings at the manor farmstead and what was to become the 'Crown' inn are shown up a short track to the south of the cross roads. Thus the layout of the village is much more recognisable, and most of these ways can be followed on foot and bridle paths today. However, one which has fallen into disuse is the way north of the river. From Berwick, the track to Norrington can be picked up, going on to join the Samways track. From there, however, it crossed fields to pass north of the church and so along a ridge and down to the Ebble at West End. Until the 1950s, Miss Parham of Norrington ensured that this was kept open by driving through with a carriage and horse. The footpath now passes through the ruined medieval village in the field south-west of Norrington, passing in front of the house, across a meadow to Twenty Acres, where it becomes a bridleway which runs through the withy beds and on in front of the church to West End.

It seems strange today that the road over the Herepath and down to Ansty was built only just over a hundred years ago, in 1896. Until then Alvediston was picturesquely described in Kelly's Directories thus:

> Alvediston is difficult to access by carriages, as it lies for the most part in a deep bottom or hollow, on the left of the turnpike-road leading from Salisbury to Shaftesbury, from which the usual mode of approach by pedestrians is the ascent by means of foot holes, in the almost perpendicular northern side of White Sheet hill; the great exertion consequent upon which is compensated by the beautiful commanding view of the surrounding country obtained, before making a nearly sudden descent on the opposite side of the hill into Alvediston below.

The views from both directions at the top are still staggeringly beautiful, changing by the season, the day and even the hour, and although most people do not enjoy the sense of achievement of having heaved themselves up on foot, the road is still a challenge, and often impassable in icy weather, especially as the northern slope may not defrost all day.

The track, now a bridlepath, which goes north from Norrington and crosses the Herepath eases its way more gently north-west down the hill, to join the A30 to the west of Ansty Coombe. In his book on Cranborne Chase, Desmond Hawkins points out that from Berwick, from which the valley road shortly joins the A30, only Alvediston and Fifield now have direct access to the other side of the Herepath, until roads go over to Wilton at Bishopstone church and Stratford Tony, by which time the traveller is almost on the A354 Salisbury to Blandford road. This may explain why Alvediston residents are more likely to have discovered the delights of Tisbury than inhabitants of other villages in the valley, especially as, from the closure of the shop and post office in Ebbesbourne Wake until the opening of the Ansty Farm shop just three and a half miles away, Alvediston found itself stranded in the middle of a circle, with shops five or more miles away at: Broad Chalke, Bowerchalke, (now closed), Fovant, Tisbury, Ludwell and Sixpenny Handley.

There may have been tracks criss-crossing the village but were they passable or safe on a wet, foggy night? In her book on Berwick's church, Hazel Giffard records an intriguing item in the will of John Gane, rector from 1674 to1738. In 1735 he left ' 'all that messuage, tenement and garden commonly called Wm. Lodge's house' to the parish clerk for a rent of 2s. [£10 in 1999] a year in return for a duty to toll the Great Bell of the church every evening for fifteen minutes at 8 o'clock in the winter months so that travellers, lost in the mist of the hills, could find their way down into the village...... Apart from the years of the war the curfew continued until the 1950s, when the resources of the fund were no longer adequate.' This anecdote from another village is relevant both because the bell would have alerted travellers approaching Alvediston from the west that they were not far from the drovers' inn above it, and because it highlights the hazards on the Ox Drove. Piles of chalk were left at intervals to mark the way, while in 1700, the Earl of Pembroke had milestones erected at one-mile intervals along the Herepath from White Sheet Hill to the Wilton hare warren, (near the race course.). A replacement for one of these, dated 1796, can still be found at the top of White Sheet Hill, marking ninety-seven miles to Hyde Park, London, and fourteen to Salisbury. Bowles illustrates the need for a high coach road, even at the expense of the horses straining to haul carriages up on to it, in his introduction to the chapter on Berwick:

'The roads in the vale are impassable for any other four-wheel carriages than those used for husbandry purposes, and are suitable only for a *sure footed* horse.' No wonder that the diarist of Ferne and later, Berwick St. John Rectory, Charlotte Grove, who lived at the same time, was such a prodigious walker, although she must have had a robust attitude to mud. Nevertheless, Bowles paradoxically writes of the village of Alvediston: 'Its general character is neatness and cleanliness combined', not a sentiment which the reforming vicar of the eighteen-nineties would share. He wrote: 'The state of the by-roads and the road communication with the centres of industrial life are matters which unless seen to will lead to the utter blotting out of villages like this one.' The Rev. Charles Ousby Trew cared deeply about the people of Alvediston and he opened their eyes to possibilities of education and self-help which were sorely needed but, for all his blusterous energy and the opening of the road to the A30 during his six-year incumbency, 'communication with centres of industrial life' has remained rather a low priority. The village has certainly not been utterly blotted out, but employment and entertainment opportunities for those relying on public transport are so limited that the balance of society has moved out of all recognition. In the 1940s Mildred Read, née Topp, who was born in 1935 and lived on the Knapp until her marriage in 1958, experienced transport problems far worse than today's:

> I went to Shaftesbury High School, and had to cycle each day to Berwick St. John to catch the bus, as we had no buses through Alvediston. When it snowed I used to walk to Berwick to catch the bus, all on my own, and thought nothing of it.

Now, the weight of traffic, frequently increased by the vagaries of sat. nav., brings anxieties about pot-holes imperilling cyclists, pedestrians and horse-riders, while much of the current discussion about communication centres around mobile 'phone reception and Broadband internet access.

~ *The Ebble* ~

ANOTHER CAUSE FOR diversion and dissension is the source and even the name of the river Ebble, Ebele, Chalkebourne, Chele, Chalke or Stowford. John Leland, (a sixteenth-century cleric who was also employed by Henry VIII to catalogue church treasures and documents prior to the dissolution of the monasteries and whose work, still in note form, provides fascinating details of the areas he covered,) and John Aubrey, (the seventeenth-century archaeologist and writer who hailed from Broad Chalke) wrote of the 'Chalkebourne'. 'Chele' was an early name for 'Chalke', as in the Chele or Chalke estate, and the name 'Stowford' is preserved in Stowford Hill, which is the steep hill running up from the river valley at a point between Ebbesbourne and Fifield. In 1997, Barbara Fergusson, a gifted naturalist, photographer, local historian, agriculturalist and general enquirer, published her authoritative book 'The Ebble River', now sadly out of print. The river as far as Broad Chalke is a winterbourne, drying out for months of the year, typically in the Alvediston area between August and December. However this varies and, after an exceptionally dry spring in 2006, when it sent shock waves around the valley by drying out in May, there were three summers of such miserable wetness that it only stayed dry for short periods. George Kellow, who has lived in Alvediston for over fifty years, quotes Sam Moxham, who maintained that he remembered a time when Norrington pond was always sufficiently full to provide trout for the permanently-running Ebble. This would have been within the last hundred years. During the past century, there have been many new demands on the local water supply.

As the Chalke Valley is full of springs, the scope for argument over the site of the source is immense, and as satisfying as the comparisons of one year's flow with another's. John Aubrey claimed that it rose at Knowle, Bowerchalke, because the springs there flow into the river at Broad Chalke all year, but the winterbourne which runs through Ebbesbourne and Fifield rises on the west side of Alvediston, or even further west. Barbara Fergusson suggested:

'There are old wives' tales, never to be totally neglected, that the river originally rose round about Ludwell, near Shaftesbury, and carved its way along the Ebble Valley through Berwick St. John and on to Trow. Relief maps show the possibility of this story. The river Nadder might well have stolen the head-water springs of the Ebble to run along its own valley further north. Springs still rise in Berwick St. John fields to collect in a stream which flows down the roadside along Water Street. This stream disappears under the ground to emerge later in Ebble Rise about a mile to the north-west. Were there once a constant stream overland from Ludwell, it would account for various enigmas recorded later in [her] text.' In 'The Donheads Past and Present' we read that six streams in those villages make up the Nadder, so it seems to have a thirsty source. However, Francis Dineley, previous owner of the Ferne Estate on the Berwick-Donhead border, vehemently asserts that 'NO ambivalence exists between the sources of the Nadder and the Ebble'!

Barbara Fergusson took Ebble Rise as the source. This field is immediately to the east of Bushy Garson, and there is no doubt of the liberality of the springs there for much of the year. The field has historical significance too, as part of the ancient manor of Trow, which was mentioned in the Domesday Book while Alvediston was absent. The water pools in the field, into a ditch and under the road, (although much of it overflows onto the road in heavy showers), and on to Norrington. Incidentally, Barbara Fergusson points out a phenomenon of the 1970s: the destruction of elms due to Dutch elm disease. There were many elms on either side of the road by Ebble Rise, which used to support rookeries. The displaced rooks had to find other tall trees, as did those in Elcombe Lane, where there was a flourishing rookery in Samways elms. Rookery shoots were an important time in the local calendar, as Frank Roberts remembers. Now the rooks have adopted ash trees and grow fat and noisy on food put out for hens in an Elcombe Lane garden.

Howard Phipps, who has published a book of his acclaimed wood engravings and coloured lino cuts entitled 'Ebble Valley', maintains that the 'initial springs rise in a field' and are 'supplemented by further streams which flow into numerous irregular basins, submerging the roots of willows and alders, to form Norrington ponds', a description which he brings to life in one of his illustrations.

However, there is another contender for the home of the Ebble's source: Berwick St.John. The V.C.H. chapter on Berwick begins: 'The ancient parish of Berwick St John . . . lay at the head of the Ebble valley', and maintains that the Ebble and Nadder watershed is White Sheet Hill, while that of the Ebble and Tarrant is the southern ridge, topped by the Ox Drove. This is Bowles' choice. In his chapter on that village he writes:

'A small rivulet, which I have ventured to call the Ebele, rises in this parish, and proceeds hence to Norrington.' This suggests that the choice of names was open to option as late as 1830. A hundred and eighty years later, Francis and Libby Dineley point out that, if the course of the Berwick stream is followed, it has a strong claim. Springs rise where the permeable chalk of Winklebury Hill meets the greensand of the valley, and the water flows down the south side of Water Street. It passes behind the cottages and forge opposite the Talbot Inn and goes under the road in front of the redundant chapel. It runs alongside Dog Lane to the end of the Priory garden, then takes a circuitous route around paddocks, either following hedge lines or dictating them until it reaches the former retting pond at the far end of a meadow by Woodlands. 'Retting' is a process in the production of linen, the soaking of flax to soften it. From this small pond the stream has been diverted into a straight channel across a meadow, bordered by three diminutive horse chestnuts, known as 'Waterloo chestnuts' because Libby Dineley grew them from conkers found on the field of the battle of Waterloo. Crossing a few more meadows and passing under a lane which leads to the Hall family's dairy at Berwick, it reaches Norrington land, flowing through a ditch until it meets the stream from the Ebble Rise springs. This Berwick stream was bubbling along cheerfully on a wet August afternoon in 2008.

Whatever the true source of the Ebble, both it and the river are inextricably entwined in the history of the area. At Norrington the nascent river fed ponds once used by the inhabitants of the medieval village, and still feeds the ornamental ponds created at the behest of Wadham Wyndham. It passes under the drive and takes a shallow channel through the field called Twenty Acres which once housed the eastern part of the medieval village, and which still shows signs of a water meadow system.

The construction and use of water meadows is described in 'The River Ebble'. Basically, the meadows were flooded by means of ditches in the fields and hatches in the river, to control the flow of the water and to allow an even spread over the field. This combined both irrigation and fertilisation, so produced good spring grazing and hay. At the eastern side of the field, by the houses known as Twenty Acres, the Ebble passes under a bridge and through the Withies, which Barbara Fergusson describes as 'a small, magical wood... . . . The footpath runs along the top of a gorge, with the Ebble lying in among the shrubs and lush plants below. Masses of bog loving plants like hemlock water-dropwort and angelica, hide the river's course from above.' She goes on to describe fungi and fauna in this naturalist's cornucopia. It is amazing to think that George Kellow can remember this area as a meadow, grazed by cattle. There is a pool at the further end then the stream, for it is no more, takes a deeper channel through Fiddle Pit, which is a good example of a former water meadow.

At the field gate, the Norrington workers who lived at the farm and at Twenty Acres used to gather on a Sunday morning, in good time for a gossip with the inhabitants of the main village before wending their way up to the church. Meanwhile the Ebble passes under the road and through 'the field in front of the church', as it is imaginatively called. This may be the field formerly known as Long Mead. The footpath runs beside the stream, providing generations of children with fun throughout the year: Pooh Sticks and river-bridging in the winter, exploration of the surprisingly deep course, mysteriously overhung with branches in the summer; and pyrites found in the dried watercourse. Four hundred years ago, this field was the stage for the grisly misdoings by Kennell, after Thomas Gawen's death, described in the chapter on Norrington. Foyle's Field is the last in Alvediston's share of the Ebble. The land slopes up northwards, making the gorge seem deeper, and there is a flat area to the east, where the river loops a little and passes into the garden of Badger's Glory in West End, and so on to Ebbesbourne. The ruins of a cottage with a well and fruit trees are tucked away on the sward. It looks ancient but it was inhabited in living memory; Sid Roberts, Frank's distant cousin, lived there. Nostalgic visits must be sad for Sid as he also lived in a cottage in the street, opposite the Manor, which has since been demolished. The Ebble flows through the valley to join the River Avon near Longford Castle at Bodenham, and so south to the sea.

To recount, running through the maps, the Ebble's source is supposed to be: between Fifield and Broad Chalke, (1576), between, and to the north of Norrington and Bowerchalke, (1611), west of Berwick with a tributary from Ebbesbourne, (1618), at Fifield, (1677), at Norrington Farm, (1773), just east of Berwick, (1811), and west of Windmill Hill, Norrington, (1842). In case the discrepancies are just attributed to naïve map production, the 1974 Ordnance Survey map has nothing west of Twenty Acres and today both west Berwick

St. John and Ebble Rise at Trow are contenders. If there were no argument, it would surely be a worrying sign of apathy.

~ *Coombes* ~

THE COOMBE OR combe must be one of the most stunning features of this area, contributing to the 'bladderwrack' effect on Andrews and Dury's map. However, the discovery of them on foot is quite startling because they are so deep and in places so narrow that they are often quite hidden until the last minute. Standing on downland at the top, one may look down onto a buzzard circling above its prey, far below. These secluded valleys, folded into the hills, serve as a reminder that much of the history of this place will remain folded away, and perhaps rightly so. Hints of life in ancient times are found in bowl barrows and field systems on the downs, with a Bronze Age field system extending from Elcombe Down into Ebbesbourne. In 1944, William E.V. Young found a hoard of sixteen bronze bangles and a bronze torque on Elcombe Down, near the boundary between the two villages.

In 2000, Martin Green published 'A Landscape Revealed, 10,000 Years on a Chalkland Farm', which gives a detailed account of the archaeology of Cranborne Chase, and particularly of Down Farm, his home in Sixpenny Handley, a few miles south of Alvediston. In his introduction he explains that, although not completely iced over during the last Ice Age, this area was deeply frozen so, as the Ice Age came to an end, (10 – 20,000 years ago,) streams which fed into the Avon and Stour became 'raging torrents by the unleashing of meltwater trapped by frost and ice around the periphery of the glaciers' which 'would erode and transport vast quantities of chalk previously weakened by being frozen to considerable depths.' Some of this material remained in the valleys where it is known as 'coombe rock'. The term 'naled' is used for what Martin Green describes as 'mounds and hollows', formed where chalk deposits gathered around frozen springs in the valleys, 'creating a strange contorted landscape'. He has an aerial view of the northern escarpment from Win Green, (south-west of Alvediston, and the highest point for miles around,) which shows the 'magnificent sculpted dry valleys' so familiar in our landscape.

Edith Olivier, in her book on Wiltshire, quotes John Aubrey, 'the most romantic of our Wiltshire historians'. Aubrey rhapsodised about the south of the county, confusingly referring to the 'downes or Salisbury Plaines' of this area, whereas the area now known as Salisbury Plain is to the north:

> On the downes, sc. the south part, where 'tis all upon tillage, and where the shepherds labour hard, their flesh is hard, their bodies strong; being weary after hard labour, they have no leisure to read and contemplate of religion, but goe to bed to their rest, to rise betime the next morning to their labour . . .
>
> The downes or Salisbury Plaines . . . are the most spacious plaines in Europe, and the greatest remaines that I can hear of of the smooth primitive world when it lay all under water . . . The turf is of a short sweet grasse, good for the sheep, and delightfull to the eye, for its smoothness like a bowling green . . . About Wilton and Chalke, the downes are intermixed with boscages, [masses of trees and shrubs,] nothing can be more pleasant, and in the Summer time doe excel Arcadia in verdant and rich turfe and moderate air . . . The innocent lives here of the shepherds do give us a resemblance of the Golden Age . . .

and so on. Sheep-rearing being the predominant farming pursuit in Alvediston now, current shepherds will doubtless recognise their qualities so fulsomely extolled, and may be glad that they do not operate in North Wiltshire, where 'the rich wett soile' had disastrous effects on the 'phlegmatic . . . Aborigines', making them 'melancholy, contemplative and malicious . . . more apt to be fanatiques: their persons apt to be plump and feggy . . . hypchondricall . . . very worm-woodish and more litigious than South Wilts.' How mercifully are we preserved.

In *Arcadia*, Adam Nicolson describes the agricultural system that operated in the chalkland areas for many centuries. The manors comprised downland grazing for sheep, arable land and woods below with lush meadows for spring grazing and hay-making in the valley. A natural symbiosis arose as flocks which grazed the downs by day were driven down to the arable fields at night, fertilising vital grain crops and helping to fix the seed in the soil. Water meadows were developed to encourage early grass, and hay also fed the oxen which drew the ploughs to cultivate arable land. 'All was connected: chalk turf and valley hay, down and meadow, the digestive system of sheep and the well-being of men, women and children.'

Incidentally, another local name for a coombe is a 'bottom', leading to interesting identifications such as 'Miss Hoole's Bottom', more romantically known as 'The Secret Valley'. This leads up to the Herepath between the tracks north of Norrington and Twenty Acres, and is part of Samways Farm. Copses of native trees, (beech, ash, sycamore, hazel, whitebeam, oak, elder, spindleberry, horse and sweet chestnut, and, until the 1970s, elm) crop up on the slopes of some coombes and on the hillsides. Young elms still shoot up but, after about seven years, have so far all succumbed to Dutch Elm Disease as the old ones did. Manwood and Elcombe Copses to the south and Crockerton Firs to the north are examples, while several lanes and tracks have high banks, topped by trees and tall hedges creating a 'tree tunnel' effect.

~ *Location and Orientation of Houses* ~

ANOTHER FEATURE OF Alvediston is worth noting. Today, with the decay and disappearance of several cottages in prime linking positions, the houses are not concentrated together along streets or lanes emanating from a discernable centre, or clustering around a church, pub or green, as dictated by the traditional image of a village. The centre is arguably at the cross-road, ('The Cross',) but this accentuates the sense of dispersal, because it is merely a 'T' junction with a track up to the 'Crown', which is hidden by a bank. The road to Tisbury goes north, while the Valley road goes east to Ebbesbourne and on to Salisbury, (along a stretch sometimes referred to, in the past, as East or Ice Lane,) and west via Berwick towards Shaftesbury. There are three dwellings at the Cross, each of which used to have a community purpose which, with the pub, would have given the village a focus as people converged on this area. However, this only applied for a comparatively short period from the mid-nineteenth century. Cross Cottage was once the Post Office, the school opposite opened in 1874, (now 'The Old School House' and 'The Old School Hall',) and the Crown started trading as a pub a few years earlier. Next to Cross Cottage, by the war memorial, was 'The Hut' or 'Reading Room', used as a village hall between the closure of the school and the time when the former schoolroom returned to that role. The Marks family bought the Reading Room hut from the diocese and transported it to Shortsmead. At one time, Bill's son Bernard lived there with his wife Margaret, and their son, Trevor, was born there. The hut is now tucked into a corner of the garden at Shortlands.

Christine Richardson, daughter of the Rev. Imrie Jones, who grew up in the Vicarage in the late nineteen-twenties and thirties, remembered that people gathered to chat on the corner of the Street. There is still a pleasant vestige of this when children wait with their parents for school buses, and there is a notice board at the bus stop. The slab of concrete is a reminder of a village scheme to erect a bus shelter in the nineteen-eighties. Unfortunately, this foundered when the council denied approval since, Alvediston being too small for a Parish Council, it does not raise a precept and so is deemed incapable of maintaining any 'public building'. The nearby public telephone doubles as a newspaper collection point, there being no house-to-house delivery. As there is currently no mobile 'phone reception the need for it would seem self-evident, but it is under threat of removal in the cause of 'improvement of services', the reason already given for limiting its use to bank cards rather than coins.

Cross Cottage faces south, The Old School House north, The Old School Hall west and the Crown east, which is typical of Alvediston. The forty-five homes are scattered over a wide area but even where they cluster together their outlooks are often distinct. It is as though the very dwellings resolutely refuse to share the same view. It would be interesting to photograph the village from the perspective of each home: so many different aspects would be covered. Despite the dispersal and the orientation of their homes, in times of communal need, (e.g. raising funds for church restoration), celebration, (e.g. village parties) or personal crisis this scattered community invariably pulls together.

~ *Enterprise* ~

WINDMILLS MAY COME under this category: in 1331 and 1360 one is recorded as part of Alvediston manor, while another was at Norrington in 1576. On his 1611 map, Speed has a large windmill symbol resplendent on a hill between

'Norrynton' and 'Burchalke', (Bowerchalke.) A survey of Norrington farm in 1664 records a windmill, and the hill on which it stood is known as Windmill Hill to this day. All local corn had to be milled at the lord of the manor's windmill, and the proceeds from this contributed to his income, as well as ensuring the dependence of his neighbours. William Day's race horse-breeding enterprise in the mid-nineteenth century is described in the chapter on Samways, and local businesses are covered with the inhabitants below, who ran them.

There have been some other forays into enterprise over the years, but not many, and generally of short duration. In 1845 a plan for a 'Direct London to Exeter Railway' was to run north of Alvediston, but would steam straight through the middle of West End. It foundered before a sod was dug, as did the 'Chalke Valley Railway', a less ambitious project for a horse-drawn tram or light railway in 1875. If the reforming Rev. Charles Ousby Trew had been around to be consulted, Alvediston might have gained 'rail communication with centres of industrial life' after all. A direct London to Exeter railway would have changed the valley irrevocably, raising the spectre of railway towns such as Gillingham, Dorset, C.O.Trew's former stamping ground. All this is idle speculation, only entertained today, perhaps, by disconsolate teenagers waiting for a bus and the hour-long trip into Salisbury, hardly a 'centre of industrial life', on a Saturday, knowing that they will be stranded if they stay there later than 5.40 p.m. For some this proves to be an impetus to spur on their studies and to gain a place in a far-flung university, but public transport remains a real problem for employment and entertainment beyond Alvediston for those without the use of a car.

The new road linking Alvediston with the A30 over the Herepath was cut in 1896, perhaps prompting a brief flash of enterprise which had certainly disappeared in a few years. The Kelly's Directory for 1898 records a 'golf ground' which opened out before the traveller once he had zig-zagged his way to the summit of the downs at Crockerton Firs.

Other references to this have not been found; possibly the challenge of retrieving golf balls from the depths of the coombes on either side cooled the zeal of the golfers, who have now been replaced by four-by-four loads of guns on commercial shoots. The Chalke valley is one of the best areas of the country for shooting so, with the pressure on farmers to diversify, the pattern of shooting has changed dramatically from rough shooting providing a welcome break in the local autumn and winter calendar into a business. Pheasant and partridge join the sheep in the fields and, while passers-by slow to enjoy the antics of lambs in the spring, later in the year they are more likely to be delayed by a plump little partridge scuttering along the road like a distracted woman trying to get her shopping done before her parking ticket runs out.

~ *Some of the Inhabitants during the past 170 years* ~

ACCORDING TO THE 1841 census, there were 250 people in Alvediston at the time; of these 115 were under 18, but this did not mean that they were unemployed. The youngest agricultural labourer was William King, aged 10! Only males were counted in the 54 agricultural labourers, but many women would have been involved as well. Apart from Thomas King of Samways, (no relation of William King's), who is recorded as a banker, all other occupations were related to the community. James Parham of Norrington and John Wright, (who farmed land belonging to Mr. Foot of Berwick St. John), were recorded as farmers and Joseph Rogers of the Manor as a yeoman. There were also: 11 servants, 3 blacksmiths, 1 shopkeeper, 3 carpenters, 1 sawyer, 1 mason, 1 gardener, 1 dairyman, 1 glover and 2 grooms. There was, in fact, only one landowner,

(Thomas King); Parham, Wright and Rogers were all tenants, and it does not seem that the village was particularly prosperous, but most people of employable age seem to have found work. There were a few women bringing up children alone, and very few older men who were no longer working: two 75 year-olds were still recorded as agricultural labourer and glover, but only 16 of the village of 250 were aged 65 or over. Even allowing for haziness about birth dates, this would be one of the most striking differences today.

The Mullins family was more enterprising than most. In 1841, the shop was run by William Mullins from what is now Cross Cottage. One of his sons, John, was a carpenter and the other, another William, became a 'carrier', providing transport, and was soon branching out into other businesses, see below.

The incumbency of the Rev. Soulieu Desprez (1862 – 79) was a time of great change, with the restoration of the church and the building of the school, both described in the relevant chapters of this book. This first resident vicar for nearly three hundred years was buried in the churchyard by the east end of the church, opposite the vicarage which he had built. Local residents subscribed to a fund for the west window in his memory.

Kelly's Directories provide interesting cameos of life. William Day's horse training establishment brought new interest, employment and life into the community. In 1867, while he and the Rev. Desprez were in action, there were two shopkeepers: William King was also the parish clerk while the younger William Mullins ran his shop with the Crown inn and his carrier's business. Some time between the 1851 census and the 1867 directory, the licence for the 'Bentinck Arms', (the inn at Bigly, on the Ox Drove), was transferred to the valley and the Crown, formerly two cottages near the Cross, came into being. The date of the original cottages is not clear. The *V.C.H.* says they 'may . . . be of 18th-century origin.' Probably earlier dwellings have been incorporated into these cottages, like others locally. Indeed, during the past thirty

The Crown in the Comptons' time, with the school in the background. (Pat Scrivens)

years there have been fires, one very serious, and many restorations and additions. The move down into the village was probably precipitated by the local stretch of the London to Exeter railway providing alternative transport for flocks and herds which had previously been driven along the Ox Drove. In the next generation, George Mullins continued the carrier business. In 1885 he is recorded as taking day trips to Salisbury on Tuesdays and Shaftesbury on Saturdays as well as running his shop. By that time Ann Compton, a widow, had taken over the Crown. Her son George, who was born in 1874, was young enough to attend school when they first arrived. He married Jane and had ten children. Ann stayed at the Crown after George took it on. Bigly continued to be farmed by the publican even after the licence was transferred. Joan Reeves, George's youngest daughter, remembers the dairy there, and the two house cows kept at the pub. When the Wilton Estate sold its property in this area, in 1918, George bought the Crown. There is no evidence of a pub in the village before this.

The Crown in the Rogersons' time, c. 1961. (Olive Rogerson)

The 1918 sales particulars describe:

Lot 119 "THE CROWN INN" (Alvediston) Situate in the centre of the Village. A FULLY-LICENSED HOUSE, Brick, Stone & Thatched, containing Bar, Tap Room, Living Room, Pantry & Four bedrooms with Detached Stone & tile Wash House & E.C. [earth closet] & Detached Brick & Thatched Stable.

Adjoining the House is a Range of Stone, Timber & Thatched Buildings, comprising Coal House, Cart Shed & Three-stall Stable. GARDEN & ORCHARD . . . containing about 0 Acres, 3 Rods, 27 Perches. The Property is held by Messrs. Matthews & Co., Brewers, Gillingham, holding over on a yearly Michaelmas Tenancy, at an annual rate of £14. 0s. 0d., the garden being Let at a further yearly Rent of £1. 0s. 0d., a total of £15. 0s. 0d.

Outgoing ~ Land Tax 14s. 0d.

In the Compton's time, the Crown was not only the base for the family businesses of inn, carrier and small farm, it was also home to

George and Jane and their ten surviving children. The influence of the church and agriculture on all walks of life in the village is emphasised by the Michaelmas tenancy; September 29th, the feast of St Michael, being the time of year most convenient for farmers to move, as the harvest should be safely in. Michaelmas was one of four 'quarter-days' when agricultural rent was due: the others being: Lady Day (25th March), Midsummer Day (24th June), and Christmas Day. These rent days still apply in farming.

Letters came from Salisbury via Swallowcliff and the 'precipitous' climb over the Herepath, while the nearest place to change money was in Shaftesbury, eight miles away. Henry Matthews was the blacksmith and otherwise people were still generally agricultural labourers, a few were servants. If all else failed, the workhouse was at Tisbury, the building on Monmouth Hill remaining until 1967. By 1875, William Mullins seems to have given up his shop, Mrs. Jane Matthews had presumably

Primitive Methodist Chapel and cottage, 1907. (Peter Daniels)

been widowed and was keeping the smithy going, residents only had to go as far as Donhead St. Andrew to change money, (still about five miles away), and the population peaked. By 1881 it was falling as the effects of the agricultural depression began to hit home. By 1880, the Samways horse trainer had been replaced by a farm bailiff, working for the new absentee owner, Frederick Gray. Postal collections, from the wall letterbox in what is now Cross Cottage, had been reduced to once daily. Perhaps the high point in the life of Alvediston was the decade between the mid-1860s and the mid-1870s.

Between 1881 and 1891, the current Elcombe House became the Police House, even appearing in the 1901 census as 'Police Station'. By 1885, William King was the parish clerk; and Josiah Sims, whose family played a major part in the village for several generations, had taken over as Frederick Gray's bailiff. He had the Primitive Methodist Chapel built in 1894, seating sixty, a capacity increased to a hundred and eight 'sittings' a few years later, which seems remarkably optimistic. However, 1880-92 was a particularly dire time in the life of the church, so perhaps he was responding to a village need as well as appealing to a wider area. Congregationalists had been well established in Ebbesbourne for much longer, and had had a chapel since 1857. By 1895, Bernard Parham, tenant at Norrington, was able to employ a bailiff too, Henry White. There was still no Post Office, but Ebbesbourne provided a money order service and there was a telegraph office at Donhead.

From December 1894, the 'Minute Book of the Parish of Alvediston in the Union of Tisbury, County of Wilts.' adds another dimension, until 1962 when entries stopped. However, it is now being used once more, for the minutes of the Parish Meetings which have taken place biannually since February 2007. The book opens with disappointing attendance caused by the stipulation that only electors were eligible, but sixteen votes were cast in favour of a parish meeting, beating those who wanted a parish council by only one vote. Then, as now, most discussion centred on the state of the roads and the problems of flooding.

Crockerton Firs, on the brow of the hill where the parish boundary crept to the north of the Herepath for a short distance, was

Cross Cottage, formerly 'Gardener's Cottage', an early post office. (Olive Rogerson)

the site of the most isolated dwellings, often inhabited temporarily by poorer families. There is still a sense of former habitation amongst the trees in the corner between the Herepath and the track to Ansty. Roy Marks remembered a tramp, Frankie Burt, living among the trees there. Just to the east, in part of a field on the other side of the 'new' road was the Poor Patch, a last vestige of common land, so there was somewhere for itinerant families to graze a few animals, cut grass and collect wood. Bill Marks was not allowed to catch rabbits commercially there. Roy also remembered a pit in this area; it may have been a source of flints. In 1903 the parish clerk was instructed to write to Lord Pembroke's agent because: 'The parishioners of Alvediston feel hurt by the damage done by the drawing of flints from the Poor Downs, and wish to know the position of the parish with regards to stopping it.' From the school log book, an erratic pattern of attendance by many families at Crockerton Firs suggests that education was not their first priority.

By 1898, Alvediston finally had a Post Office. This was probably housed in the current Cross Cottage, before moving down to what is now Street Cottage. Henry Charles Coombs was sub-postmaster, able to issue, but not to pay out, postal orders. The Post Office would have played a greater part in people's lives when few would have used a bank. George Compton had taken over the Crown from his mother and kept a small shop there too, while William Coombs had a pony-trap for hire. Letters began to come through the valley from Salisbury via Broad Chalke at about this time ~ a more reliable and logical route established just when the postman from Swallowcliff could have had an easier journey! In the 1901 census, Church Farm was inhabited by William and Susan James, described as 'dairy manager and dairywoman' respectively, while William Coombs, (a 'farmer') and his family lived in 'Little Lane'. This suggests that the lane up to Shortsmead was called Little Lane at that time and that the Coombs family lived in what was known as the 'White House' at the bottom of the lane. In the early years of the twentieth century, this fell into disuse and ruin, but it features in the watercolour reproduced on the cover of this book. By 1903 Church Farm operated as a separate entity from the rest of the manor land, farmed by Tom Henry Sims, a cousin of Josiah, and he lived in the farmhouse.

A six-year battle with the District Council began two years later. The bridge at Long Mead needed repair, but pleas and visits by the district surveyor were to no avail, and in 1911 we read that it was repaired by private subscription. What state was it in by then? In 1609, Long Mead was included among William Gould's land, so would be part of Samways or the Manor. The logical choice for the field is that which now rejoices in the name 'Field in front of the church', and the road bridge is to the west of it.

After the large-scale sales of land by Lord Pembroke of Wilton in 1918-19, Tom H. Sims and Josiah's son-in-law, Alfred Gladstone Hull each appear as 'farmer and landowner', a title which they could have enjoyed much more if farming had not gone into such a depression after the war. As much of the village became independent of the Wilton Estate, ambitious housing plans were spawned, most of which came to naught despite numerous meetings of a Parish Housing Committee. The problem of affordable housing for local people is acute today.

In 1919, plans for a war memorial cross to be raised by public subscription were more successful. Both Mr. Hoole and Mr. Sims offered sites but, after some to-ing and fro-ing, the site in the corner of the Manor orchard, next to the old Reading Room, was chosen. Some time in the 1920s, the cross of Chilmark stone was hauled over the hill from Tisbury by George Compton in his capacity as carrier. Today, a small clump of dark violets, a fitting flower, pokes through the grass on the roadside in spring, and an Act of Remembrance is held by the cross on Remembrance Sunday. Tisbury remained a vital store of goods, especially those which could arrive there by train, and there were deliveries from the 'International' Stores.

The Rights of Way Act of 1934 led to the establishment of most of the current footpaths and bridleways, and the following year the Rural District Council was asked to build four cottages. Their offer of only two was accepted and the first Council Houses appeared, two more following a few years later. More innovation was requested of the Post Office: that a telephone be installed in the village Post Office, (in the Street,) and a call box erected at the Cross. The Electricity Board was also approached about bringing 'the current' to Alvediston. Electricity was 'available' from around 1938, but did not reach the church until the 1960s.

As war loomed the plans for air raid precautions drew a full house for a Parish Meeting in September 1938. The school room would become the First Aid post, Mr. Tom Sims and Miss Parham were chosen as air wardens and Mr. J. Mitchell and Mr. W. Marks as dispatch riders, Bill's beloved motorcycle proving its worth. The First Aid Party comprised Miss Olga Hoole, Mr. Hayward, and Mrs. Gillam, (nee Sims), and the Decontamination Party: Mr. Frank Compton, Mr. A. Watts, Mr. H. Collis and Mr. H. King. These names, many still familiar locally, demonstrate the local community in action

Alvediston School group, April 1907. For names see Appendix. (Peter Daniels)

just twenty years after the end of a very different but still all too well-remembered war. Although there were fewer men to go off to fight, the war itself came closer to home, especially with the involvement of the Air Force. A homing beacon was placed on Samways land, near Twenty Acres, lighting the night sky as bright as day. Parish Meetings went into abeyance, and in March 1945 Bernard Parham retired as chairman ~ after fifty-one years! Some years later, Norrington provided another similarly long-serving chairman in Tristram Sykes.

In April 1945 the need for an extension to the burial ground was noted. As much of the churchyard is not marked by gravestones, it must be much fuller than it looks. Some stones have disappeared but many people were buried without any mark. One suggestion was to create a burial ground on the glebe land but, although this gained the approval of the clergy, Bill Marks already had an option to purchase the glebe. By the end of the year Tom Sims had stepped in with the offer of part of Church Mead for £15. This was accepted, and so burials for some years were placed up a steep bank at the northern boundary of the churchyard.

Earlier, allotments were cultivated on the glebe land, to the left of the track to Shortsmead. When the glebe was sold by the diocese, Roy and Bella Marks were able to build 'Shortlands' there, incorporating stone from the long-deserted 'White House' by the road into their new drive. Recycled materials have always been used in cottages and tracks, sometimes even from churches and churchyards before diocesan faculty arrangements regularized matters.

Family and school photographs have been carefully preserved and generously shared, both for this book and for various exhibitions. In 1907, Charlie May made a valuable record of village people and buildings. His picture of the school in 1907 shows the recently widowed Mrs. Thatcher in the year before her retirement, while the gloriously coiffed woman to the right was her assistant. Some of the little boys are wearing lace collars, one has a dress and smock like the girls', (until remarkably recently young boys wore dresses, as Joan Reeves' memories illustrate.) Their boots would have had to protect their feet in all weathers, and it is clear form the school log that ill-shod small feet often suffered. The purchase of boots told on shoe leather: Frank Roberts remembers walking from Ebbesbourne to Bowerchalke on his fifth birthday to buy a pair of boots; Reg Marks recalled Broad Chalke as the source of boots.

By 1910, sailor suits began to make an appearance in a class photo, and a diminutive Reg Marks was wearing one in 1920; (the Nellie next to him was his sister. Twenty-one years later he married another Nellie.) Roy Marks' siblings, Pearl, Stuart and Myrtle (Molly), are pictured, but he was just too young to attend Alvediston School. Cyril and Clifford Marks moved to Ebbesbourne, and Beryl Andrews' father was a carpenter. Most of the other children are mentioned in relation to the war memorial below, which makes these school photos all the more poignant. (See the school photograph, 1920, on page 144.)

On the war memorial, the list of those who served in the First World War as well as those who died is valuable, not just as a historical record, but also as a reminder of the long-term suffering of many who returned, most of whom rarely referred to the horrors they had experienced. All are named at the war memorial on Remembrance Day.

~ *The Fallen of Alvediston in the Great War, 1914-18* ~

PRIVATE WILLIAM GEORGE SCAMMELL
2nd. Battalion Wiltshire Regiment
Killed in action, 24th. October 1914, aged 20
Commemorated on the Menin Gate memorial
among those lost without trace at Ypres
parents lived at Ebbesbourne Wake

PRIVATE BERTRAM WILLIAM JAMES MOXHAM
1st. Battalion Wiltshire Regiment
died of wounds, 31st. July 1915, aged 25
buried in Lijssenthoek Military Cemetary, Belgium
lived at Twenty Acres
Possibly this Bill Moxham was in the 1910 football team photo (p.48)

LANCE CORPORAL GEORGE GRACE
17th. Battalion machine Gun Corps (infantry)
died, 4th November 1918, aged 19
buried in Englefontaine British Cemetery, Nord, France
lived at Crook Hill, Alvediston
In 1945, another George Grace was still in Alvediston

The youngest died exactly one week before Armistice Day. Not mentioned on the memorial is another who grew up at Trow, but his family moved away: Private Walter Charles Compton died of his wounds at home in Romsey on 19th. March, 1919, aged 29.

The names on the memorial of those who served and returned are:

H.J. PARHAM, Croix de Guerre   J. CARTER
WILLIAM MULLINS   JOHN KITCHEN
J.J. SCAMMELL   H.J. VINCENT
H.D. KING   J.L. ROBERTS
S.G. MOXHAM   J.T. COMPTON
G. DALTON   T.A. SIMS
E. SCAMMELL   WALTER MULLINS
CECIL MOXHAM   J.H. CHILD
V. WATTS   CHARLES ROBERTS
DOUGLAS LUSH   G.E. COLLIS

Most of these took up their lives as well as they could on the farms or working in the gardens or stables of the three big houses, as the details from the 1925 Kelly's Directory show below. However, J.T. (Jack) Compton's story was probably typical. The eldest of George and Jane Compton's ten surviving children, he played in the football team. Having overcome, (or ignored) his father's wishes that he stay at home, he joined the Wiltshire Yeomanry but later transferred to the Royal Scots, earning the nickname 'Jock'. He served at Bethune, in Northern France, and was twice

Jack Compton, 1916. (Pat Scrivens)

Alvediston Football Team, 1910. For names see Appendix. (Roy Marks]

wounded by shrapnel. He had severe injuries to his head, neck and jaw, and lost his teeth, but was sent to Manchester Hospital and retained a lifelong affection for the Salvation Army whose nurses cared for him. The 1907 school photo shows three of his sisters, Annie, Violet and Mabel, while Vera, Lucy and Frank are in the 1920 one. After the war, he took over the 'Talbot' inn in Berwick. His son, Peter, lives in Berwick St. John with his wife, Pip, and they still have Jack's beret and forage cap. The collection at his funeral was for the Salvation Army.

Hetman Jack Parham was the son of Bernard Parham, who farmed Norrington. Born in 1896, he served in the Royal Artillery throughout the First World War in France, Belgium and the Balkans, receiving the Croix de Guerre. He remained in the army, fighting in the Second World War and rising to Major General. He was fascinated by flying, becoming an amateur pilot and writing books on the subject (for example *Flying for Fun: an Affair with an Aeroplane*, in which he described, with enthusiasm and self-deprecating humour, how he learnt to fly a tiny aeroplane just before the Second World War). He was also a keen sailor and a gifted artist. He died in 1974. His sister remained at Norrington until it was sold in 1952.

Cecil Moxham appears in the 1907 school photo. Samuel Moxham was at Twenty Acres in 1945. Like the Scammells, the family eventually migrated to Berwick St. John.

Vic Watts grew up at Twenty Acres. His widowed mother, Laura, later married John (Jack) Kitchen, another war veteran, and they eventually moved to Castle Hill. She

Herbert King, brother of Olive. (Carla Allen)

became known as 'Granny Kitchen', and she became the grandmother of Frank Roberts and great-grandmother of his niece, Carol Smith, who both live in Ebbesbourne. Phyllis Watts is in the 1920 school photo.

Charlie Roberts, Frank's uncle, was a groom at Samways, and lived in the Street.

Joe Roberts lived in at least three cottages which have since disappeared: in Ice Lane, (near the forge,) opposite the Manor and in Foyle's Field with his sons Sid and Arthur. Queenie, Flora and Edmund Roberts, Joe's siblings, feature in the 1920 photo. Edmund, Winnie and their family lived at 3, Elcombe Lane in 1942.

Jack Carter worked at Norrington. Joe, Edith and Winnie Carter all appear in the 1920 photo. Charles Carter, a game keeper, lived at Crook Hill in 1925, and 'Keeper' carter at Keeper's Cottage, now Bushy Garson, in 1942.

Herbie Vincent was the brother of Elsie Moxham. He lived in Elcombe Lane before going to Cleeves, Ebbesbourne.

Walter Mullins was a groom at Norrington, and Bill appears in the 1910 football team photo. In 1925, J.W. Mullins, (Walter) was recorded as a roadman, living on Castle Hill, and W.W. Mullins, (Bill) was a carter who later became a gardener at Samways, and who lived in Ice Lane.

Herbert, 'Herbie' King was recorded as a 15 year-old farm worker in the 1911 census. He came from the local King family which seems to have been in

Henry Stanley, brother of Kate Stanley, in front of Elcombe Cottage, with Elcombe House beyond. ((Carla Allen)

the area for centuries, and the name crops up frequently: the 1505-6 Wilton Abbey records show William Kynge as bailiff to Thomas Tylden, who farmed the manor lands; there is a will of Nicholas King dated 1555; the name occurs in baptism and burial records at the end of that century, when records began. When Luke Dyer, steward for the newly-arrived Wyndham family, detailed activities at Norrington in 1669-70, the name arises again. The 1841 census shows a William King, aged 35, an agricultural labourer whose wife, Mary, came from Ebbesbourne Wake. He, however, was born in Radnorshire because his father had moved to Wales for some reason and married there, before returning to this area. Various Kings married into a number of other well-established families, e.g. Stanley, Philpot, Roberts, but they were not related to the Kings of

Samways. William King's daughter, Elizabeth, had a son called Mark King before she married Henry Luter, so the name was passed down another generation. Mark was also a farm labourer who married Kate Stanley of Crook Hill. Their children were Herbert, (who served in World War I), Evelyn, Olive, Maurice, Gwendoline and Janet, (Nellie). The two youngest feature in the 1920 school photo. They lived in one end of the current Elcombe Cottage and worked at the Manor for the Sims family. As Mark's mother lived with them, there were nine in half of what is now one cottage. Olive worked as a nursemaid to a local family and also on the land, where she was nicknamed 'Bill' because she worked as hard as the men. She married Joseph Martin and her grand daughter, Carla Allen of Christchurch, has researched the family history. The King family still has strong links with Alvediston, and members of it live in nearby villages, including Dinton. Herbert was buried in St. Mary's churchyard in August 1948.

G. Dalton: although Daltons do not appear in the 1925 Directory, Percy and Eddie were in the 1920 school photo.

Douglas Lush, like his father, Henry, was a carter at Norrington. After 25 years' service he got his wages plus a spare ½ d., a story which still rankles those who remember it. He lived in Norrington Cottages and later moved to Twenty Acres.

Tommy Sims was Thomas Henry Sims' son. The family bought the Manor but Tommy and his wife Ivy lived at Church farmhouse and farmed that end of the Manor estate. His sister, Gwen, is in the 1920 school photo. She married Mr. Gillam and later had 'Trunnions' built for herself and her widowed father. Thomas Henry was the cousin of Josiah Sims, bailiff then farmer at the manor. Josiah's grandchildren, Peggy and Jack Hull, are in the 1920 photo, and it is through Peggy that we can identify all the children. Her daughter made this photograph available. There is more information about the Sims family in the chapter on the Manor.

J.H. Child: no further information has been forthcoming.

G.E.Collis: a George Collis is thought to have served in the Navy. A relation of his, Joe Collis, is fondly remembered for his antics at the Vicarage, having lost his leg in a football accident, (see the chapter on the church.) Prior to his accident it is said that he was farm foreman at Norrington, although another informant maintains that he was only thirteen when he suffered his accident. He and his sister, Ivy, appear in the 1920 photo. Dave Collis is the greengrocer in Tisbury.

Although they do not feature on the war memorial, the Topp family also has strong connections with Alvediston, and members now live in Broad Chalke as well as Salisbury. Bowles has details in his chapter on Berwick St. John, where they rented Higher Bridmore Farm. The 'visitation book' of 1623 recorded three generations in that village, including John, who was 46 at that time. Joan Topp's marriage to Francis Mayo in 1613 is among Bowles' extracts from the registers. They were sufficiently important to have a coat of arms.

Most of this information has been gleaned from local people in conversation, correspondence and at the local history exhibition held in the church in 2000. Jim Collins, (who was born in Berwick, grew up in Elcombe Lane and later moved to a newly built council house in Alvediston, while his father worked at Samways), has a remarkable memory of the people of the village. He was able to list almost all the occupants of houses in 1942, and many subsequent ones too, providing a valuable resource for others to add to and amend! He now lives in Ebbesbourne Wake.

St Mary's Church

~ Introduction ~

THE STORY OF the church in Alvediston reflects national and local history in its cycles of development and neglect of both the fabric and the people. It certainly belies any concept of a golden past and a gloom-ridden present for church commitment in this village and stands, as it has done in various guises for nine centuries, as a visible witness to the Christian faith. Visitors often comment on the peaceful atmosphere in and around the church and gain strength from it as do locals, but, as so often happens, this peace is not an absence of discord but something which has grown through turbulent as well as gentler times and through centuries of worship by ordinary, fallible people. Some families with still-familiar names have served the church for generations while some shorter-term residents have also influenced the history of the church.

In his *Highways and Byways in Wiltshire*, of 1924, Edward Hutton found little of interest in the church,('an old but not very fine cruciform building with western tower,') except for 'the tomb to be found in the south transept'. Nikolaus Pevsner was, if anything, less impressed, clearly not being an admirer of the energetic Victorian diocesan architect, T. H. Wyatt. Finding some evidence of the 17th century in the tower arch decoration and a small window above the south door, he dismisses it as 'mostly 1866'. However, the Wyndham monuments, especially the one in memory of John and Alicia Wyndham, by Rysbrack, are commended.

According to the *Victoria County History* of Wilts., the earliest evidence of a church appears to be twelfth century, but only the font and the nave are believed to originate from that period. The chancel is probably thirteenth century and the transepts fourteenth, the south one possibly built by John Gawen, who was building Norrington at that time, and who may well be commemorated by the recumbent figure of a knight beneath the south window. By 1585 the church was described as 'down' and extensive repairs were carried out in the following century, including the building of the tower. The early seventeenth century was tumultuous, with changes in building design reflecting the swings from Puritan emphasis on the word, (massive pulpits eclipsing the chancel), to the rise of ceremonialism as Charles I tried to re-impose Catholic tradition and the altar became the focus in worship. However this was resolved in St. Mary's, the church pre-Wyatt appeared to be seventeenth century. Wyatt built the vestry to the south, the choir vestry adjoining the rebuilt north transept and incorporated thirteenth century features into the chancel along with unmistakably Victorian features throughout, including the tiles in the chancel, which seem to have been his particular trademark around the diocese.

Charles Bowles, in his *Hundred of Chalke* of 1830, provides a fascinating view of the church at that time. Although somewhat hazy in his history, (he airily describes the font as 'of great antiquity, coeval with the Saxon times; at all events, as old as the Normans,') inclined to hedge his bets on the provenance of the knightly monument, (suggesting two other contenders as well as John Gawen: John

*Watercolour of Alvediston church from the south-west, c. 1805, by John Buckler
(Wiltshire Heritage Museum, Devizes)*

de Berwick or Roger Hussee,) and indulging in a diatribe against the abuses of the church hierarchy, he nevertheless gives a useful description of the building pre-Wyatt.

~ *The Porch* ~

BOWLES DESCRIBES A large porch, noting that most of the churches in the Chalke Hundred had larger porches than would have been built 'in more modern times'. In the Middle Ages, when few people were literate, both the design of the building and the rituals were used as visual aids in services. Marriages were largely conducted in the porch, as were the first part of baptisms and the now obsolete practice of 'Churching of Women'.

Sir Roy Strong, in *A Little History of the English Country Church*, provides details of the baptism ceremony which seem positively gruesome today. When just a few days old, the hapless infant was taken to church by the midwife and godparents for a series of rituals beginning in the porch, where the priest would first enquire whether the child was a boy, (to be held to the right) or a girl, (to the left.) He then placed salt in the mouth, (for exorcism), signed the forehead with the cross twice, and then spat into his left hand and moistened the ears and nostrils in illustration of Christ's healing. After signing the right hand with the cross and intoning: 'May you remain in the Catholic faith and have eternal life for ever and ever. Amen', he invited them all into the church where, at the font, the godparents renounced Satan and all his works on the child's behalf. Signing with the cross, (using holy oil), on the breast and between the shoulder blades was followed by the now naked baby being both rotated and completely immersed in the water of the font three times to the words: 'God the Father, God the Son and God the Holy Spirit'. Unlike today, when the water in the font is heated by the boiling contents of a flask, giving rise to billows of steam and agonised gasps from the unsuspecting baby's nearest and dearest, neither the church nor the water would be heated. It then fell to a senior godparent to retrieve the baby so that the head could be signed with the cross with the most holy oil, chrism. For this reason, the garment, (a cloth or hooded robe), that was used to wrap the child in afterwards was called a 'chrisom'. This was to be worn until it was returned by the mother at the churching ceremony, forty days later for boys and eighty days for girls. Somehow, the screaming and shivering infant was then expected to hold a lighted candle in his right hand while the words: 'Receive a burning and inextinguishable light' were said, and the godparents were told to bring the child up in the Christian faith. While the spirit of many of these rituals remains in the baptism service, the practice has changed radically. Perhaps it was for the best that the mother was still confined to her bed during all this. It is to be hoped that infant mortality was not inadvertently increased by the church's desire to save infant souls.

The Churching of Women was a gentler service. The mother, accompanied by a group of women friends, knelt before the priest in the porch for a blessing, prayers, the recitation of the 23rd. Psalm and responses, followed by sprinkling with holy water, a symbol of cleansing which referred back to ancient hygiene practices. They all then went into the church, led by the priest, and the service concluded at the altar. The chrisom cloth was returned and an offering of money made. The spirit of this service remains in acts of thanksgiving for the birth of a child.

~ *The Memorials* ~

BOWLES DESCRIBES THE recumbent knight as being 'placed on a raised tomb' in the south transept, which was still known as 'Gawen's aisle' in spite of the four grand Wyndham monuments on the walls, and he believed that the knight-figure was moved from a niche in the south wall of the aisle. Contrary to common myth, there is no evidence that crossed legs or dogs signify a connection with the Crusades, but a knight sometimes had a dog, (as in this case), or a bear at his feet. Bowles also records two brasses which have rarely been seen, because they were hidden by the Victorian altar. These finely decorated memorials have recently been restored by William Lack, with the help of Michael Stuchfield and grants from the Monumental Brass Society and the Francis Coales Charitable Foundation and fixed in the north chapel, where they are more visible. In spite of the fact that the Frys were Quakers, Bowles, who lived near the Fry family home a century or more later, does not question the position 'over the communion table'. From the Reformation until the late eighteenth century, (with a gap when Charles I tried to restore 'the true former splendour of uniformity, devotion and holy order'), the chancel was treated with less reverence. The altar was moved closer to the people so that they could see everything that the clergyman was doing during communion: a reaction against Roman Catholic mystery. The altar was called the 'table' and was sometimes even rotated so that the people could sit around it on three sides. In the early eighteenth century, there was thus no problem over brasses being placed on the east wall of the chancel. They read:

> Here lieth the body of FRANCIS FRY, Gent. who died the 16th day of December, 1710, in the 81st. year of his age.
> Here lieth the body of JANE, the wife of FRANCIS FRY, Gent. who died the 1st. of September, 1703, in the 60th. year of her age.'

His comment is:

> This Francis Fry, it is believed, was tenant of the Norrington Farm; he was of the family of Fry of Ashgrove, who gave the ground of Chevicombe Bottom in the Donhead St. Mary parish, as a burial ground for the Quakers. Of the same family, is the husband of the philanthropic Mrs. Fry, who, like a second Howard, has visited most of the gaols in England and Ireland, instilling religious principles into those females who were found inmates.' [Another coincidence is that Dr. Hugh Pelly, of Ebbesbourne Wake, is a descendent of Elizabeth Fry.]

Bowles notes the 'four very handsome mural monuments of marble, ornamented with pillars and festoons of fruits and flowers, to the memory of the Wyndham family'. One, dedicated to the memory of John and Alicia Wyndham, was erected by their son, Baron Finglass, who recorded the fact with a flowery commendation to himself, only outdone by the testimony on an enormous monument to himself to be found by the west door of Salisbury cathedral, both made by the famous Rysbrack. Bowles tells us that John and Alicia were buried in

Monument to John and Alicia Wyndham in Alvediston church, by Michael Rysbrack (Fritz Curzon)

a tomb surrounded by iron rails 'on the outside of the Norrington aisle'. This can be seen in the Buckler picture, on page 55, but it must have been too close for Mr. Wyatt's vestry, because all that remains is a worn stone with an inscription in memory of John on the ground just outside the vestry door, and a stone slab in memory of Alicia Wyndham which, like the stone on the aisle floor commemorating Gertrude Gawen, has been partially obscured by pews. Gertrude was Thomas' first wife, and he was also buried in Alvediston, in 1656, as was his second wife, Ann, in 1678, twenty-five years after the family's loss of Norrington. It is good to know that, although only recorded in the register, these burials seem to have passed off without incident. All these monuments are recorded in more detail in the chapter on Norrington.

Bowles records another floor slab that was partially obscured by a pew in the north transept or 'Gold's aisle'. As the stone may have been for a Gould and these pews were provided by the third Thomas King of Samways they may have contributed to the Gould family's sense of grievance against the Kings, (see Samways chapter.) However, the famous Gould stone, whose fate is also described in that chapter, was still on the north transept wall, as were large, marble memorials to three generations of the King family of Samways, and two small ones to members of the Laws and Rogers families, tenants of the Manor.

An inventory of 1928 mentions: 'Inset on the north wall of the sanctuary, apparently a grave slab of small dimensions, bearing a double floriated cross and floriated edging ? date' and 'This was unearthed when foundations of Priest's Vestry were being dug in 1865.' It is to be found just above the small alcove to the left of the altar. At least something from the past was carefully preserved. It is thought to be a thirteenth century coffin slab for a tiny coffin made to transport the heart of someone who had died elsewhere, perhaps abroad. This was the time of the Crusades, when knights had to be ready to fight for the king, in return for land. This coffin slab is of an earlier date than the recumbent knight in the south aisle, but both bear witness to the fact that landowners and their responsibilities were far from parochial. The other possible use for a tiny stone coffin was for the burial of a baby, but it is thought less likely in this case, as it is too elaborate in design.

The most recent memorial, to Anthony Eden, Lord Avon, was commissioned from the sculptor Martin Jennings as part of the latest fund-raising efforts. It is on the north wall, opposite the door, and was unveiled by Clarissa, Countess of Avon, on 30th. September, 2008.

~ *The Plate and Bells* ~

IN 1553, THE last year of Edward VI's short reign, a royal commission reviewed all the 'plate, juells, bellis, and ornaments' of the country's churches and chapels. This seems to have involved a major overhaul, justified by the young king's fanatical Protestantism, and executed by his greedy and scheming Protector, the Duke of Northumberland. Each place of worship was provided with plate for the new service of communion, in which the wine as well as the bread was given to the congregation, but the excess from the sale of their previous goods went to the king. Thus, 'there was delivered to William Goulde and Nicholas Martin, one cup or chalice, by indenture of eleven ounces and a half, and three bells, for the use of the inhabitants of this parish; and there was remaining for the King's use two ounces', (Bowles.)

Researching the provenance and date of the chalice and small paten currently in use is characteristically complicated. In 1977, Robert Hawkings recorded them. The chalice is 6 ½ inches high and weighs about 7 ¾ Troy ounces, which are heavier than imperial ounces, i.e. about 9 ounces or 241 grams. Therefore, the *V.C.H.* suggestion that it dates from 1521 and is the '11 ounce' one left in 1553 looks doubtful. Bowles thought it must be pre-Reformation because it held less than one pint of wine, not enough, in his estimation, for the Alvediston congregation once they were allowed to partake. J.E. Nightingale, F.S.A., in 'The Church Plate of the County of Wilts', (1891), describes 'a good Elizabethan cup without any hallmark or inscription,' similar to many unmarked chalices of that era in the diocese.

The 4 ½ inch diameter paten carries its age easily in its battered, bent and scratched surface. It is marked 'P P' with a pellet below and perhaps a crown above. Nightingale thought that the mark resembled a York one of 1608 but believed that the paten might have belonged to the Elizabethan chalice. It is generally thought to be seventeenth century, and Nicholas du Quesne Bird, researching Channel Island silver in 1994, suggested that it was made by Paul Priaulx who worked in Salisbury and was the son or grandson of a Guernsey merchant.

According to the *V.C.H.*, there was a pewter flagon in 1640. In 1865, to mark the restoration of the church, a new, 12 inch silver flagon and 6 inch diameter paten were commissioned by Rowland Williams. He was an interesting character, rector of Broad Chalke from 1858 to 1870, with a year's suspension from 1861, due to the Bishop of Salisbury's disquiet at his theology. It was generous of him to offer this flagon and paten to Alvediston so soon after his troubles. Certainly, he was much loved by the people of Broad Chalke, where his rather unconventional views seem to have been quite acceptable. Today, a small, glass cruet with silver mouth-piece, handle and base holds sufficient wine for the regular congregation.

While there may be doubt and discussion about the provenance of the older vessels, there is no doubt that they have passed through the hands of numberless priests and people as they muddled through their lives throughout the centuries, and that most people would count it a privilege to be able to share their use.

According to the *V.C.H.* there were four bells in 1553; Bowles mentions three. There were still three in 1830, but the sixteenth century ones must have disappeared and have been replaced in the following century, when the church was restored and the tower built. They are marked:

Prayse GOD 1630. I.D.
1640, [with the 4 upside down,] T
Thomas King Churchwarden. James Wells. Aldbourn. Wilts. fecit 1811.

They still hang in the tower, but the tower currently needs restoration, so they may not be used. Previously one could be tolled, not rung. The dates of the first two would suggest that the seventeenth century restoration and building of the tower took place in the earlier decades.

~ *The Clergy* ~

ROBERT STALLARD HAS researched the church in the prebend of Chalke. He explains that, in Saxon times, priests would visit outlying villages to preach at a place marked by a cross. There was a priory at Wilton from 800, and the abbey was founded after Wilton was razed to the ground by the Danes in 871, in the first year of King Alfred's reign. In 955, Alvediston was included in the Chalke valley land granted by King Edwy to the Abbess of Wilton.

Bowles and the *V.C.H.* differ in their histories of the early clergy. According to the latter, records show that John of Grimstead had the patronage or 'advowson' of the church, together with the manor which he also owned, and that he passed them to his son, Andrew, on his death in 1288. Although a vicar was drawn from this family in 1331, by 1299 the Abbess of Wilton was the patron until 1448, when she granted the whole prebendal estate of Chalke to Henry VI, who gave it to his newly-formed King's College, Cambridge the following year. The Oxford Dictionary describes a prebend as the part of the revenue of a cathedral or collegiate church granted to a canon or member of a 'chapter' as a stipend; also as the portion of land or the 'tithe' from which this stipend is drawn. A prebendary, therefore, is the one who holds the prebend and is an honorary canon. The prebendal estate of Chalke included the parish of Alvediston, and King's College retains patronage to this day, in spite of numerous changes to groupings of churches and parishes, apart from a brief spell back in the hands of the monarch, Edward IV, from 1461. He returned it to Wilton Abbey, but it was restored to King's College in 1475. There have been times when this little church and congregation have indeed been rather 'lonely and half lost', as Hutton described Alvediston, although the distance from its patron may have nothing to do with this. Indeed, the Collegium Regale from King's College choir gave a concert at Sandroyd School in April 2011, some proceeds from which were given to St. Mary's church restoration fund.

The regard in which the clergy were held in the early sixteenth century makes twenty-first century politicians positively glow in comparison. G.R. Elton, writing in 1955 about late medieval and early Tudor clergy makes some all-too familiar points:

Popular opinion all over Western Europe, though it preserved some respect for the Church as an institution, often treated its members with ribaldry. The literature of the later middle ages is full of stories which rely for their point on the peccadilloes of the priesthood; the hero of one discreditable adventure after another turns out to be a monk or clerk in secular orders.

The wealth of higher clergy, the greed of almost all, the startling poverty and ignorance of many parish clergy, the worldliness within the monasteries and the abuse of the collection of tithes compounded the indignation. The Church held about one third of all the land in England, but its administration thereof was generally so bad that anything awful could be believed of the those entrusted with its care ~ and the cure of souls. 'All in all, men were tired of being ruled or badgered by priests', (Elton). As he explains, once standards have fallen below tolerable levels the reality of what is going on matters less than the public perception of it, and it is that perception which forces change, sometimes in extreme directions. The Reformation in Henry VIII's reign was not motivated by doctrinal or intellectual argument so much as by anti-clericalism which was convenient for Henry when desire for a divorce from Catherine of Aragon brought him up against the Pope. Henry wanted a Church which would be his puppet, and Thomas Cromwell ably assisted him in increasing his power over both church and state. The monasteries were so weak and held in such disrepute by the time that they were dissolved that opposition was muted, especially in the south. In 1541, the manor of Alvediston, which had been part of the Wilton Abbey estate for almost six hundred years, was summarily passed to the Herbert family, (later Lords Pembroke.)

Henry's personal attitude to religion seems to have been overshadowed by his personal ambition, giving Protestantism a hold over England more by default than by design. His heir, Edward VI, however, was a passionate Protestant, so his commissions were instigated by religious motives even if executed by ambitious Protectors. By 1553, the year when church plate was 'rationalised' in the king's favour, there had been no sermon at St. Mary's for two years and services continued on a very irregular basis.

The sixteenth and seventeenth centuries were plagued by strife in the name of religion as Tudor and Stuart monarchs switched the country from Catholic to Protestant with alarming regularity, and the fact that a leading family, the Gawens, was staunchly Catholic must have brought the turmoil home to the tiny community in no uncertain terms. Mary's five years of fanatical Catholicism were followed by Elizabeth's forty-five year reign, characterised by 'caution and circumspection', (Elton). At first the Church favoured Catholic views on doctrine and on the pope's supremacy which brought it into direct conflict with the House of Commons. Elizabeth had to tread a line between the two that would not threaten her position. Before long, she had to agree to acts of supremacy, (making her supreme governor of church and state), and uniformity, ensuring that Protestantism was uniformly practised by fining those who refused to attend their parish church heavily. Threats from Spain throughout her reign only strengthened this legislation. Hence the Gawens' persecution.

The line of vicars was broken in 1584, a time which has already been noted as a low point in Alvediston church's history with the virtual collapse of the building, and a combined benefice was created, 400 years before the time that we now associate with a plethora of benefices, teams and general reorganisation. As ever, Broad Chalke became the centre and the vicar resided there, while Bowerchalke and Alvediston became satellite chapels, served by curates who did not usually live in Alvediston. In 1592, the recusant Thomas Gawen lost Norrington with two-thirds of his property after 215 years in the family, confiscated by the Crown and leased to a Protestant. By 1601 he was imprisoned in London for his faith and the reign of James I, a Scottish Presbyterian whose mother, Mary Queen of Scots was a Roman Catholic, began with the devastating events following the death and burial of Thomas Gawen. The story of Catherine Gawen's attempted retrieval of Norrington, her determination to bury her husband with his ancestors and her feisty defence in subsequent court proceedings makes fascinating reading now but at the time the community must have been riven with fear, suspicion and despair. During the 17th century Catholicism regained ground with James I and Charles I, and the Gawens were restored to Norrington but then the Civil War and the Commonwealth brought new uncertainty to Catholics, with the Gawens finally ousted in 1654. Meanwhile the Pembrokes, who owned the manor, found themselves increasingly at odds with the very monarchy to whom they owed their wealth and prestige, and ended up on the side of Parliament.

The unfortunately named vicar, John Sloper (perhaps unfairly putting one in mind of Obediah Slope of Trollope's Barchester novels set in this area 200 years later) presided at Broad Chalke for over fifty years from 1640 and sometimes cared for his chapels well, but in 1668 he was chided for providing neither curate nor services for Alvediston, and the old vicarage was 'much in decay'. It was demolished in the following century. The church was rebuilt during the 17th century, but it is not clear exactly when. The Restoration of Charles II and abdication of (Catholic) James II followed by (Protestant) Dutch William of Orange and Mary brought the century to a close. It is tempting to wonder how clergy maintained their integrity and got on with their job of the care of souls in their parish when the doctrines of the Established Church kept changing so radically. Interestingly, Ebbesbourne Wake remained separate from Alvediston for 380 more years. As an impoverished and probably undernourished curate was expected to walk over from Bowerchalke along muddy tracks and paths to take a service, 21st. century clergy shortages and the logistics of travelling up and down the Valley between services do not seem quite so grim, (especially if William Young's stories of the hapless cleric being refused admittance to the church on arrival by the choleric last Thomas King are to be believed.) Charles Bowles had very little good to say about prebendaries, and he chose the introduction to his *Ecclesistical History of Alvediston* to express his ire on the subject.

> This church is . . . part of what originally constituted the *prebendaryship* of *Chalke*, with its appendages; an office which entitled the person holding it, to certain portions of tithes within the parishes of Broad Chalke, Burgh Chalke, (or Bower Chalke,) and in this parish, and to nominate vicars in each place . . . The appointment of prebendaries, generally speaking, belongs to the diocesan' i.e. the bishop, 'and they were wont to assist him with their advice in the chapter room, when the good of the church was to be consulted; they were allowed commons from his table, or lived in community with him; and places or stalls, were provided for them in the cathedral or mother church, whilst seats were allotted to them in the chapter house, when matters, where their attendance was deemed essential, were to be discussed. These places, or stalls, in the cathedral church, still remain, bearing the name of the prebendary who has the right to use them, when present, but it seldom happens that such prebendaries are seen there. Peradventure, 'the prebendary might be on a journey,' or more happily situated in a rectory, or vicarage, with a wife and family, who, perhaps, would not willingly allow him to be absent, more particularly so, as the diocesan, in these our days, does not require the advice of such coadjutors.' He goes on to explain that prebendaries appointed by a religious house, such as Wilton Abbey, or another body, e.g. King's College, were in all other respects the same as the bishop's appointees. Clearly he was unimpressed by the systems of the church at a time of widespread laxity and lassitude.

Three years earlier, an anonymous writer chose Christmas Day to secrete a diatribe against the church in the Ebbesbourne Baptismal

Register, thirty-eight pages after the current entries:

> I trust the various abuses of the church will be rectified before this
> book is filled up to this. December 25, 1827. There are few parishes
> where the poor can be more abused than they are here. A few, when
> compared to the number of the poor, live by their labour and ill use
> them, why is this so?

Forty-six years and over three hundred entries later, the Rev.
Tupper Carey resolutely inscribed baptism details around the earlier
entry without obscuring any of the words. Mrs. Jill Painter happened
upon the protest in 1999; since then it has appeared in both editions
of Peter Meers' book on Ebbesbourne and now in this one. Such
publicity, albeit tardy, highlights the desperation felt at the time, but
Tupper Carey's lavish lifestyle during his thirty-six years' incumbency
does not appear to have abated after 1873.

In 1861, (the same year as Tupper Carey arrived), St. Mary's
had its own curate, who shortly afterwards became a vicar, and the
new vicarage was built in 1862. In the last sixty years change has
accelerated, with Alvediston joining Berwick St. John in 1945 (after the
departure of the last resident vicar), a new benefice of the parishes of
Ebbesbourne Wake with Fifield Bavant and Alvediston being formed
in 1963, and this being combined as one parish in 1970. (As an aside,
the confirmation of this in a letter to Alastair Fergusson, Secretary
of the Parish Church Council, quotes the Church Commissioners'
telegraphic address as 'Energetic – London – SW1.') When the
Chalke Valley West Benefice was formed in 1981 (from Broad Chalke
to Berwick St. John) the rector's patronage passed to the Bishop of
Salisbury and then, in 1995, the Chalke Valley Team Benefice was
created from Charlton All Saints to Berwick, with thirteen churches
and one redundant church spread along a distance of twenty miles.

~ Tithes, Clergy and Landowners ~

IN HER INTRODUCTION to *Tithe War 1918-1939 The Countryside in Revolt* (published by Media Associates) Carol Twinch explains how, in the past, a very complicated system of tithe-paying was in force. Each pocket of land was expected to raise money for the church. Originally based on Old Testament directions, it became a means of supporting monastic houses and the work of the clergy. All this was thrown into disarray at the Dissolution of the Monasteries, but, some 170 years later, Gilbert Burnet, then Bishop of Salisbury, chaired a committee which, in 1704, created 'Queen Anne's Bounty for the Augmentation and Maintenance of the Poor Clergy' to regularise tithing and to ensure that the proceeds went to support clergy. (All too recently Charles II had cheerfully used the proceeds to support his mistresses and their children!) The right to receive the tithe became firmly fixed in both civil and ecclesiastical law as a form of property tax but it was effectively regarded as a tax on agricultural land. The original intention that all should give one tenth of their produce to God as an 'offering' could be more easily avoided by those whose assets could not be mapped, and the tithe produced enormous friction between farmers and clergy, especially when there was a slump in agriculture or poor harvests, and naturally farmers often found imaginative ways to circumvent it. By the 1830s the situation was bitter and chaotic, not helped by both agricultural profits and standards in the church being exceptionally low nationally.

Charlotte Downes, née Grove, wife of the rector of Berwick St. John, found herself caught up in conflicts of loyalty on all sides, and her husband was: 'very fatigued and discomforted.' As part of Trow was in Berwick parish, the Rev. Downes came up against William Wyndham of Dinton, (owner of Norrington and a friend of the Grove family.) In April 1831 she wrote: 'Mr. Wyndham trying to alter the tithe of Norrington'. And in November: 'Mr. C. Bowles came here to settle the dispute of tythe between Mr. Wyndham and my husband.' This was the Charles Bowles who had just written the *Hundred of Chalke*, in which he described his attempts to research the tithe situation in Alvediston. He got so entangled in the web of conflicting information and interests, figures, responsibilities, acreages and field names that he concluded:

> The parliamentary survey should be searched, and from it something more satisfactory may be gained, and it might be worth the vicar's while to look into the matter.

It did not help much that there was no vicar of Alvediston at the time.

In 1836 the Tithe Commutation Act set a 'rent charge' on land based on a calculation of profits received from it, and no other business was expected to pay it. Also, it was levied indiscriminately on landowners, whether Anglican or Non-Conformist. In 1837, Charlotte Downes noted the friction between her husband and her land-owning father and brother, of Ferne, on the other side of Berwick. For Alvediston in 1842 the rent charge of £80 was levied; 19 years later this became the curates' salary, rising to £100 in 1867, supplemented by £16 per annum from King's College.

~ Information from the 'Church Book', 1799 – 1943 ~

FROM 1799 WE have a 'Church Book' to refer to; the problems encountered may seem mundane after the religious crises of the previous few centuries, but calm can turn to stagnation and there are always petty arguments and mysterious feuds to deal with. The accounts for the year 1799 -1800 were drawn up by the church warden, Thomas King, whose family feature large during the next forty years. The rate collected was £5. 4s. 4 ½d. This was before civil and ecclesiastical government were separated.

Bread and wine for the year cost 7s. 4d.; the clerk received wages of £1. 6s.; the churchyard was cleaned for 3s., the surplice and napkins were washed twice at a cost of 1s. 3d.; a besom, or broom made with bound twigs cost 2d., while the church book cost 6s. and £1. 8s. was spent on binding and repairing the Monitor's Bible and Prayer Book. Expenses for a visitation, by a bishop for confirmation, were £1. 4s. 6d. , while 8s. 10d. were paid for sparrows and 6d. for three stoats. A few years later, 6d. was paid for a 'Hedg Hog'. Since Henry VIII's time, various species of wildlife were considered vermin and prices were set for the bodies or heads of animals believed to threaten grain harvest e.g. 12d. was paid for the head of a badger in 1532. Hedgehogs were thought to milk cows lying down at night. The law was repealed in the 18th century, but evidently habits and means of remuneration died hard in Alvediston, so the custom remained. While most expenses are far greater now, it is worth noticing that some of the duties are undertaken voluntarily today, and any church warden rash enough to pay for the destruction of badgers and hedgehogs would risk the force of the law and wildlife charities.

In 1815-16 a new pulpit was erected and King himself paid for the painting of the church and for new pews. It was this Thomas King (who died in 1825), who left a bequest of £500 for the poor in his will, as indicated on the board to the south of the font:

By the will of the late Thomas King Esq. the interest of 500 pounds 3 pr. ct. con's [i.e. £500, 3%, consols] is bequeathed to be distributed by the minister and church wardens of this parish of Alvediston annually upon the 21 day of December among such of the labouring poor of the said parish as have not directly or indirectly received the relief from the Poor Rates the year preceding [21st. December is St. Thomas' Day].

This fund proved to be providential for a large number of residents over the years and continues today, amalgamated with Ebbesbourne Wake's Poor's Charity, and with a different remit, suitable for changed circumstances. Clearly the King family deserved a reputation for local service and generosity, yet the final Thomas King of Samways let the side down very badly, according to local legend recorded, gleefully, by William Young of Ebbsbourne Wake. As Young asserted that the King Fund was set up in response to a deathbed panic by 'wicked Tom King', who actually died in 1863, it is worth viewing the rest of his accusations somewhat circumspectly.

The true story behind the disappearance of Gould memorials during the 19th century is also difficult to unravel. Young would have us believe that 'wicked Tom King' was responsible for the removal and/or defacement of every reference to the Gould family in stone or register, due to Josiah Gould's claim to Samways, which he took to court. Charles Bowles refers to the north transept as 'the Gold's Aisle, under which are the remains of that family, and of their successors in the possession of the estate, the Kings,' and he describes 'a single stone in the wall, having on it a cheveron between three roses, the arms of Gold or Gould, empaling a fesse dancette, the arms of West de la War.' In fact the stone recovered from Ebbesbourne Wake churchyard in 1933, restored and placed near the font is commemorating the marriage of William Gould of Alvediston with Eleanor Chadwell of Ebbesbourne Wake in 1610 (a union which, according to the registers quoted by Bowles, produced eight children between 1611 and 1630.) In 1934 Lt. Col. J. Benett-Stanford of Pythouse, Tisbury, who had been consulted about the stone, wrote a memo to the Rev. Mr. Imrie Jones:

> I have gone very closely into the History of Wilts. and find the stone with the heraldic marks on it, now in the garden at Ebbesbourne Wake Vicarage, undoubtedly in 1810 was in the N. wall of your church.

By the accounts you so kindly showed me, the restoration or damage to your church was done in 1866.

Now it behoves you in the interests of archaeology to find out if there is any old man in the village who can give you any information as to why what the builders call rubbish, and which you and I call archaeological remains, were hauled to Ebbesbourne Wake.

It is tantalising that he does not identify the arms more closely and that we do not know if Mr. Jones discovered any information – or indeed if he heard similar tales to those written down by Mr. Young. Certainly, during the years of the last Thomas King's churchwardenship, records are very scanty, but there appear to have been services of Holy Communion four times a year. Mr King appears to have been church warden as late as 1855, and was among those called together in 1863, shortly before his death, to plan the refurbishment of the church.

In 1855 things were definitely tightened up. Joseph W.G. Rogers (a tenant of the Manor, whose memorial is to the right of the organ,) examined the accounts and he became parish churchwarden while James Parham, Norrington's tenant, the minister's warden. A named curate, albeit frequently changing, appears as chairman of the vestry. The sole control of the King family, whether benign or not, which had lasted for about sixty years, was finally broken. Lest it be thought that small congregations are a recent phenomenon, although ninety-two people turned up on Census Sunday in 1851, in 1864 only fifteen out of a congregation of eighteen received the sacraments at Communion which was celebrated monthly and on Easter, Whit and Trinity Sundays. Other weekly services would be Matins or Evensong.

In 1861 the Rev. Philip Soulieu Desprez was appointed first resident curate and then vicar, and the new vicarage was built. His successor wrote a note in the 1887 inventory under the title 'Benefaction... A Miss Rogers, sister of Mr. Rogers then residing in the Parish, seeing the forlorn state of the Parish without a Resident

Minister, sent a cheque of £500 to the Bishop of Salisbury (Hamilton) towards the building of a Parsonage. As her means were very small the family urged the Bishop to return it to them but the Bishop (acting as trustee) told them he had no power to do this. The sum was therefore offered to the Ecclesiastical Commissioners who met it with a similar grant. King's College also assisted – Lord Pembroke gave some land and the parishioners also assisted and the sum of £1,600 was thus raised and a Vicarage House was thus built in the year 1862 and first inhabited by Rev. P.S.Desprez who subsequently built the stables etc. with a balance from the House': a case of the Church of England being shamed into action by the exuberant generosity of a spinster lady in the face of opposition from her appalled family.

The following year 'it was resolved that steps should be taken to restore Alvediston Church and that a subscription list should be immediately entered upon for that purpose.' With William King as clerk, William Day, George and Henry Parham, John Matthews, John Rogers, Mr. Desprez, Mr. Mullins and Mr. King subscribed and the first job was to repair the roof temporarily and to put up a fence on the west side of the churchyard. Mr. Thomas Henry Wyatt, the diocesan architect, was engaged and the church was transformed. This Mr. Wyatt was from a long dynasty of architects, whose work has floated in and out of favour with the years. He was first cousin twice removed of James Wyatt, mentioned below, and one of his larger commissions locally was the Italianate church of St. Mary and St. Nicholas, Wilton. More often, as here, his style was Gothic. During the restoration the east window, inscribed 'To the glory of God and in memory of Sidney Lord Herbert, this window was erected by his widow' was included as a reminder of the Pembroke ownership of Alvediston Manor. This 1st. Baron Herbert, or Lord Herbert of Lea was half-brother of Robert, 12th. Earl of Pembroke. Their father George, 11th. Earl, was responsible for extensive alterations at Wilton House in the early years of the 19th century, engaging the architect James Wyatt. His second wife, Catherine Woronzow, was daughter of the Russian ambassador to London and she had five daughters and one son, Sidney, born in 1810 and remembered here. He rented Wilton House from the 12th. Earl who lived abroad. Sidney became Secretary of State at War at only thirty-five and was instrumental in Florence Nightingale going to the Crimea to organise nursing for wounded soldiers. He married Elizabeth à Court and had four sons and three daughters. He died in 1861, (a year before the 12th. Earl, who had no children), so two of his sons, George and Sidney, became 13th. and 14th. Earls of Pembroke respectively.

Thomas Wyatt removed the Wyndham tomb and railings, built the vestry and choir vestry, rebuilt the north transept and gave the chancel 13th century features, (and the floor his trademark tiles,) while the whole church was refurbished, including new pews. Only the tower and the window over the door escaped his attentions, hence the disgust of later observers.

The west window, depicting the Sermon on the Mount, with the words: 'Blessed are they who hunger and thirst after righteousness' across the top, was erected later, in 1881, by public subscription, in memory of Philip Soulieu Desprez, who died in 1879, having presided over the building of the vicarage and school as well as the restoration of the church.

An Aylward harmonium was installed; (did it, one wonders, cause the sort of distress and fury which Thomas Hardy describes in 'Under the Greenwood Tree'?) Coal first features in the accounts, firing the new boiler. At this time, too, in addition to churchwardens, two 'overseers' were appointed, often two or three of these offices were held by the same man, eg. Mr. Rogers from the Manor was church warden, overseer and waywarden in 1864. Overseers had to enforce the Poor Law and were entrusted with the dispersal of relief for the poor, while, in the last resort, the local workhouse was in Tisbury. The waywarden's responsibilities were roads, bridleways and footpaths.

Thus it is clear that whatever local government there was at parish level was still firmly in the remit of the church.

Once again, things go quiet under two vicars from 1880-92, the last ten years probably not being very satisfactory if the experience of teachers under the Rev. William Aron Woods are anything to go by, but then the parish was firmly taken in hand by a new vicar, (who rejoiced in the name of the Rev. Charles Ousby Trew,) his dedicated wife and two daughters. Formerly headmaster of Gillingham Grammar School, thirteen miles away, Mr. Ousby Trew must have been struck by the contrast between a growing railway town and a tiny, isolated village, so he set about pulling Alvediston into shape to face the 20th century. He very quickly called a vestry meeting which Messrs. Parham, Sims, Thatcher (schoolmaster and organist) and Mullins attended. Mr. Parham was elected churchwarden and Mr. Mullins, clerk. (In the 1881 census, William Mullins was landlord of the Crown, his mother, Sarah, had kept the shop at the Cross, and he had previously been a carrier. Although born in Alvediston, he does not appear in the 1891 census, by which time Ann Compton ran the pub, but he evidently returned later and played an important part in the village.) The meeting was adjourned for a month by which time word of the new vicar's arrival had got around and he noted 'a large number present.' However, 'No accounts were presented nor could they be found.' Moreover Mr. Mullins complained that the previous vicar owed him over £10, a considerable sum, 'and it was decided he should be written to.' By the following year the accounts had surfaced, were presented and passed, but in 1894 Mr, Ousby Trew paid the balance of £6. 10/3d. with the ultimatum that he 'could not in future be responsible for the churchwarden's accounts.' However, he and his wife continued to subsidise most of their initiatives.

One of his first jobs was to oversee the entire renovation of the vicarage which, although only thirty years old, had been left 'completely out of repair.' Meanwhile, the first record of the King Charity (in

1893) showed that almost half of the forty-one recipients were unable to write their name, so signed with their 'mark', a cross. Writing of the fourteenth century, Ian Mortimer calculated that 'only' a twentieth of the rural population could read. Progress over five centuries seems slow. The vicar records that on his arrival 'the school was condemned but by prompt action was placed in such a condition as to have honourably passed in October 1893' . . . 'Mr. and Mrs. Thatcher worked at it continuously.' The church and school both benefited from decent leadership and co-operation. Other educational initiatives included a night school, (which failed in a year), a Reading Room, (possibly the Meeting House recorded as being built and opened in 1894, and later known as the 'Hut'), a weekly children's service and a Sunday School in the Vicarage with Mrs. Trew. On the practical side, the Trews initiated and heavily subsidised: a Penny Bank, a Clothing Club, a Coal Club, branches of the Church of England Temperance Society, the Girls' Friendly Society and the Mothers' Union; accounts for the 'Sick and Needy' and for a school piano were set up, while the King Charity, 'found to be in a state of deficiency', was sorted. The guidance for the trustees included:

– tickets should be on a house of business preferred by the recipient' i.e. a type of voucher system was used rather than cash.

– the remaining members of a family should not be cut off because one had received relief

– everyone in the parish except the Trew, Sims, Parham and White families were eligible

– up to twenty should be children

– the length of residence should not be a consideration

– illegitimate children should not be recognised, nor their mother, (a new condition which seems draconian today, but should be seen in the context of late Victorian morality. Needless to say, plenty of children born out of wedlock had always been quietly incorporated into extended families.)

Others who contributed to the various accounts were Lord Pembroke, Mr. and Mrs. Gray of Samways, William Wyndham the owner of Norrington and his tenant, Mrs. Parham, G.B. Matthews of the Manor, a Miss Crosier who does not appear on the 1891 census, and King's College. It is clear that the wealthier members of society took their responsibilities to the poor seriously, or could be lent upon to do so, but that the paternalistic attitudes which could bring much good to communities when outside help was lacking also left poorer people at the mercy of the consciences of the more powerful.

One other organisation which flourished was the Guild of Ringers, whose rules were, unsurprisingly, drawn up by C.O.Trew.

RULES OF THE GUILD OF RINGERS

No person who is not a member is allowed in the belfry.

No talking, smoking, drinking allowed.

All reasonable care to be taken of the bells.

All members to obey the senior member present.

Each member to be a confirmed member of the Church of England, attending service once at least on Sunday, and if possible a communicant.

Any member may be suspended or, if the offence be sufficiently serious, expelled for any breach of the above laws.

Members of the Guild who duly agreed to the rules were: Charles Ousby Trew, William Mullins, James Pothecary, (the Samways shepherd), Sidney Johnson, A. Mullins, John Topp and Charles Stanley (who, in the 1891 census, were aged 12 and 13 respectively and who were both agricultural labourers.) Frank Roberts has a marvellous story which must date back to about this time and illustrates either the need for a guild of ringers or, if from the Ousby-Trew era or later, the rapid waning of interest. On Sunday Mornings Joe Roberts, Frank's great-uncle, used to feed one herd of cattle at Elcombe Farm, walk up to Bigly to feed another, then hurry down to clean up and be at church by 10.40 to chime all three bells, one rope in each hand and the other looped over his foot.

Church business included general repairs: new lamps, prayer, hymn and carol books, Bibles and hassocks; bell inspection, ropes and repairs; heating apparatus and harmonium repairs. Sunday services were held at 11.15 a.m. (Matins with a short sermon), 6 or 6.30 p.m. (Evensong), with Holy Communion on the second Sunday at 8 a.m. and on the fourth at 11.15 instead of Matins. Sunday School was held in the Vicarage at 10.30 a.m. and 2.30 p.m. except when there was an afternoon Children's Service. (This hectic church schedule was all held in one tiny village, but at least the vicar only had a few steps to travel. Now we get two services per month, taken by a rapidly dwindling clergy team covering the whole valley, or lay people.) Offertories were taken for the first time to meet expenses.

There seems little that the redoubtable Rev. Charles Ousby Trew, aided by his wife, did not think of and the reforms are recorded with dizzying intensity. However, changes were afoot in the wider world. At a vestry in 1892 'Answers (were) given to Questions in the *Salisbury Times*.

What is the feeling about the Parish Council Act?' Trew's summary of the response perfectly evokes English parish politics: 'At first there was no interest, then great enthusiasm, then, after the act was explained the interest waned and now it is a matter of utter indifference.'

2 The provision of allotments: it seems that many were available at a reasonable rent. They were situated on the small glebe land, where the bungalow 'Shortlands' now stands.

3 Small holdings: there were several but some people were

waiting for the outcome of the parish Councils Act before committing themselves. (In 1894, the death of a Mr. King led to the reversion of land to Lord Pembroke, which he offered to let in small holdings.)

4 Water; there was a 'considerable number of deep wells but some cottages were deficient.'

5 Parish needs for a parish meeting or parish council. Again, the Rev. Trew makes pertinent comments: 'It is extremely doubtful whether even a Parish Meeting would be representatively attended and very uncertain whether a Parish Council would be elected or not. The state of the by-roads and the road communication with the centres of industrial life are matters which unless seen to will lead to the utter blotting out of villages like this one.

It is worth mentioning that a well-attended Parish Meeting was held early in 2007 in the 'Crown' inn, the first of biannual meetings. The state of the roads continues to be a much-discussed problem, but, in spite of potholes and flooding, communication with 'centres of industrial life' is possible, while communication via broadband and mobile phone is more contentious.

In November 1893, a Parish Meeting was held in the school, so presumably some consensus was reached before the Parish Councils Act was passed two years later. The meeting mainly recorded protests: at the threat to the individuality of the parish and against Tisbury Highway Authority for refusing to repair the Down and Church roads. A collection of goods and money was made for Salisbury Infirmary and 'only 2 expressed a wish for the Reading Room and no-one wished for a Night School' so the Rev. Ousby Trew's plans for adult education were being eroded. Finally, the power of the church in local affairs was curbed in 1895, as they were separated into ecclesiastical business (to be dealt with by the Vestry) and non-ecclesiastical (to be dealt with by the Parish Council or Meeting.) This arrangement holds today, except that the Vestry is called the Parochial Church Council, comprising members from Ebbesbourne Wake, Fifield Bavant and Alvediston, and now held with Bowerchalke's P.C.C. Anomalies remain, however, as the two semi-detached cottages at the top of Castle Hill are under the Parish Council of Alvediston, in spite of adjoining West End, which belongs to Ebbesbourne Wake Parish Council! Village priorities are demonstrated in a sad little note recording that, at a Vestry meeting called for April 13th. 'not a single person attended. C.O.Trew Vicar.'

However the new, secular Parish meeting got off to a flying start with Mr. Parham as chairman. Another disappointment for C.O.Trew followed when his 14 votes for office of parish councillor were dwarfed by the Non-Conformist Mr. Sims' 22. Notwithstanding, he assiduously recorded developments, notably that the new road over the downs to Tisbury 'which had been agitated for' was agreed at a cost of £100, half of which was subscribed locally. The Kelly's Directories prior to this graphically describe the reason for the agitation:

> [Alvediston] lies for the most part in a deep bottom or hollow, on the left of the road leading from Salisbury to Shaftesbury: from which the usual mode of approach by pedestrians from Tisbury via Swallowcliff' [*sic* and incidentally, the route for the post] is the ascent by means of foot holes in the almost perpendicular northern side of White Sheet Hill, the great exertion consequent upon which is repaid by the beautiful and commanding view of the surrounding country obtained before making a nearly sudden descent on the opposite side of the hill into Alvediston below.

As the vicar noted in 1898 that 'the cure of Ansty necessitated the Celebration Sundays being the 2nd. and the 4th.' one imagines that he was mightily relieved by the provision of a road. Things moved swiftly and the new road was opened for traffic in 1896. In the same year, 16 out of the 39 residents receiving the King's Charity had to mark with a cross rather than a signature. There was still a long way to go on the literacy front.

Two reports about the Golden Jubilee celebrations ring a now familiar note. At a meeting at the Vicarage, with Mr. Parham in the chair, 'suggestions for a general feast, and a bonfire were well received ~ and a suggestion by the Vicar for the supply of the village with water was heartily approved. On minor points much discord was manifested and the meeting finally broke up without any plan.' Nevertheless, in the event, a supper for the whole parish was held in the loft at the Tower, (the current name for Samways) and there was a bonfire on Middle Down. Special services were held in church on the previous Sunday and there was a Flower Service to raise funds for sick children at Salisbury Infirmary, (a regular recipient of funds and goods in those pre-N.H.S. days.) 'A small committee carried all out satisfactorily.'

In 1898 Mr. Sims was re-elected as district Councillor and events were summarised thus: 'Sundry improvements were mooted at the parish meeting but little done. Some perturbation was caused by the statement that the Tower Estate had changed hands' (a rumour which proved groundless, but which would affect many families). One of the vicar's last duties was to officiate at the marriage of Miss Parham of Norrington, and then he departed in August for Upchurch in Kent. Ironically Upchurch almost adjoins Gillingham, so the headmaster of Gillingham School in Dorset moved to the rapidly expanding Gillingham in Kent after six years' striving to ensure that a tiny village was not 'blotted out.' One hopes that his efforts in Kent were appreciated. It is easy to imagine that he was discouraged by local intransigence and bewilderment but he clearly cared deeply and Valerie Trew, researching family history in 1999, came across references to the marriage of Winifred Trew (presumably one of the daughters) after their departure from Alvediston, and reports that a few sprays of white geraniums 'sent by the parishioners of Alvediston, Wilts.' were tucked into the ribbon of her bouquet, and that the bride and groom received a present of photographs of the parish of

Alvediston 'with signed address.' Such personal tokens suggest that the family was held in real affection and possibly, as so often happens, the parish appreciated his worth more after he had left than when he was serving it.

This detailed record of six years of parish life is included because it covers so many aspects of life in Alvediston at a time of change and just before the turmoil of the early years of the twentieth century. It was also a time when the authority of the church was coming into question nationally as the Christian faith was facing unprecedented challenges theologically, morally and culturally. Queen Victoria was an aging recluse who, in spite of the fervour of the Jubilee, was losing respect and her entirely different son was waiting in the wings, espousing the new freedoms that would characterise the Edwardian era. The Rev. Charles Ousby Trew battled onwards for the church and for what he believed were the best interests of the local people as a 'Christian soldier'.

The new incumbent was the Rev. Arthur Wilfrid Baynham, another Oxford graduate who had served as a chaplain in Her Majesty's Services in India on the Bombay Ecclesiastical Establishment. At this time the church building, windows, pews, pulpit etc., plate, bells and clocks (which have since disappeared) were insured for a total of £1,000. Half yearly income totalling £53. 3s. 8d. came from Queen Anne's Bounty, the three main landowners, (all of whom were absentee at this time,) the church commissioners, rent for glebe and a contribution from King's College. Expenditure on a church clock, insurance, heating, lighting and 'sundries including sick relief', but not the vicar's stipend, came to £9. 8s. 3 ½ d.

Rev. Baynham's period of office was characterised by energy on the church fabric and furnishings front. In June 1899 'a handsome oak and walnut Eagle Lectern was presented to the church by Mrs. Parham of 3 Mount Ephraim Rd. Streatham and used for the first time on Whit Sunday. The lectern is the work of Mess. Wippell &

Co., Exeter.' The old lectern, recorded in 1887 as having brackets for candles, was offered to Fifield Bavant church two years later, but a more modern one is in place there now.

The choir numbered fourteen and included several still-familiar names: Jack and Ernest Topp, Charles and Walter Stanley, Albert and Walter Mullins, Alfred Coombs, Joseph, Charles and George Compton, Edmund Jones and Walter Smith, with Mr. Thatcher the schoolmaster, who was the organist. On Easter Day, 1900, the choir wore cassocks and surplices for the first time. New gates were made and installed by Osmund of Tisbury in 1900-01 and at that time the coal merchant was changed from Alford of Tisbury to the local George Compton. With the coal-fired boiler and oil-lamps, cleaning was quite a task, and Jane Topp became the first paid cleaner in 1901. She was also responsible for washing all the choir surplices.

As church heating remains a perennial problem, it is worth noting how it was tackled a hundred years ago. 'Hot air heating repaired in 1902,' we read in the Church Book, 'and thereby resulting in half the consumption of coal. Lighted on Sunday a.m. and well filled up and allowed to burn out, in this way the furnace gets well heated and remains hot all day. The principle of it is that the cold air comes in thro' the grating in the floor and comes hot into the Church through the gratings above.' While the current system leaves much to be desired, the temperature is at least marginally raised by the mere flick of a switch.

In January 1903 the Rev. Mr. Baynham left for Somerset. In his retiring statement he noted that the Vicarage was insured for £1,000 at a premium of 16/5d., the Church for £1,200 at 10/5d. and the School for £400 at 6/3d. which may be worth comparing with current prices for a little idea of inflation. His successor, Rev. George Wynne, very soon set about making his mark by commissioning a cross and pair of candlesticks in brass from a Mr. Ramsden. Ramsden and Carr went on to become famous for their work in silver as well as brass, and were

Arts and Crafts design candlesticks by Omar Ramsden and Alwyn Carr, 1904, made for Alvediston church, and now in Wiltshire Heritage Museum, Devizes.

therefore increasingly unlikely to undertake such work as this. The design was agreed by the Vestry in May, and he wrote in August that he hoped that the commission would be ready for the Bishop's visitation in October, 1904, for a confirmation. These large, splendid but somewhat impractical and ornate items adorned the altar for many years and can be seen in the photograph of the interior of the church at this time. By 1997, a smaller, simpler cross and candlesticks were always used and the safe storage of the now valuable 1904 set became impossible, so they were sold at auction to help finance repairs. Fortunately they were bought by Devizes Museum and may be seen there.

Mr. Wynne noted that, as well as the church wardens, 'about 15 other parishioners ~ quite a gathering' turned up for the Easter Vestry in 1906, but did not disclose the reason for the excitement, and things

Revd. and Mrs Wynne outside the Vicarage. Mr Wynne was vicar, 1903-10. (Pat Scrivens)

returned to normal in subsequent years. By the time he left, in 1909, only one King's Fund recipient could not sign his name. In January of that year Mr. Thatcher died; as well as being the local schoolmaster, he was the church organist and had been church warden for nine years, providing a valuable link between two prominent local institutions. A reading desk was donated to the church in his memory and is to be found in the choir vestry, where it now holds a notebook for prayer requests.

During the next decade, there were four vicars and at least one lengthy interregnum, not to mention the local reverberations from the First World War. Of the twenty-two men currently living in the village who served, three were killed, as was one other whose family had moved to Romsey, dying of his wounds at home. The lives of others and their families were irrevocably changed. As the church clerk, William Mullins, was called up in 1916 there was not even continuity in that role.

The Rev. W.H. Courteen arrived in 1918, as the servicemen began to return. In spite of all this upheaval, the names of inhabitants receiving the King's Charity scarcely changed, while Mr. Parham of Norrington and Mr. Hoole of Samways were churchwardens together from 1912 until the church book ended in 1943.

The Rev. E. Imrie Jones followed in 1928, having previously been incumbent at the thriving village of Imber which, being in a prime position on Salisbury Plain, was evacuated in 1943, and subsequently destroyed, despite promises to the contrary, (see *Little Imber on the Down* by Rex Sawyer.) Mr. and Mrs. Jones are remembered well by a number of local people, Mr. Jones rather more fondly than his wife. Their children were Harry, who was ordained and served in parishes in Devon; Christine, who lived in Salisbury and was buried in the churchyard in 2004; Trevor, who was killed in an air raid in Romsey in the war and David, who emigrated to Australia. Christine remembered the Vicarage being freezing cold, and another abiding impression was of 'clearings' at various points around the village, e.g. at the crossroads and near the church gate, where people met for a passing chat. Because almost everyone worked locally, had little or no transport other than their feet or bicycle and no television to distract them they could spend far more time with their neighbours. Mr. Jones would do his parish visiting on his pushbike with one of his children perched precariously on the bar. On arrival at the chosen house, he would simply prop his bicycle up against the wall, leaving his offspring straddled. Harry apparently used to organise children's parties in the village hall with such military zeal that his sister still remembered them with some embarrassment seventy years later.

Other stories from the vicarage at this time come from Dave Collis, now the Tisbury greengrocer, who was brought up at Crookhill and whose uncle Joe Collis worked in the Vicarage garden. He had lost a leg due to a football accident and wore a wooden 'peg' leg. To avoid trampling worked ground, he put a plank across the garden when he was digging it but unfortunately, he once forgot where he was, stepped off the plank and his wooden 'leg' sunk eighteen inches into the soil. To extricate it he first had to take it off. Another of his jobs was to mend the vicar's pushbike. Again, absent-mindedness got the better of him when he forgot to put new brake blocks in properly, so the hapless Mr. Jones took off down the hill at reckless speed to be faced with the split-second decision of whether to ride 'smack into the gate' or to land in the deep mud beside it. Oral history being what it is, both outcomes are recited, with equal hilarity, and the impression is that Mr. Jones took it all in good part. Not all clerical misadventures could be excused by Joe's absent-mindedness, however. The evening routine at the vicarage was that he should pump water to fill the tank before knocking off at 5 p.m. However, he had a little cocoa tin which he used to push through the kitchen window to young Reg Marks, (who worked in the house briefly until he managed to extricate himself under the pretext of 'toothache' one day and refused to return.) Upon Reg filling it with water, Joe would retrieve it and pour the water all over the tank so that it would look as if it was full to overflowing and then take himself off home avoiding Mrs. Jones' lengthy list of jobs which he was inclined to supplement with notes such as 'and make a few bricks in your spare time!' History does not relate how often he got away with this ruse. He is remembered riding a fixed wheel bicycle and local boys used to help to push him along. Christine Richardson remembered Joe's successor too, either Mr. Coombes or Mr. Mullins. The vicarage children used to enjoy taking his tea out to him, served in a cup and saucer. They watched, intrigued, as he held the cup in one hand and gestured with the saucer, pointing out fields where he had worked. Many of those employed as gardeners in the country were retired farm labourers. The 1925 Kelly's Directory gives both C. Coombes and W.W. Mullins as carters, the former also ran the Post Office with his wife.

Mr. and Mrs. Jones never really recovered from the shock

of Trevor's death, and Mr. Jones used the pretext of his increasing deafness to hasten his retirement in 1942. The Rev. Mr. Rae took over for two years until he, too, retired. Remembered most for his tendency to enjoy a tipple and for his humming, he was known as 'Hummer Rae'.

~ *1945 onwards* ~

FINALLY, THE REV. Mr. Poole both came and went in 1945. Thus, after eighty-four years and twelve clergy, the line of resident vicars ended once more, at a time when the whole country was facing readjustments after the Second World War. However, some things retained their usefulness, e.g. the King's Charity which still had twenty-eight people on its books in 1946, receiving between 5/- and 14/- per annum. Miss Cooper, the retired schoolmistress who became the first female church warden in 1948, moved into the former vicarage with Betty Wynne, daughter of a former vicar. Pat Scrivens remembers her mother, Dolly Lodge, doing Miss Cooper's laundry. Collecting it would not have been too unpopular a job with the Lodge children, as Miss Cooper used to leave a little gift out with her laundry. Pat also remembers picking primroses from the bank behind the Old Vicarage on Good Friday, to decorate the church for Easter. Violets were collected for the new innovation of a Mothering Sunday service in 1945. The churchyard was extended in 1948, courtesy of Mr. Sims, hence a number of graves from the following years are up a steep bank along the northern boundary of the churchyard. Primroses still flourish, the first ones appearing along that bank, as do snowdrops, cowslips and ox-eye daisies. As ever, churchyard maintenance periodically became a problem and in 1953, Mr. Topp organised a group of helpers aided, some years later, by the introduction of a motor scythe. Over the summer months this became

St Mary's Church, c. 1960, soon after George and Pay Grant arrived at Church Farm, with one of their Welsh black cows seen on the right of the photograph. (Pat Scrivens)

a regular village activity, until Alastair Fergusson and Anthony Bullen (who lived on either side of the church) undertook to mow half the area each, carefully circumnavigating cowslips, and their successors continue the tradition of maintaining the churchyard. All these people, and those who have cleaned, arranged flowers, laundered linen, played the organ and acted as sacristan and sidesmen and women, as well as those who have served on the Parochial Church Council, the earlier Vestry and as churchwardens have contributed to the life of the church and community in an invaluable way.

The church and social life of the village remained inextricably linked, although there was a slight tussle over the schoolroom. Len Frampton had rented the school house for many years and the schoolroom had been used on an ad hoc basis with church permission. However, by 1954 the social committee, comprising:

Peter Topp, George and Tony Lodge, Mrs. B. and Miss B. Marks, J. Whaten, Miss Hayward, Mrs. Lodge and Mrs Moxham (mostly familiar names today) had been going for six years and wanted to buy the room as a village hall. Mr. Frampton agreed to buy the house from Salisbury Diocesan Council of Education, which was prepared to sell the schoolroom for £100 plus expenses. This sum proving hard to raise, the Church Commissioners loaned £150, to be repaid in annual instalments of £30, but they stipulated that it should be called the 'Parish Room' rather than 'Village Hall', to denote the continuing church connection. Diocesan aspirations for its use included services, meetings, conferences, 'physical and mental training and recreation and moral and intellectual development through the medium of reading and recreation rooms, library, lectures, classes, recreations and entertainments...' Memories of the Rev. Charles Ousby Trew's ambitions are stirred on reading this, but local recollections are of darts, table tennis, dances and wedding receptions: in reality, a village hall, and as such it was known.

To return to the church itself, twentieth century advances were impinging gradually. In April 1957 'a discussion took place about installing electric light in the church. It was decided to leave any discussion until after the Fete which would take place on Aug. 3rd.' By August, it was hoped to have an evening service if the new occupants of the vicarage, Mr. Cathcart Kay and his mother, would let the church have a supply of electric current from his house. The church electricity supply continues to be closely dependent on its neighbours: strenuous efforts to establish why the entire supply to the house to the west dipped significantly whenever lights or heaters were turned on in the church proved inconclusive to the end of the century, and Jill Bullen's printing work was frequently impeded. The heating system cannot work fully as the supply is too low, (albeit just within the legal limit).

By the 1960s, there was concern at the decline in numbers at services due to the departure of several church-going families and disaster struck the ailing heating system during the arctic winter of 1962-3. The pipes froze and the whole system collapsed. Ominous little notes such as: 'General Dewing had been able to remove the heavy black pipes which were in front of the recumbent figure of a knight in the Norrington aisle' almost restore one's faith in the much-maligned faculty system. Pevsner had noted depairingly a little earlier that the fourteenth century monument was 'displayed in the south transept behind heating pipes.' Whether the dog at the knight's feet lost his nose during the installation or removal of these pipes, or in some other misadventure is not clear. Although the faculty process causes anguish and frustration to many a P.C.C. it can check some of the more cavalier 'improvements' to churches, much as the early heating may have been appreciated. With a new system now an imperative, electricity was finally installed for both heating and lighting, followed by experimentation with several organs, the penultimate one being a Compton Mellotone with 'two manuals, pedals, balanced swell, separate damp-chaser and loudspeaker; overhauled recently; suitable church or home' as advertised in the 'Church Times' of November 8, 1974. Unfortunately, the purchaser found that, on removal from the damp atmosphere of the church, substantial repairs were required so the tone of his correspondence waxed increasingly peevish. Most recently, a fine two-manual pipe organ, built by Brian Daniels and still tuned and serviced by him (2011) was installed in 1975, and this has proved a success.

Many of the names occurring at the end of the church book are familiar today, and these people are either still part of the community or remembered with great affection. Mrs. Dolly Lodge, daughter of George and Jane Compton of the Crown, was a church warden and also, with Mrs. Mullins, cleaned the church and arranged flowers for many years. George Kellow was another church warden who kept the old boiler going for winter services and who, until recently, cleaned the church with his wife Mary and daughter-in-law Pat Scrivens (née Lodge.) The Topp family also helped in many ways. Major-General Richard Dewing, CB, DSO, MC, and his wife, Nell, moved to the village when Church Farm was sold, and renamed the farmhouse Church Cottage. Alastair and Judith Fergusson, writing in 2000, remembered them with great fondness. He was born in 1891, fought and was decorated, in both world wars, and later ran a market garden in Suffolk with his wife. They landscaped the garden at Church Cottage, and were also remembered for their hospitality and humour, in spite of suffering the bereavement of three of their four children, and for his 'characterful' Jack Russell, 'to whom he talked vociferously while they walked together every day.' Also, 'Mrs. Dewing (Nell) was the Treasurer of the PCC for many years. She had an excellent system for the safe keeping of church collections, based on a Fortnum and Mason's biscuit tin', which continued to be used for many years after they moved to be near their surviving son, in Scotland. Tristram Sykes of Norrington first became church warden in 1959 and held that post at his death in 2006, together with several other crucial jobs in the parish and the team benefice. Anthony and Jill Bullen were church wardens and fulfilled many other roles in the church ~ Jill's flower-arranging and printing skills were much appreciated. Judith Fergusson played the organ and was P.C.C. secretary, Alastair was treasurer. Mrs. Annabel Hillary and Amanda Vesey are also remembered for their contributions to church life, as are many more. Anthony Eden, Lord Avon, lived at the manor for his later years and his grave to the south of the church is frequently visited. This has now been supplemented by the memorial to him opposite the door. Today a large proportion of residents has a strong commitment to the church and, although services have to be adjusted to cater for declining numbers of clergy, they are much appreciated by the congregation. The side chapel is ideal for quieter, more meditative occasions and many visitors appreciate the fact that the church is kept open. It has also been used over the years for concerts and exhibitions, and in 2007, fund-raising for major restoration work was launched, under the chairmanship of Robin Garran, with a party in the candlelit building. With grants, donations, concerts, an Open Village day and a great deal of work by Robin and members of the community, sufficient was raised to restore the roof and windows, undertake internal decorations and replace electrical fittings, with the hope that the church will continue to be loved and used by many generations to come. Most recently, Christmas Eve 2010 saw the first Carol Service for many years. A wooden crib had been made by Richard Trahair to house figures donated by the Rev. Roger Redding, who blessed the crib and led the service in a full church. Despite snow, ice and treacherous conditions eighty-five people walked, slid or were shuttled to the church where candles and mulled wine helped to ameliorate the bitter cold.

Alvediston Church of England School

IN 1870, UNIVERSAL primary education became compulsory under the Education Act. Prior to that, schools were set up on an ad hoc basis: a local woman might take children into her home for lessons or teach them in part of the church, as Susannah Young the blacksmith's wife did in Ebbesbourne Wake until the National School opened in 1851. Sometimes a 'School House' was purpose built. Charlotte Downes, (nee Grove), set up a school in her husband's parish of Berwick St. John in 1835. In the *Victoria County History*, (*V.C.H.*) we read that there was a day school in Alvediston in 1818; fifteen years later, twenty children are recorded as attending school in the village, and in 1859 an inspection reports that thirty infants were taught in a cottage by Miss Kate Carley, the twenty year-old adopted daughter of Joseph and Harriet Pike. Mrs. Pike was mistress of the school in Ebbesbourne, and Miss Carley, an ex-pupil teacher, was recorded in the 1867 Kelly's Directory as mistress of a National School, so the idea of schooling was not a novel one. However, the Education Act came at a crucial time for rural villages, as agriculture entered a protracted decline from the mid 1870s. The school and teacher's house still standing on the cross roads near the Crown inn were built between 1870 and 1872 at the instigation of the first resident vicar for nearly three hundred years, the Rev. Philip Soulieu Desprez. From October 1874 until its closure in July 1922, we have two schoolbooks chronicling the education of local children, the vicissitudes of the

Date	Teacher	Vicar / 'Correspondent'
1874	K. House	Rev. Philip Soulieu Desprez
1875	Miss Louisa Hancock	
1879		Rev. Desprez died
1880	Miss Hancock married	
	Mr. Young;	Rev. William Aron Woods
	– Mrs. Young	
1883	Miss Florence Thick, (locum tenens)	
1884	Miss Mary Ann Edmunds	
1886	Miss Harriet Mary Forth, Jan. – Feb.	
	Mr. J.M. Tucker, Mar. – Dec.	
1887	Mr. William Pinyon, Jan. – Sept.	
	Miss Annie K. Schollick, Oct.	
1888	Mr. William Henry Pimlott, Feb.	
1891	Mr. W. K. Woods, Jan. – Feb.	
	Mr. and Mrs. Thatcher, Mar.	
1892		Rev. Charles Ousby Trew
1898		Rev. Arthur Wilfrid Baynham
1903		Rev. G. Wynne
1907	Mr. Thatcher died	
1908	Mrs. Thatcher retired,	
	Miss Dorothy Cooper	
1909		Rev. W. A. Keith Douglas
1913		Rev. J.H. Batten
1915		Rev. J.A. Alexander
1918		Rev. Wilfred Henry Courteen
1922	School closed	

teachers, the influence of weather and illness and the significant effect of individual clergy on the Church of England school.

The book starts with 'Particulars as to the size of Alvediston

School'. The School Room was 28 by 16 feet, reaching 15 feet at its highest point down to 10 feet 10 inches at the sides. This total area of 448 square feet for up to 50 children compares with primary accommodation guidelines for a school of 90 pupils in 2007 of approximately 500 square metres, (well over 5,000 square feet), of which more than 3,000 square feet are to be dedicated to teaching purposes, and the rest to a multitude of other needs for the smooth running of a twenty-first century school. The brand new school opened in Broad Chalke in 2007, attended by a number of children from this village, illustrates the vast changes in provision in a hundred and thirty-four years.

The first entry in the Alvediston School book reads:

Very good attendance. Visited by the Revd. P.S. Desprez on Monday, Tuesday and Friday. Tuesday afternoon taught 3rd. class simple Addition ~ Wednesday afternoon took the eldest children to Church, being Harvest Thanksgiving ~ Thursday morning gave an Object Lesson on Tin to the first, second and third classes ~ Friday afternoon taught Standard 1 simple subtraction. Oct. 10th. 1874, K. House.

This demonstrates several strands typical of education at the time. The first, obviously, is the importance of the local clergy and of the church calendar, which was closely allied with the local economy of agriculture. Much of this still pertains to country church schools. However, the sheer pressure of dealing, as a lone teacher, with children of so many ages, stages and abilities at the same time and in the same room, albeit divided into numerous classes and 'standards' is the stuff of nightmares. Managing to insert some simple addition and subtraction into the day must have seemed like an achievement of some magnitude. 'Object lessons' feature regularly, and covered such diverse subjects as Cocoa, Copper, Silver, a Cup and Saucer, a Teapot, the Horse, a Book, a Slate, a Desk, a Sheep, a Buttercup etc. but it is not quite clear what lesson was drawn from them. Other subjects included History, covering topics such as Ancient Britain, the Battle of Hastings, the Conquests of Ireland and Wales, Joan of Arc and the wars of the Roses, while Geography tackled 'Possessions in Asia and British North America' with a confidence about the place of England in the world which was natural to the time but quite alien today. Her Majesty's Inspectors were assiduous in their annual examination, accompanied by the local vicar and another clergyman from a neighbouring village, usually at this time the Rev. Tupper Carey from Ebbesbourne.

By November 1874, discipline was being exercised: ('Gave Crook Hill children a lesson after school, being a punishment for loitering about on the road') and attendance was reduced by the elder children being 'kept home for potatoeing' (sic). In November this would be for digging potatoes; April saw another dip in attendance for potato planting.

'Miss Louisa Hancock entered upon the duties of School Mistress of Alvediston School on Feb. 1st. 1875' wrote the vicar with justifiable satisfaction, for Louisa Hancock gave the new school over seven years of service before moving on to Ebbesbourne Wake school in November 1883. Mr. Desprez visited most days and sometimes Mr. Carey came over to see how the new school was faring. The first 'Harvest Holidays' were taken from 23rd. August to 4th. October, although attendance had dropped during the previous week as children were already helping in the cornfields, and some years the first week or so after the harvest Holiday was disrupted by children finishing gleaning well into October. The dates of these holidays varied from year to year, reflecting the community's deep relationship with agriculture and the weather. Although this was one of a series of disastrous harvests, haymaking and harvest generally took place much later than today.

The verdict of the inspection a year after Miss Hancock's arrival was:

> The present teacher has shewn (sic) much aptitude for her work. The children are in good order and have passed on the whole a fair examination. The Reading of the Second Standard and the Arithmetic of the First and Third Standards were weak today. The keeping of Registers needs attention.

Checking the registers to ensure both regular attendance and good timekeeping by pupils was an important part of the vicar's role, and one which led to truculence and acrimony in future years.

On or near St. Thomas' Day, 21st. December, numerous children were absent for a village custom. The distribution of the Thomas King Charity, (the background to which is given in the chapters on the church and Samways), was decreed on this day but, it being a charity for 'the labouring poor', it had become an important day in the village calendar and the children's involvement is variously, and none to enthusiastically, described as 'going to the Vicarage to receive charity' (1875) and 'begging' (1876). Carol singing for financial reward seems to have been an enterprising later development, but not one which endeared itself any more to the teachers. The interdependence of church and school is also illustrated by the note, '2 boys given a lesson for bad behaviour in Church on Sunday.' As if trying to keep village children in order for five days a week was not enough, the hapless teacher was expected to take responsibility for discipline in Sunday services, entailing keeping them back after school. Nonetheless, the H.M.I. report in 1876 was more guarded than the previous year, with 'weak' and 'fair' appearing, and an injunction that the pupils 'be checked in their tendency to give and receive help during the examination.' January 1877 saw the peak in average weekly attendance: 53.2, particularly surprising as January attendance was usually adversely affected by illness and the weather. The challenges of teaching that number in a small area must have been exacerbated by the heating arrangements, consisting of a coal-fired and frequently bilious stove.

On the death of the Rev. Desprez in 1879, his daughter, Fanny, became the official 'correspondent' or church representative until the appointment of the Rev. W.A. Woods the following year. His twelve-year incumbency does not appear to have been a happy time for either church or school, as evinced by the trail of teachers. His relationship with the school seems to have combined intransigence with neglect and some distinctly eccentric ideas. In the summer of 1880, a measles epidemic wreaked havoc among the children, causing Miss Hancock to close the school for three weeks, and even after that she reported 'the few children who were present very dull.' Measles, mumps, chicken pox and whooping cough were not just unpleasant rites of passage, they could be a real threat to health when there were few effective medicines and no antibiotics to counteract the more severe symptoms.

During the Harvest Holidays Miss Hancock married John, the only son of James and Mary Young, of the Ebbesbourne family associated with both blacksmithing and education. John himself was a gardener and 'tail-docker' (presumably of horses.) It is thought that he was gardener Ebbesbourne Vicarage for the Rev. Tupper Carey and his successor. Louisa was his second wife.

The Rev. Woods took the ravages of measles to heart and, in October, a mere four months after the outbreak, suggested that the schoolroom be sprinkled occasionally with disinfectant. 1880 was an eventful year for the school mistress: measles, marriage, the death of her mother, then snow in October and November. With December came an outbreak of chicken pox and the treacherous weather persisted throughout the following January and February. Possibly the appearance of supply teachers at intervals during the next eighteen months indicates that Mrs. Young suffered miscarriages, but her husband was ill too. In July 1883 Mr. Woods alerted Messers. Gray (of Samways) and Parham (of Norrington), recording pedantically:

'Mrs. Young the schoolmistress of the Church of England School of this Parish has complained to me that the drainage of the School house is defective and she alleges that her husband's health suffers thereby.' Rapid response was not much in evidence; a month later we read: 'School visited by F.Gray Esq.' but there is no evidence of action on the drainage front. When term began at the end of September, three children were 'absent with ringworms.' This seems to have been the final straw, and Mrs. Young took herself off to Ebbesbourne Wake School, where one hopes that the drains were kinder to her husband's health. As her son, Bertrum, was born sometime during that year, followed by Ethel and Janet, and as Mrs. Young became the longest-serving teacher at that school, staying until the 1920s, it would seem to have suited the whole family. However, tragedy struck in 1918, just a month before the Armistice, when Bertrum was killed in France. His memorial can be found in Ebbesbourne church.

Miss Florence Thick arrived as 'locum tenens' until Miss Mary Ann Edmunds took over. Three trends are clearly illustrated: first, family mobility, especially as the agricultural slump began to bite. The roll changed constantly, e.g. in 1883, one child left in January, four were admitted in February, four left in March and six in April, while in June we read: 'Monday morning one boy left for the fields', which introduces the second trend: the interdependence of school, agriculture, church and village. For example in 1883, term started on January 1st., there was a day off for Good Friday then three days' Easter holiday, Harvest Holidays were from mid-August until the end of September and Christmas holidays began on St. Thomas' day. The school attended church on Ash Wednesday, Ascension Day and for Harvest Festival. At some stage, a week's holiday at Whitsun appears and various full or half holidays were given for church or village events, which were communal affairs, families rarely going on an outing, while family holidays would be unheard of. The final trend is the effect of the weather and seasons on attendance. There is frequent mention of heavy rain, flooding and snow preventing children from getting to school, while parents clearly expected a certain laxity in attendance when haymaking, gleaning, potato planting and harvesting etc. called. Roy Marks recalls that children many decades later were given official 'exemption' at busy times in the agricultural calendar.

Miss Edmunds introduced both stricter discipline and more singing. Some song titles make strange reading today, e.g. 'Is this my cross O Lord', 'Humble is my little cottage', 'Then I won't be a dunce'. The vicar was called in to help with discipline problems and a catalogue of accusations and counter-accusations appears in the school book: (The boy kicked the mistress, the mistress had 'struck him on the head with a stick', the boy's testimony was 'utterly false', he and his mother were suitably contrite . . .) and presumably order was restored. In spite of these contretemps, the vicar risked enrolling two of his sons at the school. Their arrival is duly noted: 'Master Wilfrid Wentworth Woods and Master Percy Sinclair Woods' were clearly felt to raise the tone of the establishment, although it is not clear how long they remained to do so. Other children came and went with rarely a mention of their name, and not a 'Master' or 'Miss' between them.

With four 'Standards' as well as infants to be educated, Agnes Coombs was appointed monitress in 1885. Some practical lessons included 'How to light a fire' and 'How to make a plum cake', with regular needlework classes for the girls. The latter was provided rather erratically during the school's history, but Joan Reeves, who narrowly missed going to Alvediston School, having been born in 1918, is emphatic about the importance of needlework in schools. Clothes had to be made, altered and mended when they were only rarely bought. Although the discipline, 'general tone' and progress were all commended in the annual inspection, Miss Edmunds resigned at Christmas 1885, after two years at the school.

1886 opened with a temporary teacher for a few days, after which, on 12th. January, a new arrival burst on to the scene: 'Today I Harriet Mary Forth (late Colonel Forth's daughter) took temporary charge of this school. I found the children very well behaved.' Unfortunately the children may have found Harriet Mary Forth's behaviour somewhat erratic, if her handwriting and comments are anything to go by.

For some undisclosed reason the school was shut for a week after her first day but, on its re-opening, she underwent dramatic changes in her perceptions. The first comment of the day is: 'I find the children very forward in their reading and Dictation especially', but then the writing becomes quite wild and emphatic: 'Mrs. Woods [the vicar's wife] visited the school and brought some work for the children to do (nightdresses) H.M. Forth', with a further change in the script: 'I regret very much coming to this school'. Quite a day. It is not clear whether the vicar's wife, the nightdresses or growing acquaintance with the children were her undoing. Little else is recorded except weekly average attendance in wildly differing scripts until 24th. February:

> Gave up temporary charge of Alvediston School. Fear from never having taught in a school before I have done little or no good. I have never struck a child. H.M. Forth. Late Colonel Forth's daughter.

Poor woman – and unfortunate children. The selection process seems to have been sadly defective.

On 15th. March the first male teacher began a stint of only six months. His tenure is marked by very neat records and an almost complete absence of sewing. Attendance was affected by potato planting, hay-making, wild strawberry-picking, wet weather and social attractions laid on by Club Festivals in both Ebbesbourne Wake and Berwick St. John. An 'interval for recreation' from 3 to 3.10 p.m. was instituted, but such latitude was soon abused. Mr.

Tucker recorded: 'It having been brought to my knowledge (through a conversation with the Vicar) that some of the boys during the interval allowed for recreation in the playground, were in the habit of using obscene language', the alleged ringleader was punished and threatened with dismissal. By 29th. September, Mr. Tucker had had enough; he submitted his resignation for the end of the year.

Meanwhile, his choice of poetry: 'I love to see the Busy Bee', 'I'm only a little Sparrow', 'Battle of Blenheim' and 'Deserted Village' and songs, e.g.: 'The Minstrel Boy', 'Ye mariners of England', 'A Little Cock Sparrow', 'Hearts of Oak', 'Home Sweet Home' and 'The Labourer's Toil' is revealing. Sparrows, (a common species then), battles, patriotism and the due place of the working classes were natural themes in those times.

Relations with the vicar were deteriorating rapidly. Mr. Woods complained that registers were unmarked and his instructions to have attendance numbers recorded on a slate in the school were ignored. Mr. Tucker countered that he could not comply without a clock, which had been required at the last school inspection. By the time he had checked with the clock in the school house, 'the time during which the registers should have been marked had expired (10.20)' and he 'could not conscientiously mark them'. One wonders what current Health and Safety regulations would make of a teacher being forced to leave about forty children unsupervised, or with a monitress scarcely older than the charges, in a small room with a solid fuel heater while he popped next door to check the time! Subtle hints via the singing of 'A Neat Little Clock' seem to have fallen on deaf ears. In the long clock saga, there never seems to have been a suggestion that the teacher would own a watch. By the mid-nineteenth century, watches were becoming more generally available due to the Industrial Revolution, but many could not afford them until they were mass produced at the end of the century. Anyway, the children needed a clear clock to learn to tell the time.

The next school report was unsurprisingly damning. The

premises, instruction, lack of Needlework and Object lessons, standards of Arithmetic and the School Drill all came under attack, although the children's behaviour was commended. This provoked another spat between vicar and teacher conducted, as usual, through terse comments in the school log. Mr. Woods demanded an explanation for the early dismissal of the children on two successive Fridays. Mr. Tucker's excuse, (that he had to catch a train unexpectedly both days and that it was too wet to send a messenger to the vicarage) seems pretty thin, but he produced a trump card with:

> I notice that the foregoing is not a verbatim copy of the Report in its entirety, as required by the Education Dept. and no provision has been made by the managers for instruction in Needlework since the exam.

Mr. Woods' selective record of the school inspection was not denied, and a rash of needlework classes with Mrs. and Miss Woods occurred at the end of November, but relief is palpable on December 17th. 'Gave up charge of this School. School closed for Xmas holidays. J.M. Tucker.'

The next teacher, 'William Pinyon, 2nd. class certified master', started in January 1887 and lasted for nine months. He found the children 'very backward' and numbers were low. The highest roll was twenty-seven, compared with forty-plus a few years back. This probably reflects the ravages inflicted upon agriculture at the time, due to imported wheat, dairy and meat, together with wet summers and poor harvests. Census returns show a marked decline in population: 281 in 1871; 236 in 1881 and 195 in 1891.

Mrs. Woods appeared occasionally to teach the girls sewing but, in her defence, she had a large family. The 1891 census lists five children from the eldest, William, described as a 'tutor', Clara (20), Mary (19), Cecil (10), and Eustace (9). Masters Wilfrid and Percy, whose arrival in school was greeted so effusively by Miss Edmunds in 1884, are conspicuous by their absence. Given the closeness in age of the other progeny, one may assume that they and perhaps others were between Mary and Cecil. They were probably away at school. Mr. and Mrs. Woods were only 44 and 40 respectively at this time, and the sole residential help recorded at the vicarage was the unfortunately named servant, Ellen Smallbones. The picture which begins to emerge may be Dickensian, but was probably also one of total exhaustion. For more about the Woods family, see Appendix on page 356.

For a short while, Mrs. Gold, 'seamstress', took needlework lessons. She was probably from the local Gold / Gould family, but after her things lapsed again. Under Mr. Pinyon, 'Object Lessons' and 'Drill' introduced a sense of order and compliance with inspectors' expectations, although there was 'one case of irregular attendance and non payment of school fees by a family in receipt of Parish Relief'. It is not clear how much was due for each child, but it must have been difficult for some families to pay up. There is no apparent reason for Mr. Pinyon's departure, but he gave notice as early as June of his 'resignation at the end of ensuing quarter'.

Annie K. Schollick, who took up the mantle on October 24th., had beautiful handwriting but, by January 1888 the H.M.I. report reiterates the need for 'a clock (not necessarily an expensive one) [which] should be procured without delay'. The following indicates the growing tension and frustration as yet another teacher was ground down.

11th. Jan. I have given the mistress a month's notice. W.A. Woods.

I find that I have dismissed the school fifteen minutes before the proper time. I sent out to enquire the time but was unable to learn it ~ hence the irregularity.

23rd. Jan. Dismissed children at 11.40 a.m. through ignorance of the correct time.

> 24th. Jan. Visited by the Rev. W.A. Woods and Mr. W.K. Woods'
> [the son recorded as 'tutor' three years earlier]. The vicar desired to
> check the registers but as they were not closed he was unable to do so.
> Registers closed by the Tower clock. I find it very difficult to work in
> strict accordance with the routine owing to the managers not having
> provided a suitable clock which they have been instructed to do in the
> reports of H.M. Inspectors.

She went on to complain about her authority being disputed by the
vicar in front of the children and of the deleterious effect on school
discipline.

Annie Schollick's nerve seems to have suffered under the stress.
A few days later she received 'a most insulting letter' from a mother.
She sent both the pupil who delivered it and her sisters home, but then
was not sure if she was justified in doing so, so sent a letter revoking
her action. Convinced that she could disprove the letter's accusation,
she was relieved by a letter of apology from the mother a few days
later. She seems to have been a conscientious teacher who might have
made progress with the children and their parents, but her sense of
isolation cannot have been eased by frequent visits from the vicar and
his son, once with 'a gentleman', presumably the teacher-elect.

> 6th. Feb. Dismissed morning school according to the time given to
> me at the village inn. The Tower clock does not strike at present.
>
> 10th. Feb. Very good attendance this week. Average 26.4. The
> Rev. W.A. Woods visited the school this p.m. and told the children
> they were to have a week's holiday 'while something was done about
> it.' I protest against being compelled to give up charge of this school
> on one month's notice.

'School closed for one week for repairs and cleaning. Heavy
snow this week', was the clergy comment. How he managed to avoid

getting a clock for so long, (at least two years already), and how he imagined that successive teachers could keep the records, which he checked so rigorously, without a timepiece in the schoolroom beggars belief, and also reminds us that the discrepancies between teachers and educational authorities which can cause anguish today are not new phenomena.

Along came William Henry Pimlott. With renewed zeal, 'W.A. Woods visited a.m. and p.m.' on the new teacher's first day, 20th. February, and a week later, while Mrs. Woods tried again with the sewing class. On March 1st. five boys and two girls were given work after school for sliding on the pond during school hours. This reminds us both of the severity of winters at that time and of the dewpond situated behind the Manor and later filled in after dry summers.

Songs included 'Ring the Bell Watchman' and 'Grandfather's Clock'. Perhaps Mr. Pimlott, like Mr. Tucker two years earlier, was trying the subtle approach, but still there is no sign of a school clock. His records seem quite impressive, with various exercises in Mathematics, English, Geography and Object lessons, although mysterious 'business' sometimes entailed his leaving Miss Pimlott in charge while he disappeared elsewhere, and the H.M.I. report was disappointing in both exam results and discipline. However, despite Mrs. Woods' efforts, the standard of needlework was such that the withdrawal of the grant was threatened, which would have spelt the end of the school. Mrs. Woods continued to make sporadic forays into the school, but in July 1890, we read, 'Needlework not taken this afternoon. Object lesson on 'Frog' given instead.' Versatility was essential. Mrs. Mullins took up the challenge, briefly. That November, the H.M.I. report was uncompromising:

'I regret to be able to give a favourable report of this school which though small fails to reach the required standard of efficiency.' Reading was 'very fair', writing and arithmetic 'indifferent' and infants 'extremely backward.' Eleven children were absent, but only three reported ill, and 'no specimens of knitting were shown.' This was the final straw; a formal warning of withdrawal of the grant for the next year unless there was an improvement was meted out.

In January 1891, Mr. Pimlott disappeared from the record, perhaps to pursue his 'business'. W.K.Woods ('undergraduate of the University of London' by this time) took charge. Mary Stanley, the eighteen year-old daughter of William Stanley, a carter, helped with the infants' class, and Mrs. Woods made one last effort with needlework. The school limped on. It is not clear what happened to W.K's. undergraduate studies or whether a clock had finally been provided.

Flora Thompson, in *Lark Rise to Candleford*, gives a detailed account of life in an isolated rural community in Oxfordshire during the 1880s and 1890s. She believed that there was more literacy among the working population than might appear. She also noted that there were few clocks but, as watches became more prevalent, they were taken to the fields by the men, whose womenfolk were left without. Many more of her observations tally with evidence from Alvediston, including the trend of working families to move to villas in the suburbs as employment became more and more scarce towards the end of the century and beyond. This is exemplified by many families who ended up as far away as Poole and Bournemouth, whose descendants have made valuable contributions to this book.

However, a new age dawned in March with the arrival of Mr. and Mrs. Thatcher, who served the school, church and community for many years and brought much-needed continuity. There were only eighteen pupils, and they immediately set about improving their concentration in spite of set-backs. Whooping cough wreaked havoc in June and July, and towards the end of the outbreak Mr. Woods was due to send disinfectant 'as the closets were offensive.' How different from the national strategies to deal with the threatened swine 'flu pandemic in 2009. There was a half-day holiday on August 3rd. for the flower Show at Wardour Castle as 'cottagers of this parish attend and show there.' This must have been quite an expedition as the road over the downs had not been made. Four days later, Miss Woods requested a half-holiday for children from her Sunday School to go to tea at the Larmer Tree, some miles in the other direction. By the end of August almost all the boys were away in the fields, harvesting. Officially, there were only two weeks' harvest holiday that year, due to frequent school closures during the previous months, but the start of term on 14th. September was largely ignored by the boys and the school tottered on with half-days until the 25th.

Drawing lessons were proving to be a problem in both Alvediston and Ebbesbourne schools, and they had to be officially excused by the Education Department, until the following March, when Mr. Thatcher was able to introduce map drawing. Heating was a worse problem, which Mr. Woods managed to ignore. There was insufficient coal in December, and the 'master provided fuel' when school reopened in 1892. Roof repairs were 'urgently needed,' and schooling in the first two months was virtually wiped out by influenza. Mr. Thatcher carried on heroically, in spite of delays with money and erratic attendance of pupils: 'The older children are taken to work, as early as possible, the boys leading horses and the girls weeding', while '2 fresh scholars, girls living in Crockerton . . . left after being here only one day.' Being church organist, Mr. Thatcher tried to introduce 'musical drill' for the first time, with a harmonium 'which is all to pieces; bellows broken and every part generally dilapidated.' The half-day allotted to allow the Master to 'vote for M.P. at Berwick St. John', (currently Thomas Grove) must have come as a blessed relief.

Even more blessed must have been the arrival of the former headmaster of Gillingham School to replace the Rev. Woods as vicar. The Rev. Charles Ousby Trew visited the school in July, a month before his induction, bringing 'copy books, drawing books and a quantity of other useful books for school purposes; grammars, geographies, histories, spelling books etc.' After years of neglect and under-funding, Mr. Trew launched a new era and used the pulpit to enjoin parents to ensure regular school attendance. Infants were separated by a screen, and equipment for drawing, sewing and writing 'to the extent of four pounds, everything needful being provided' was recorded by C.O. Trew with justifiable glee. Two new blackboards followed, the roofs and fences were repaired, the exterior repainted, the drains cleared, (previously 'all pipes stopped and completely foul'), and double the usual amount of coal was delivered, all by early October.

Mr. Trew was a great instigator. The committees which sprang up like dandelions after rain were doubtless intended to share responsibility, although the candidates deemed suitable to serve on them were few, and he remained the driving force on each. The Committee of Management for the school consisted of Mr. Gray of Samways, (who spent much of his time away on his other estate in Sussex), and Mr. Parham of Norrington as before, but with the addition of Mrs. Trew and of her husband as ex-officio chairman. A ladies' committee was set up 'to watch over the welfare of the girls in school and to assist, if needful, in superintending the needlework.' The novel approach of award was introduced, with prizes for attendance, the best copy book made by a boy and best garment worked by a girl, unaided, and each in their own time, with another for the infant 'who shows up the cleanest and best kept books.' George Compton from Trow, whose younger brother Walter was to die of wounds incurred in the First World War, won one of the earlier infant prizes. Valiant efforts were made to raise the tone of recreation activities. A magic lantern featured quite often; there were concerts, 'tableaux vivants', lectures from such worthy organisations as the Temperance Society, meetings of the National Labourers' Union, vicarage tea parties for church-attenders, (even on Christmas Day) and conjuring tricks for children, while funds were raised through rummage sales. The school room doubled as a Reading and Recreation Room with night school, attended in the first flush of enthusiasm by ten young men and boys, whose education had undoubtedly suffered from the disruption of previous years.

The war against truancy continued apace, although one mother, covering all eventualities, 'stated child was not well, was under age, and learned too fast.' Mr. Trew was to be informed immediately whenever attendance fell below twenty; he tried naming and shaming late arrivals on a notice posted outside the front door and he often appeared in person at 9 a.m. to check attendance. Tea at the vicarage was offered as an incentive. With improved heating the vicar strove to encourage attendance in wet weather if the children were 'properly clad' and soon a ventilator was put in the ceiling, which may have extracted some of the steam and smoke. Inspectors' reports improved dramatically but it was some time before the school's finances were on a sound footing and the gallant Thatchers had to accept salary limitations until that time even though their workload must have increased dramatically. The Church school magnanimously granted a half-holiday in July 1894 when 'a new building for worship' was 'opened by the non-conformists of the village', the Sims family at the Manor. Only five years earlier, Mr. Pimlott had referred to 'the Dissenters of this Parish' whose particular offence was to take children off to Wardour on an excursion. Although Wardour has always been a centre for Roman Catholics, he is more likely referring to the Sims, as the chapel was stronger than Catholicism. Object lessons were still a serious part of the curriculum; those 'sanctioned and signed by H.M.Is.' for the year ending 1895 were: 'Bread, butter, sugar, tea, water, ice, Pig, Horse, Dog, Cat, Lion, Ink, Stinging Nettle, Summer, Ball, an Indian Rubber Ball, an Umbrella, the outside of a house, a railway station, a grocer's shop.' As ever, the content of these lessons is most intriguing.

The school became central to all the villagers, regardless of age, as meetings were held there to determine the recipients of the King's

Charity and to discuss the Parish Council Bill. It was used as a polling station for the election of a district councillor and as a venue for fund-raising events to set up a new Post Office in 1894. This was sited in the thatched cottage opposite the school.

Unfortunately, the first six months of 1895 were blighted first by terrible weather and then by severe colds and influenza. In April Mr. And Mrs. Thatcher succumbed, and the entry for 15th. May reads: 'School closed on account of the burial of the daughter (M.E. Thatcher aged 26 years) of the Master and Mistress. School children attended the funeral.' Mary was the only child living with them at the time of the 1891 census. As far as we can tell, there is no grave with her name in the churchyard, but many people were buried without visible record. The vicar closed the school for two days. Apart from the usual magic lantern entertainment on Christmas day, little else is recorded until the new year.

On January 6th. the children gave a concert of songs and the following day Mr. Trew gave a 'magic lantern entertainment to the children and their friends as they acquitted themselves well in the previous night's entertainment.' Although 'lads misbehaved themselves' and the harmonium was 'injured' by them, necessitating the closure of the Reading Room for a night or two, 1896 was a good year for the school, with little illness in the winter and the average attendance rising to 35.2 in May, 93% of all children of school age in the parish, and about double the numbers in 1893. One unfortunate was absent on an inspection day 'thro' want of boots', which reminds us of the constant battle against poverty and its practical effects. The appointment of Edith Brockway as school cleaner and fire-lighter must have been a great help to the Thatchers, but it should be noted that she did not leave school for another seven months when she became eligible 'being over 13.' However shocking it seems today to employ such a young child in the school, it was common to work before and after lessons.

The next year did not begin so auspiciously. Mr. Thatcher was ill, there were problems with the school house drains, *vide* the Youngs' troubles, boys were wreaking havoc when the school was open for their education in the evenings and there was 'exceedingly rough and stormy weather' in March, followed by measles. However, improvements included the provision of an enamelled jug and two cups for drinking water, and a 'tripod stand and basin with soap and soap dish for washing hands'. Also 'Thick the carpenter' overhauled all the desks and seats, and mended a window, while Randalls of Tisbury installed a 'Cheltenham' stove in the school house kitchen, replacing an open fire there whose smoke belched through to mingle with other pollutants in the school room air. Most craftsmen could be found in local villages: the Thick family is still one of the longest-standing in Ebbesbourne, Mr. Young the blacksmith mended the school bell and John Gold (or Gould) bravely tackled the drains. Needlework materials came from Mr. Hibbert of Tisbury and stationery from Mr. Gale of Salisbury.

At 12 o'clock on June 16th. 1897, the children were 'marched up to the Vicarage' and each presented with a commemoration plate and mug for Queen Victoria's Diamond Jubilee. Mrs. Trew organised it, Miss Winnie Trew made the presentation, and her father announced a holiday until June 28th. Even absent children were not forgotten. Six months later Winnie Trew was in the local limelight again. 'Jan. 3rd. 1898 Dramatic and living waxwork entertainment given to the parishioners by Miss Trew and Miss W. Trew and young lady and gent. friends. Children sang three of their songs. Admittance free.' Sometimes one wishes that cine cameras had been invented to capture these moments in grainy film, but then perhaps parishioners would not have been so cheerfully entertained by dramatic and living waxworks, nor by the 'itinerant exhibitor of dramatic pictures' of the Holy Land, Canada and general interest who had appeared a month earlier. However, it is heartening to know that village halls still provide a variety of local entertainments without the trappings of 21st. century sophistication.

At the end of February 1898, the three young Comptons at Trow developed whooping cough. Although they were kept in quarantine, five weeks later the whole school was closed for three weeks on doctor's orders 'on account of general sickness prevalent amongst the children.' Efforts to get going again at the end of April were further hampered by a day off for Miss Parham's wedding. A week later, school was dismissed at 9 a.m. because so few children had staggered in after a 'meat tea . . . given to most of the parishioners and their children in the loft attached to the Tower Farm,' (Samways). Beneficial as the food and fellowship may have been after weeks of sickness and isolation, the teachers must have despaired of educating their charges, especially when, at the end of May, thunderstorms so severe that a man and several sheep were killed by lightening between Alvediston and Salisbury, led to more absences. Further disruption occurred in September when: 'The autumn manoeuvres of the army [were] held in the neighbourhood: troops continually passing. No school this p.m.', and the next day: 'Thousands of troops passed through the village this a.m. and transport wagons passing all day rendered the road impassable for the children. No school.' The road surfaces were treacherous at the best of times, so this onslaught before the winter rains must have been unwelcome, but probably not to the little boys, many of whom would have marched off to war and unimaginable experiences only sixteen years later.

However, the greatest disruption to the routines of the past five years came with the Rev. Charles Ousby Trew's decision to move to Upchurch, Kent in August, although it is comforting to note that a school clock was firmly ensconced by then. Mr. Parham took over as treasurer and correspondent until the Rev. Baynham arrived in November 1898. By this time, schools were receiving more prescriptive guidelines from the education authorities, but Mr. Baynham seems to have been a genial soul. Christmas parties at the Vicarage were now gladdened by his appearance as Santa Claus to distribute presents from the tree, while Lady Pembroke's prizes for needlework and attendance were awarded at the same time. The choir took on a new lease of life with surplices, at least partially funded by a concert given by local people of all ages. On 19th. July 1899 we read that a school holiday was granted because 'the vicar, the master, [also the organist] and adults in the choir were taken by the vicar to Bournemouth for a treat.' Mr. Baynham was assiduous in his school duties, always teaching the older children Scripture and the Catechism from 9 to 10 a.m. on Wednesday, Thursday and Friday unless there was a church service. In May, an outbreak of Scarlet Fever in neighbouring villages and other fever scares prompted a visit from the unfortunately-named District Insanitary Inspector, who declared the premises satisfactory. Over the summer major redecorations took place, so the reforming impetus was not lost under the new vicar. At the beginning of the autumn term Mr. Baynham noted there were 'fifty-six children, thirteen of whom are babies'. At a rough count in early 2009, there are twenty-seven children.

1899 ended with another Christmas party at the Vicarage, where the family and a friend waited on the guests. It fell to one of the three Miss Baynhams, Beatrice, to distribute presents from the tree, dressed as a fairy. The new year and new century arrived without recorded ceremony, and by the beginning of February severe snowstorms and frosts were causing problems, with even worse to come when a violent storm and heavy rain, combined with melting snow, caused floods. The following month Mr. Thatcher slipped on more ice and 'severely injured his left wrist.' Accident and emergency treatment came to his home in the form of Dr. Bluche, who set the bones and told the patient to rest it completely for a week, after which he reappeared in school, complete with splint and sling. In April the Dowager Countess of Pembroke gave the school a picture of her late husband. Links with the Wilton Estate were very real, even if the children had never seen Wilton House or the earl, they would realize that much of the land, many houses and the pub belonged to the Pembroke family, and they would have Lady Pembroke to thank for school prizes.

May brought celebrations for Queen Victoria's eighty-first birthday and for the news of the relief of Mafeking in South Africa after a seven month siege by the Boers. The soldiers practising manoeuvres in the area eighteen months previously may have ended up fighting in the Boer War of 1899-1902. In July, probably the first Alvediston and Ebbesbourne Wake Flower Show was held, diplomatically, in a field in West End. The children were encouraged to show wild flowers. October saw a bit of a damp squib on the political front. The school room was 'granted to A. Morrison Esq. Cons. Candidate for South Wilts. For purpose of stating his political opinions.' It was just as well that his prospective audience consisted only of the Rev. Baynham, his daughters and Mr. and Mrs. Parham since 'neither the candidate nor any of his agents came.' Perhaps they had got wind of the level of political fervour in the village. Later that month, the Compton family of Trow, who featured regularly and favourably in the school chronicle, left the neighbourhood. George, with William Mullins, had left school a year earlier. Walter, who died of war wounds in 1919, was still a pupil. The better-known George Compton remained at the Crown, where he and his wife Jane brought up a large family.

The syllabus begins to look a little more familiar, even if the content was not: reading, writing, recitation, arithmetic, geography, elemental science, singing, drawing, needlework, the study of common things, (probably 'object lessons 'under another name), and P.E. History was introduced in the 'Vth. Division.' Absentees were still a headache and there was particular concern over one family from Crockerton, whose 'residence is a lonely house in a clump of trees on the top of the down north of the school 1½ miles away.' No great distance to walk in those days, but Crockerton was always isolated.

Near the Poor Patch on the other side of the newly-opened road to Ansty, beside the old coach road, these dwellings were crudely made and frequently deserted as families moved in search of casual work.

1901 opened with such arctic conditions that the bell's axle was frozen solid in its sockets. Although plagued by the weather, smoking chimneys and foul drains, a few brave souls gathered in February to select a committee to plan the next flower and vegetable show which was to incorporate Fifield Bavant with the two other villages, an arrangement which still pertains today. The harvest festival seems to have been particularly successful. Children brought fruit, vegetables, flowers and corn to decorate the church; 'a bright service' took place at 3 p.m. with the Rev. Jacob, rector of Fifield and vicar of Ebbesbourne preaching. It seems odd that the tiny hamlet of Fifield had a rector while its larger neighbour only had a vicar, but this reflects ancient status.

This year the H.M.I. report was genuinely complimentary: 'This little school is well equipped and most carefully taught' was a verdict which says much for the Thatchers' dedication and clergy support. This was a peak in the school's history, but at Christmas, only two months later Mr. Thatcher retired, aged sixty-five, and his wife Eliza must have found taking over the whole school daunting.

Early in January 1902, 'Mr. Parham, Norrington, gave a treat to the children of his workmen, as they were required to be at Norrington at 4 o'clock, opened afternoon school and registered 1.30 p.m. dismissed school at 3.30 p.m.' Local farmers and employers would have no compunction about organising a treat which 'required' disruption to the timetable. Employment, education and entertainment were all integral to village life and hierarchy. The very next day, measles struck again and it was a month before the school was back to normal. Mr. Gale, stationery supplier, sent a copy of his 'Model Course of Physical Training' with the next consignment of exercise books, blotting paper, slate pencils, sponges etc. Slates were in use right through the school's history, as we learn from Reg Marks' memories. As Mrs. Thatcher was the sole teacher, the screen dividing infants from older children was removed, but in spite of the excuse of bad weather, she managed to raise average attendance to 27.1.

In May there was a playground accident of sufficient gravity to merit record in the school log, a rare event in those pre-litigation days. Two brothers 'seriously hurt themselves', one suffering a 'deep cut on the forehead showing the bone and had to be taken to the doctor', who lived in Donhead, so the jolting journey cannot have been pleasant. The following month we read: 'Mistress away with consent of managers attending Annual Mtg. of Women's Union. School taken by Mr. Thatcher.' This single reference to the Women's Union raises questions. Was the Women's Union political, social, educational or religious, like the Mothers' Union? Mrs. Thatcher may have been rather isolated socially, being better educated than most village women, and may have been more open to new ideas. Of these there were plenty at that time. Emmeline Pankhurst's Women's Social and Political Union was formed the following year. It was a time of burgeoning political interest among women but whether Mrs. Thatcher had any affiliations with the movement or even attended Women's Union meetings regularly is unknown. (The burial of Mary Ann Pankhurst, 'servant for 53 years and friend to . . . the Rev. W.A.K. Douglas' in 1912 might prompt suggestions that Mrs. Thatcher was also her friend, and that they shared political sympathies, Unfortunately, as the Rev. Douglas did not arrive until 1909, such surmise is impossible.)

June 1902 saw the coronation of Edward VII, whose mother had died unnoted in the previous year. His own poor health was cause for concern. Accordingly, 'a meat tea [was] given to all the inhabitants of the village, no other festivities owing to the King's illness.' Nevertheless, he surpassed expectations, both in longevity ~ reigning until 1910 ~ and in effectiveness, for he worked much more conscientiously than his mother and others expected from his track record during her reign. These years were characterised by unprecedented upheavals in attitudes, expectations and world politics. Meanwhile, back in the classroom, there was consternation when some of the elder boys were absent for the Religious Knowledge examination by the rural dean and diocesan inspector, due to the call of the hay harvest, while in July an Inspector for the Prevention of Cruelty to Children paid a call with the local policeman, (P.C. May, father of the boys involved in the playground fracas, who lived in the Police House, now Elcombe House,) to examine the children of a particular man. However, they left without further ado. The authorities voiced concern over attendance during harvest: 'Some of the children attend school so irregularly that the managers ought to call the attention of the attendance committee at once. The plea of 'distance may hold good in the winter time, but the attendance is as bad during the summer.' Mrs. Thatcher is more prosaic: 'T.Butt Esq. Sub. Inspr. Came in the morning at 10.30 a.m. Work carried on as usual. Left at 12.30. Half holiday given to the children in afternoon.'

One eight year-old girl was 'unable to walk or even stand for any time.' Although Mrs. Baynham provided her with a basket chair in November 1902, five months later 'the invalid scholar . . . was taken to Salisbury Infirmary during the holidays' and passes out of the picture. The 1907 school photograph shows another little girl perched awkwardly on a high chair to bring her level with her standing class-mates. Facilities to help disabled children must have been pitiful and the prospects if they could not be kept at home even worse. Although average attendance reached 33.9 in November, a government report described it as 'truly deplorable' soon afterwards. The 'school continues in a very fair state of efficiency, but his cannot be maintained unless the Managers give the Mistress some assistance and the attendance be improved.' The grant for the year was only £65.

1903: After Christmas Mr. Baynham appointed an ex-scholar, May Jenkins, as monitress, on a salary of ½ crown (12 ½ p!) per week.

One afternoon in March, all forty children turned up, but by then Mr. Baynham had left. The Sims family, staunch non-conformists and builders of the chapel, begin to feature more in the annals of the school. In May 'the Misses Sims with teachers and children subscribed to obtain a football', delivered by Miss May Sims a week later and strictly for the pupils only. It is extraordinary to imagine a time, only a hundred years ago, when the purchase of one football for forty children was so momentous. Some of the young men in Roy Marks' photo of the 1910 football team would have used that ball. More familiar names appear in the October prize list; Gwendoline Sims, Annie Compton, Caroline Stanley and James Roberts. The names Moxham and Mullins occur in later lists.

From 1st. October, 'the County Council took over the school for educational purposes.' Just before the end of term, a rubber stamp for marking books with 'Wilts. County Council Church School' arrived from Birmingham, to clinch the change. Other things did not change: chicken pox kept children away for a minimum of three weeks; truancy was tackled with 'enquiry notes concerning 'Reasons for absence', but one remained unanswered, probably because the recipient at Crockerton Firs was unable to read; and the fire smoked so badly that it had to be put out for four days in December.

1904 began with influenza and bronchitis, followed by bad colds and sore throats in April and yellow jaundice in May. The 'dirty condition' of three siblings merited inspection and the drains needed to be cleared of mud to 'act properly.' If nothing else, this record explodes any myth of blissful cheer and health in 'the good old days', while the challenges faced and material expectations bear little comparison with today's. There was some light relief for the monitress, presumably still May Jenkins, and five scholars on 13th. July when they went to Bournemouth for a day trip, exciting enough in itself, but made more exciting by a train derailment. (This derailment occurred two years before the famous railway accident at

Salisbury, when twenty-eight people, mostly Americans, on the boat train from Plymouth to London were killed.) They did not get home until early the following morning and were consequently 'too tired to attend school.' It is interesting to speculate how quickly and effectively the news reached village families. A day trip to Bournemouth sounds tame in comparison with the exotic travel available to children today, but instant communication has effectively brought far-flung corners of the globe closer than Bournemouth was in 1904. Limits of local horizons are further highlighted by the Assistant Director of Wiltshire County Council's demand that a good map of England and Wales be requisitioned.

Although 'major drain work' was carried out by Mr. Mills of Broad Chalke during the summer, and the start of term was delayed for a week while ventilators were fixed, the chain of the bell proved harder to mend, giving another excuse for late arrivals and truants. On December 21st. Mrs. Thatcher noted: 'St. Thomas's day. The children of the village have been for many years past in the habit of going on this day to the better class of houses singing and soliciting money. Many absented themselves this a.m. but the custom is gradually dying out. Formerly a holiday was given.' Carol singing in school hours may have been on the wane, to the teacher's evident relief, but the King's Fund continued to be administered on that day for many years.

At the end of January 1905, the bell was finally repaired by T. Young, probably Edward Thomas, the last blacksmith Young in Ebbesbourne, and father of William, archaeologist and local historian. With only an unqualified monitress to assist her, Mrs. Thatcher sometimes took the infants for reading. In June May Jenkins was replaced by assistant teacher, Miss Alice Gertrude Silvester. If May Jenkins took up the assistant director of education's suggestion that she become a pupil teacher, she would probably have gone to the College of Sarum St. Michael in Salisbury Close, immortalised in Thomas Hardy's 'Jude the Obscure'.

April saw the arrival of the former church harmonium to replace one which was 'useless and worn out', although church damp caused a rapid turnover of instruments, so the improvement would be limited. Measles and mumps wreaked such havoc among the forty pupils in June and July that the school was closed for two weeks. During the holidays 'a change was made in the offices. Movable pans being substituted for the pits formerly in use. The pans are to be regularly removed and emptied by the cleaner and replaced.' This brave soul was Mrs. Brockway, perhaps the mother of the first, young cleaner. How the 'offices' were cleaned prior to this does not bear thinking about. On the first day of term no children turned up to benefit from either lessons or new 'offices' because Mr. Sims took two wagon loads to Salisbury Race Plain for a Band of Hope treat. Most of the pupils belonged to this largely nonconformist organisation which existed to discourage the consumption of alcohol, but they probably associated it more with treats and outings. However cynical one may feel today, the motivation of real concern for the lives of working people should not be underestimated. Meanwhile the C. of E. was represented at the rummage sale held in the empty school by the vicar and the Parham ladies.

The County Council in Trowbridge was exercising more authority. Timetables had to be sent there for approval although the diocesan inspector still examined the children on the Bible and the catechism, i.e. the religious doctrine of the Church of England. The December Inspector's Report is a tour de force: 'The school is doing fairly well, on the whole, so far as the mechanical work is concerned. The question of intelligence still calls for attention. The infant class has improved, and now that the children are no longer left in the hands of a young girl their work should soon become satisfactory.'

However, on 19th. January, 1906, we read: 'The continual wet weather since the Xmas holidays has lowered attendance. Children living at a distance get wet through going home and are obliged to stay away next day to dry their clothes.' There was still snow in March, and soon afterwards someone from 'The Royal Commission on the care and control of the Feeble minded' visited but, as he sent no report, one can only assume that he felt his services were not required. However inadequate the provision for children with special needs may be today, help and understanding was certainly sparse then. Head lice were a problem, as ever in schools, but they were recorded differently, e.g. 'Twice had to caution several boys that they must come cleane (sic) to school' and six months later there was more concern about the unclean state of certain heads. Other hygiene efforts included the occasional white-liming of the walls of the 'offices'. Another outbreak of whooping cough in the autumn kept some children away for five or six weeks.

1907 opens with notice from the Rev. Wynne of an extra week's holiday 'owing to a death in the School House,' that of Mr. Thatcher, who had brought welcome strength and continuity to the school, church and community for sixteen years, remarkable at a time of great upheaval and poverty in the agricultural community, which forced families to move around in search of work, while Mr. Wynne was the fourth vicar in those years. The following Monday Mr. Thatcher's widow wrote bravely: 'Commenced work again after the Christmas holidays. In the morning there were thirty-six children present and in the afternoon thirty-eight.' By the end of January she had to take sick leave and Annie Maynard took up the reins for a month, with more frequent visits from Mr. Wynne. On the last day of May, 'perfect attendance' of forty-two is recorded. Mr. Wynne took five boys to Swallowcliffe to be examined by an H.M.I. John May passed at standard 5 for 'total exemption', his brother Edgar, Jack Compton and Herbert King passed the 4th. standard for employment, 'All four boys gone to work.' Presumably the fifth had to return to school. A school photograph was taken this year (see page 44).

The younger woman could be Miss Taylor or Miss Silvester, who took over in July. This difficult year for Mrs. Thatcher ended with

Schoolmistress Mrs Thatcher and pupils at Alvediston School, 1906. (Peter Daniels)

two problems, one a minor security matter, the other a family tragedy. In November 'the vicar sent a lock and chain to be put on the gate of the playground as the cleaner complains of outsiders getting into the boys' offices in the evenings.' Evidently their proximity to the pub was proving a little too convenient. A month later: 'On Saturday last [a girl] was severely burnt . . . her sister is absent from school to attend to her, as there is no mother at home.' Today a burns victim would be treated at the regional burns unit in Salisbury, a half-hour drive away.

1908 saw attendance climb to forty-eight in mid-June, and numbers remained in the forties even after five children left for work. However, when a doctor announced that he was coming to 'inspect medically the children' only eleven presented themselves. It is not clear how many were due to be seen or whether some children (or parents) took fright at this innovation and felt the pull of field work. On October 15th. 'The mistress Eliza Thatcher' wrote, 'having reached sixty-five years of age today ceases to hold office.' She arrived seventeen and a half years earlier with a husband and a daughter, and left alone for an undisclosed destination, without delay it seems, for Dora M. Cooper, 'a late Salisbury T.C. [Teaching College] student' took over the next day. Miss Cooper remained for fourteen years, until the school closed, so, apart from eight chaotic years there was reasonable continuity throughout the school's history.

One of Miss Cooper's first actions was to divide the school with a curtain 'as a help towards keeping silence.' Another was to institute a new form of prayers which caused a minor rebellion by several older boys who kept clear of the school until prayers were safely over. However, the new teacher reported that the mother of two miscreants was 'extremely anxious for Harry to start work', reflecting the hope of many a parent over the years that employment would steady their offspring. One thirteen year-old from Amesbury stretched the facilities by requiring standard VII studies, but six days later started work at Norrington, which must have been a relief all round. The intervention of Mr. Wynne served to placate, or at least call into line, any awkward parents and prayers resumed as Miss Cooper wished. Soon the boys were directing their energies towards subscribing for a new football, but Harry's foray into work did not last long. Within three months he, with another aspiring employee, had returned to school.

Meanwhile, Miss Cooper was reviewing the timetable and presented experimental schemes for Geography and History which illustrate changes in priorities and perceptions.

Geography:- stories of children of other lands, the earth and planetary systems, land and water, day and night, seasons etc.

– Lower School:- concentrating on the local landscape, extending to England generally, its chief physical features and large towns and ports e.g. London, Portsmouth.

-Upper School:- British Isles in more detail. Europe. 'British possessions – their use, extent, how obtained.' Study of chief in more detail e.g. India, Canada, Australia. Physical geography.

History:- 'How the British nation grew up, and in her turn founded daughter colonies.'

    -Lower School:- 'Stories of great persons and events,' e.g. King Arthur, Alfred, Canute, Magna Carta, Nelson, Florence Nightingale, Grace Darling.'

    -Upper School:- 'Simple general outline of English History in chronological order. Lives of great men and women and epoch making events which illustrate such facts as:- Growth of our parliament, acquirement of colonies. All to give some idea of their responsibilities as citizens of a great race.'

When Dr. Brown reappeared in December to examine fourteen children, eye-testing was included, making the whole process so long that afternoon school had to be cancelled because he 'ran on until 2.35 without dinner.' She was distressed by the muddy state of the playground and by the habit of begging or playing truant on St. Thomas' day, but at least the King charity money was distributed at 6 p.m. to avoid interfering with the school.

The new year, 1909, started with good attendance, but mumps soon put paid to that. The clock broke and had to be sent away for eleven days for repair. Miss Cooper was keen to introduce new ideas: five years earlier, a map of England and Wales had been ordered; now she sent off for one of the world, also a pair of scales and equipment for brushwork and modelling, but her request for geography books was refused and her verdict on the first brushwork lesson was not encouraging. This was the year of the great gardening experiment, for boys only. The education Committee took a while to catch on to the idea, but she persevered and by April a gardener was coming over from Shaftesbury, an area was pegged out and tools and seeds requisitioned. Measuring rods arrived via Tisbury, at a cost of 6d. (2 ½ p) to be paid at the station and 6d. delivery. Seeds came, and three stone (19 kilos) of potatoes were 'brought by Smart from Tisbury, 1/1d. for carriage and 3d. for conveyance from the station. The next day another 6d. was paid for tools to be delivered and, under the Shaftebury gardener's eye, seeds were sown on May 3rd. and 6th. He appeared several times in July, and at the end of September the gardens were 'examined and approved' by the County instructor, whose enthusiasm rather got the better of him. He recommended that:

a) additional tools and watering can be requisitioned
b) a small bed be made for cuttings of currants, raspberries and gooseberries
c) if possible the land behind the school be made into a fruit plantation
d) a four foot brick pit be dug for rubbish and be emptied periodically.

Unfortunately, by November 5th. the gardening class was 'temporarily suspended as there are less than six boys to attend' and a month later there is a sad little note: 'Gardening tools sent to Barford St. Martin.' One can almost hear the titters in the background as the Education Committee's, and probably many of the locals', prophecies were fulfilled. How irresistible it must have been, en route to the Crown, to lean over the fence in the company of friends and assess the new, young teacher's efforts. Other innovations met with more success: a 'small contribution' was sent to the Willis Nature Study Exhibition in Marlborough, many miles away over Salisbury Plain, the playground was cleaned, renovated and later gravelled; needlework materials were sent from Tisbury and 'weighing days' for the girls were instituted by the Education Committee. Another school photo was taken in June, and the school was closed for an afternoon in late November for a farewell tea and entertainment for the Rev. and Mrs. Wynne.

1910. Health and Safety issues were tackled. In February we read: 'School scrubbed. (It is necessary to keep record of this as it was not always regularly done.)' Head lice were either proliferating or treated more stringently, with regular medical checks and the exclusion of new arrivals with 'unclean heads' for a week, which cannot have helped their integration. When the school pump 'gave out', water for both school and house had to be drawn from the well, an extra task which lasted for weeks. Desks which 'failed to satisfy modern requirements', e.g. by having no foot or back rests, could be dispatched to the vicarage for teas and entertainments once new ones, requisitioned three months earlier, arrived. In August Mr. Foyle of Broad Chalke 'overhauled' the school, installing wash-hand basins in the lavatories and repairing the roof and railings.

One afternoon the school was closed so that Miss Cooper and her assistant could go to needlework lectures in Tisbury. Apart from gleaning new ideas, she may have welcomed the rare opportunity to meet other teachers. Plans for May were disrupted by the death of King Edward VII. The school was dismissed on the 13th., after lessons on both Edward and the new king, George V. Empire Day was still celebrated on May 24th.; the school was decorated with daisies, the elder children had a lesson on 'The Empire' and the day ended with a rendition of the Empire Song and the National Anthem. This was the education of children who were to live through and in many cases, fight in the First World War. It is so tempting to assess history from a twenty-first century perspective, or to dismiss the decisions and attitudes of previous generations through ignorance of their lives. When autumn term began, only three children turned up, the rest being enticed by military manoeuvres in the area. These continued for several days, and Miss Cooper clearly lost her battle to attract attendance. At the opposite extreme, 'Observation Walks' on the downs or among copses, and the call of the land in October to cart mangels (large beet used for cattle food), continued unabated.

In January 1911, all the pupils were involved in an entertainment consisting of 'three costume action songs and a Fairy Nursery Play.'

Fortunately influenza did not hit until ten days later. On March 21st. there is an interesting note: 'A lesson on the 'census' given this morning. Its methods, purpose etc. Special attention being given to the correct filling in of 'column 10.'" This described the profession or occupation of adults, so clearly the teacher wanted to ensure that local families had help via their children when battling with the complexities of these forms, for in earlier years the information had been compiled by a designated recorder.

The educational year ended on March 31st. even though the Easter holidays were from 13th. – 24th. April. Accordingly on April 1st. the 'standards' were reorganised, while, 'Two children over 14 are remaining in school for a time', which must have put a strain on the teacher, however young they seem now. Miss Taylor appears to have returned. During her absence Annie Compton, who had recently passed her 'Labour Cert.' allowing her to leave school, was employed as a monitor, and she was called on again five months later, when Miss Cooper was ill and Miss Taylor had to take charge. This year Empire Day could be celebrated with more panache, with flags as well as daisies, and a lesson on 'The Empire, what it is, and how it can be kept', introducing a tiny note of anxiety on the subject. The last mention of this day is in 1920. In mid-June there was a week's holiday for the coronation of George V. Afternoon school was delayed one day during the previous week as so many children were needed to take tea to the haymakers, so probably most of them spent the week in the fields. There is no mention of festivities or outings to join with other villages.

This was a time of national growing tension and frequent change at the vicarage. Agriculture reflected the uncertainty and Miss Cooper noted on 20th. October: 'This week the last of the Michaelmas moves have taken place. Eight children have left and at present only two have been admitted, which makes no. on books only 35, the lowest number reached for some years.' (Michaelmas, or St Michael's Day, occurs on 29th. September and is traditionally the time when agricultural moves

Village outing in a charabanc belonging to Reginald Stephens of Shaftesbury.

are made.) Two infants appeared a week later, which boosted numbers and morale a little. This year's health initiative from the medical officer was to send 'Instructions concerning teeth' and a specimen toothbrush to the school. Ringworm was the only outbreak to affect attendance over the summer. On St. Thomas' Day, Miss Cooper admitted defeat, writing: 'As children always absent themselves for carol singing on this day, school was closed for Xmas holidays until Jan. 8th.'

1912. 'The safe return of their Majesties King George and Queen Mary from India' was marked with 'a short thanksgiving' led by the Rev. Keith Douglas on 9th. February. Almost a century later our octogenarian Queen undertakes gruelling foreign tours, but the travel arrangements would bear no comparison. Also, contemporary film shows King George and Queen Mary in full royal regalia: enormous crowns, long ermine-trimmed trains, and quantities of highly decorated layers underneath, so their survival in the steaming heat of India, as much as their safe return, was worthy of thanksgiving. The school room continued to be used for local entertainments, sometimes involving school closure all day for the preparations. Temperature records were sent to Trowbridge for the first time, none too soon since 84 degrees Fahrenheit, (46.5 centigrade) was recorded the previous July. A glance at the garb worn in contemporary school photographs is salutary. However, the next H.M.I. report criticised the heating arrangements, so both extremes must have been unbearable.

In October, the mistress and her assistant accompanied the choir on an outing to Bournemouth. The remaining pupils had the day off. The Education Committee was beginning to revel in the joys of circulars. Some arrived in November:

1. 'Revised suggestions' on Arithmetic and English.
2. Report on School Gardening, (which must have been a bitter pill).
3. Report on Rural Education.
4. 'Circular stating that salaries will now be paid on 15th. of each month.'

These were received without further comment.

During the winter of 1912-13, 'constant smoke from chimney, accompanied by showers of ashes, [blew] into the room with every strong wind.' Thus began a long, frustrating saga.

In April Miss T.A. Young replaced Miss W.H. Taylor, who appears to have been much appreciated in almost six years as assistant teacher, because the Rev. Batten presented her with 'a handsome fitted attaché case, for which managers, parents and children had subscribed.' If this Miss Young was local she may have been Annie, sister of William E.V. Young the local historian, or Agnes, a cousin, since there is no record of a Miss T. Young in 'Ebbesbourne Wake Through the Ages'. Soon after her arrival Miss Cooper had to take extended sick leave for a 'complaint of the eyes'. The school was closed for two weeks, then a supply teacher was brought in until 2nd. June. However, the rot had set in as first haymaking, then wheat harvest took a toll on attendance right through to the holidays, when the usual cleaning and repainting took place. 'Also the hat pegs were altered according to H.M.I's. recommendations', but not quite. In November he noted that 'there are still pegs less than 12 inches apart.' He also suggested that Miss Young pay 'a visit of observation' to a larger infant school, so perhaps she was less experienced than her predecessor. She duly went off to Mere for two weeks while Olive King was employed as monitress. Generally, the inspector was positive in the circumstances.

'Owing to illness the Head Teacher was absent for six weeks in the early part of the educational year. The school suffered in consequence, but since her return in June the discipline has much improved and is now quite satisfactory. The children are, generally speaking, painstaking and careful in the writing exercises, needlework is being sensibly taught, . . . and the first class reading is very satisfactory.' There was a lack of original thought in composition and arithmetic teaching was too formal, but 'The small class of Infants is being kept fairly well employed . . .

'Premises. The Cloak-room has been re-coloured and some of the pegs have been moved but not to avoid the over-hanging of clothes. The urinal is in an unsatisfactory position. There is no washing bowl in the receptacle provided for one on the boys' side; soap, a roller for a towel and a towel should be provided in the boys' lavatory.' The state of it can be imagined.

In January 1914, coal was delivered from the Ebbesbourne Co-operative Society. Forays into the co-operative movement do not seem to have lasted long. Peter Meers notes in 'Ebbesbourne Wake through the Ages vol. 2' that it was in action in the 1890s, but seems to have disappeared again by 1897. There must have been another attempt, but throughout the war the coal deliveries proved woefully inadequate.

Also inadequate was the provision for children with what are now called 'special needs'. The terminology, too was harsher. Miss Cooper had a temporary triumph with one 'mentally deficient boy of nearly 11 years of age' when she moved him from the Infants to Standard 1, 'tho' not at all capable of Std. 1 work, he is too big to be retained among the infants.' Ten weeks later he 'made a perfect attendance this week. The first time in his life', but after the harvest holidays the best that could be said if him was 'still attending v. irregularly.' It is tragic that, while we may wince at earlier classifications, there are still horrific numbers of children who slip through every educational net.

The last excursion to Bournemouth for six years, organised by the Band of Hope, took place in July. There is little comment on the First World War. Of course, for several months it was not expected to be more than a temporary skirmish and, by the time that this was clearly not to be, life at school was so grim that Miss Cooper probably needed all her energy to keep some semblance of control. Through the school log we have a vignette of life on the home front with rapidly diminishing numbers of active, reliable tradesmen, craftsmen, builders, labourers and farm workers. Their return for leave was often blighted by incomprehension of trials which they could not begin to describe and which were not aired in the media, so what may have passed for complacency at home was more likely exhaustion from the grinding efforts to keep going through local exigencies. While the correspondent, (the ever-changing vicar), the medical and attendance officers wrangled over whether chicken pox had so decimated numbers that the school should close, Miss Cooper used the log to vent her frustrations, albeit with commendable economy:

November 27th. 'Smoke and ashes blown into the school this week have rendered the room scarcely habitable. The flames at times blow out beyond the guard.'

December 4th. The H.M.I. visit. 'He arrived in the midst of a cloud of smoke and commented strongly on the state of the chimney.'

The 'occasional holiday' granted 'to enable Head teacher to purchase wool etc. for working classes' indicates that women were getting together to knit warm clothes for soldiers.

At the end of January 1915, well into the coldest term, a cowl was fitted on the chimney. Mr. Foyle of Broad Chalke was evidently still in business. When Miss Cooper fell ill for the whole of February, Miss Young had to manage with the help of older girls. Immediately on her return the head alerted the correspondent to the need for more coal; it ran out six days later and it took another two before a mere two hundredweight was delivered. Whether this was intended for the school house as well or not, cold and anxiety cannot have been conducive to convalescence or getting the school back in shape. Mrs. Hoole from 'The Tower', (Samways), brought some cheer and an afternoon off school with a tea for all the children. On April 1st. shortly before the beginning of the summer term, thirteen hundredweight of coal was delivered. The date may have seemed inappropriate, but heating would still be needed. As the war progressed, supplies would frequently appear quite randomly, just when the recipient was at boiling point, and then prove to be other than ordered. By then there were only twelve children in the Infants class and twenty in the Standards, of whom the 'mentally deficient' one rarely appeared and was definitely not within earshot when the Medical Inspector came.

In September, the Diocesan Inspector reported: 'The papers of Group I were rather weak, but the oral work was well done, and Group II has improved since last year. The hymns were reverently sung' and the school as a whole was graded 'good' with 'very good discipline and tone.' This must have come as a relief as the premises caused more problems:

Oct. 9:- 'The school cleaner's daughter being ill the school did not receive its monthly scrubbing.'

Oct. 23:- 'There being no water in the school pump the scrubbing had to be again deferred. The school cleaner declined to fetch water from the well.'

Oct. 30:- The school was scrubbed and the chimney sweep came, apparently in that order!

Nov. 5:- A 'continuous current of smoke into the room' made it 'evident that the sweep has choked the cowl on top of the chimney.' This was reported to the correspondent and ten days later,

Nov. 15:- The cowl was cleared and 'Fire now burns cleanly', but another whole year had passed. Perhaps all the experienced sweeps had gone to war.

The first reference to the shattering events in Europe occurred fifteen months after the beginning of hostilities, but it was still oblique and reflected the local impact. 'Goods requisitioned in September received this week. Part of the delay caused by congestion of railways in Salisbury district,' and the roof was leaking. The training of troops was well under way in a huge training establishment in and around Fovant, just a few miles away, admittedly in another valley (that of the Nadder), but still much more accessible since the road over the downs had been built twenty years earlier, while Salisbury Plain was swarming with troops. Alvediston itself had already lost two young men in action: Privates William Scammell on 24th. October 1914, and Bertram Moxham on the last day of July 1915. How soon their deaths were confirmed to their families is not known.

Just before Christmas, reality began to be recognised in the life of the school. A collection in aid of a prisoner of war whom the children were 'adopting' raised nearly 10/-, (50p), enough to send a parcel weighing sixteen pounds, (about seven kilos), containing food, books and knitted articles to Private A. Simpkins, 8909 Gothingen Camp in Hanover, Germany. The children also wrote letters to him. Mike Longstaffe has discovered details of several Arthur Simpkins from Wiltshire who could have served in the Wiltshire Regiment, as this one did, but closer identification is not possible. However, he received three medals: the 1914 Star for service under fire in France and Belgium, 5 August – 22 November, 1914; the British War Medal for service abroad; and the Victory Medal for military and civilian personnel who served in a theatre of war. It would be nice to know if he got home and ever had any more contact with Alvediston. The children had several 'talks' on the war, and drew maps of Europe, showing which countries were allies and which enemies. The relevant approaches, sea-boards and frontiers were also marked; as the war progressed, names of far-off places would become eerily familiar, and the war became the subject of compositions and songs such as 'Prisoners' National Anthems' and other with patriotic themes. By this time the fate of those injured, captured or missing was pressing, as well as bereavement. However, carol singing on St. Thomas' Day continued unabashed. 'It is the usual custom, which it seems impossible to break' is the teacher's weary comment.

1916 started with the lowest roll for seven years: only twenty-seven. It could be that, as wage-earning men-folk disappeared across the Channel, their families had to move away in search of work or to be nearer relations and facilities. Damp was appearing in a corner of the school room and the bell was out of action for six weeks. Mr. Foyle was finding it difficult to get work done due to the shortage of men. Snow lasting into March and the wretched chimney problems made matters worse. The cowl 'choked' again on the 24th. causing the chimney to catch fire and quantities of soot to fall, 'since then,' we read, 'the fire has drawn better.' Miss Cooper's optimism is commendable. On May 5th. Miss Young left to get married, thanked by yet another new vicar, the Rev. Alexander. With the rapid turnover of clergy during the war years, the vicarage and its incumbent feature less in school life. This could be a bane or a blessing, depending on the characters involved, but in spite of Wiltshire County Council's control of education, the vicar was still the local 'correspondent' in charge of the other 'managers', landowners or farmers. Trowbridge seems distant today, but a hundred years or so ago, with minimal and slow communication, it was almost foreign, certainly the counties of Dorset and Hampshire are much closer than Trowbridge.

As there was no suggestion of another assistant, Miss Cooper was left to manage alone. Desks were rearranged and valiant efforts made to follow timetables. In less than four months, including the harvest holidays, the attendance officer changed three times. A map rack took three months to arrive and water jugs even longer. However, a nurse was now visiting monthly and there was a blitz on head lice. Children suffering from these were 'dirty', or had 'verminous heads', while one poor family was marked 'XX'. Letters were sent to offending parents, but there would have been even less that they could do to eradicate them than today, when products regularly come on the market and 'nits' as regularly get the better of them. Perhaps the heavens took a hand in trying to stop carol-singing / begging on December 21st. for: 'One of the worst floods that can be remembered ran over the village this morning. Sixteen children managed to come in the morning, but the roads became impassable and they had to be taken home in a cart. None arrived in the afternoon.' Surely enough excitement for one day. The floods, at least, can be imagined, especially after the winter of 2006-7. With farms running on skeleton staff, farmers may have had to cut down on clearing ditches.

1917 did not have a propitious start. The school was closed one day in January for the teacher to go to the dentist, and then in the following week because she was ill. By February the cleaner was ill, so the premises did not get their monthly scrubbing, and a week later, 'Severe frost froze water in school jugs to a solid mass and when thawed one of them leaked, a hole having been forced through the bottom.' How frustrating, having waited months for them to arrive! The diocesan inspector hit upon a fuel economy: to combine his visit with one to Berwick, which would seem eminently sensible, war or no war. The coal ran out for a few days at the end of February, but there was more snow to come, so more absentees due to soaked clothes and feet. However, fires were discontinued on April 5th. a month earlier than the previous year. One boy requested 'war exemption', to start farm work, but was turned down.

Miss Cooper had a little cheer in August, when her salary rose to £120 per annum, backdated to June, but she had to wait another month for the first payment. The wet summer brought a late harvest, just when food production was causing concern. In the autumn the children collected between six and seven hundredweight, (about three hundred to three hundred and fifty kilos) of chestnuts in two months and, in response to an urgent letter from the Education Committee, they began collecting blackberries. Two half-holidays a week were granted for this, so on 15th. October they sallied forth 'in bands of 4 to pick at certain definite places in the district.' Three days later: 'Ch. taken blackberrrying on Gallows Hill. Berries weighed, packed and sent to station: 26 ½ lb. [nearly 10 ½ kilos] sent.' A card of congratulation arrived but also urged even more effort. The children rose to the challenge at Manwood: 'All picked steadily and the result was another 42 lb. [19 kilos] of berries.' It is interesting to speculate how children would rise to a national food crisis today. Would they be allowed to roam the hedgerows, even in 'bands of 4', without the supervision of one adult (CRB checked) per band, or the written authority of each parent and full insurance cover? All this might cloud the vision of rustic co-operation.

To remind us of the harsher realities of the time, notice of a dentist's visit to Berwick was received. After a day's delay, Miss Cooper fumed: 'Nine children (6-8) and their parents walked over to Berwick St. John, a distance of 2 miles, in heavy rain, merely to find that no dentist arrived, or any explanation of his absence.' Perhaps it was as well that they had the diversion of blackberrying because, when he finally came to the school almost a month later, he treated all nine in an hour, 'most of them having one or more teeth removed. The treatment was evidently painless as only one small child cried, and that was merely from fright.' No sympathy wasted there. Meanwhile, two boys were 'set to work' with hoe and spade to clean up the muddy school yard after adverse comment from the County Sanitary Inspector.

1918 dawned. 'The war' was blamed for delays in the delivery of stationery. On two occasions the temperature inside the school was only 34 degrees Fahrenheit (1° C) at 9 a.m. and once it just touched freezing, 32 degrees. When asked to light the fire earlier, the cleaner blamed the arctic conditions on 'bad coal'. Miss Cooper lost her voice and had to take a week off, and yet attendance was almost 100%. Perhaps even school was preferable to the bitter cold at home or worse, in the fields. The 'bad coal' ran out on March 30th. and by snowy mid-April with the children, who had been so brave during teeth-pulling, 'crying with cold', the school was closed for three days until ten hundred-weight of coal was delivered. Even with the fire lit the 9 a.m. temperature only read 48 degrees (less than 9° C) on April 22nd.

Deliveries of vital school materials reached crisis point. On May 3rd. Miss Cooper wrote: 'In spite of the fact that Messrs. Arnold were especially requested to forward goods requisitioned by April 7th. they have not yet arrived, and as for the last year or two, only the barest necessities have been ordered, the school is practically without books or working material.' Empire Day was celebrated with special lessons, an address from the vicar and a rendition of the National Anthem, but without flags and daisies. Was the concept becoming embarrassing or had the lassitude of war depressed such frivolity? The summer may not have brought much relief; in July wet and stormy weather kept the Higher Bridmore children, (who were just in the Berwick St. John parish,) at home.

September begins with a sorry rehearsal of building woes. The railings kept collapsing. The school had been scrubbed but the windows not cleaned during the holidays, and the school 'offices' had not been lime-washed. The managers' application for an efficient stove was delayed while they awaited a surveyor's inspection. Worse still, the earth buckets in the closets required 'attention' and the one for the house was leaking badly. All the windows needed new ropes, so presumably could not be opened, and the chimney and cowl needed to be swept. By the end of the month there was still no sign of the requisitioned goods and, even before the fire was lit, soot was pouring down the chimney and blowing around the school. The first fire was lit on October 4th. 'Result ~ Room full of smoke and ashes,' Miss Cooper wrote acerbically. Three days later: 'The smoke was so thick in the room this morning that the time could not be read from the desk. When it cleared slightly (it never quite cleared) everything was covered with soot and ashes.' Whatever effect can this have had on young lungs? A fortnight later, the cleaner once more excused herself from the monthly scrubbing due to a conveniently ill child. Her reluctance to clean may be unsurprising but poor Miss Cooper was drained of sympathy. 'She gets the money for doing it, whether it is done or not.'

The infamous influenza epidemic of 1918-19 swept through the village at this time and the mistress promptly succumbed, but had to drag herself back to the still-unscrubbed school after eight days as no supply teacher was available. November brought the county surveyor to inspect the stove and the first scrubbing for three months, but no mention of the end of hostilities. Nineteen year-old Lance Corporal George Grace died on November 4th. so any good news that filtered through may have been tempered tragically with bad. Others, like Private Walter Compton, whose family had moved to Romsey, returned wounded. He died at home in March 1919.

On 3rd. January, 1919 there is a gleam of better things to come. Villagers gathered in the school for an entertainment including three 'items' by the children, one of which was a sketch from 'Oliver Twist'. Three weeks later the bell, a constant source of irritation, 'fell from its fastenings' into the school house garden. After this dramatic collapse there is no further record of it being mended. Finally, with children once more crying with cold in temperatures of 38 - 39 degrees F. (3 - 3.5° C), the new stove arrived. After several days' holiday while it was fixed, the stove was lit on February 7th. and 'all seemed satisfactory'. Miss Cooper must have been loath to get too excited, but the stove proved its worth in the continually cold weather, heating the premises to a glorious 57 degrees F., about 14° C. and all continued to 'seem satisfactory', as long as there was coal ~ which ran out at the end of April, plummeting the temperature to 40 F. (4.4° C) again. Bureaucracy continued to frustrate: on March 21st. when it was still bitterly cold, a 'Telegram came from H.M.I. Purdie Esq. at 10 minutes to noon, requesting that Jack Moxham be at once sent to Berwick for a Lab. Cert. [Labour Certificate.] He went as soon as possible but when he got to Berwick was told that H.M.I. had left at 12.30 p.m.' Miss Cooper had a way of writing 'H.M.I.' which left the reader in no doubt of her opinion of him.

At last new hope dawned on July 4th. when 'The Rev. W.H. Courteen came in this morning about 10.15 & read the King's Proclamation concerning the Peace just signed. The children stood to hear it, & at the conclusion sang the National Anthem.' What did they understand by this and what did they feel? In fact, of course, the Treaty of Versailles was signed on 28th. June. Perhaps the slow and limited communication, tortuous though it seems today, enabled children to be shielded from much of the horror, and to enjoy more innocence and freedom. It seems extraordinary, having read of the privations of the war years and indeed, of life in general, to question the value of modern advances. However, with many children today suffering anxiety from news over which they have no control, the march of progress has brought its own problems.

This year there was more activity during the holidays as men returned from the war, and trades and crafts began to creak into action again. The interior of the school was distempered and varnished, new cords were attached to the windows, the 'offices' were lime-washed and the railings were repaired and creosoted, 'paint being practically prohibitive in price.' Unfortunately, delivery of requisitioned goods had not improved much; the autumn term started with no sign of any, even after ten weeks' wait. Benjamin Sims left for Shaftesbury Grammar School and when attendance dropped to seven due to measles and feverish colds, the school was closed for three weeks. Fortunately, health had been restored before the first celebration of 'Armistice Day' on November 11th. 'The King's Letter was read to the children. At 11 o'clock all work was suspended. The children knelt. The mistress read the Collect from the Burial Service, after which the children remained reverently silent. Hymn 437, ['For all the saints who from their labours rest'] was then repeated.' Familiarity over almost a hundred years makes it difficult to imagine the impact that this first simple ceremony had on awed and sketchily-informed young children. Today, some local children join the annual Act of Remembrance at the memorial, just a stone's throw from the school. Three days later, awe and formality were thrown to the winds when a 'Peace Tea' was held for the children in the Reading Room, followed by dancing and games. Expenses were covered by 'various subscriptions.' The younger children must have been especially impressed by such a treat after five years' austerity.

Early in 1920 pupils acted 'The Babes in the Wood' for an evening audience. Some supplies, including a fireguard, were beginning to get through but orders were incomplete, and Miss Cooper resorted to buying exercise books and ink herself 'as county supplies are exhausted.' In July, the Diocesan Inspector's Report was encouraging:

'For a very long time the mistress of this school has been single-handed. She has accomplished her difficult task remarkably well' and was especially commended for religious instruction. The verdict, 'It is a school in which good work is being done,' must have brought balm to her exhausted spirit, although modesty prevented any exuberance.

Alvediston School photograph, 1920. For names see Appendix. (Jean Heaney)

Two excursions to Bournemouth brought more treats. It was now six years since the start of the war, and the children's horizons would have been severely limited. Even the cleaner seemed more co-operative: the school was scrubbed over the summer, although the 'offices' had to wait for a lime-wash.

Term started in September with a worrying development for the future of the school: all pupils over eleven years were to attend school in Ebbesbourne or Berwick, leaving only seventeen in Alvediston. It must have been heart-breaking for Miss Cooper. She was running a school which was well-regarded, had staggered through the rigours and deprivations of the war and had maintained an excellent attendance record. Now she watched this like a hawk. It often ran at 100%, but on September 17th. she noted: 'A Fete at Ludwell rather spoilt attendance this week. 95%.' A month later we read of a familiar woe. 'No coal or wood yet received for the school. Temp. on 2 mornings this week 48 degrees [9° C] at 9 a.m., not rising above 52 [11° C] all day.' How she must have dreaded the onset of winter weather and illnesses. A new timetable was imposed and the first cases of mumps reported. Coal was not delivered until the end of November and on December 3rd. there was still 'No wood for the fire. Some lent by mistress and cleaner, just enabled fire to be lighted. Usual work carried on.' The last sentence became a mantra in the log, but, by mid-December, when a fire could not be lit and temperatures dipped to 34 degrees, (only just above freezing,) even Miss Cooper had to admit defeat. The children were sent home, but not for long. In response to a report to the vicarage, the correspondent 'very kindly' brought some wood for the fire, which was successfully lit at 11a.m. and school resumed as normal in the afternoon.

The speed of health intervention is illustrated by the reference, in January 1921, to a visit from a mother asking if anything was to be done about her son's eyes, which were 'reported faulty' a year earlier at the medical inspection, without any further steps being taken. There is no record of action in response to this request. The two tons of anthracite delivered in February were virtually useless without a supply of wood and the cleaner had to be chivvied to pay attention to the stove. Conditions concerning the 'Employment of Children' were read out; presumably the powers that be wanted to reduce the diversion of pupils' energy to the fields, but their injunctions were probably ignored by many parents as well as children. With the new school year, which began in April, the 'organisation for 1921-22' was recorded. Even after children over eleven years had left, the sole teacher had six different grades to educate from 'Standard V' to '3rd. Class 1 Infants' and only eight girls and nine boys in total.

Another frustration arose when the village milk lorry took to loading and unloading churns outside the school from 9.45 – 10 a.m. The clattering of these metal containers made 'drill' in the playground impossible, and the timetable had to be adapted. As so often happened, the weather became bitter in mid-April, with snow and winds, but finally some wood was delivered for the fire. On May 18th., 'A local wedding affected the attendance this morning.' This may have been

Jack Compton's, home after war service, as he was married in Berwick St. John in 1921. Empire Day was not celebrated, but on 27th. May, 'Privet Hawk Moth hatched from chrysalis that we have kept since last July.' In mid-July the temperature twice reached 84 degrees Fahrenheit, 30° C, which must have been as unpleasant as the cold. A school manager as well as parents pressurised Miss Cooper to end the summer term early so that children could go 'leasing', presumably gleaning. The cleaner promptly complained that she could not do the summer 'scrubbing' because there was no water. Over three weeks later, there was enough rain water for this exercise, but the windows remained untouched and the 'offices' were not lime-washed, yet again.

'Drill' was taken seriously. The County Drill Organiser visited in September and 'explained certain positions of the new Syllabus which had been misunderstood and promised to send a Book of Games.' The Diocesan Inspector seemed to appreciate aspects of education which we may associate with more modern times: 'This very small school was inspected on Sept. 30th. A very simple lesson with direct personal application was given to the Infants. Repetition was intelligently said. In the Upper Group the lesson drew on the understanding, and the children were very attentive. Throughout the whole school there is a happy relationship between the teacher and the children.'

In November, about a year and ten months after a medical inspection had shown that two children had sight problems, they were summoned to a clinic in Tisbury. It must have been a particularly dry summer, as by Armistice Day there was still no water available to the school and most of the local wells were dry. A week later there is a surprising note: the Education Committee Meeting at Trowbridge reported Alvediston to be one of the four 'cleanest schools in the County, over the longest period'! This, after Miss Cooper's constant battles with the cleaner, either says a great deal about her determination and standards, or not a lot about the state of other schools in the county.

When term started in January 1922, seven of the fifteen children were felled by whooping cough, so it was promptly closed again for three weeks. In early February the school dentist came to examine all the children over six years. Does this indicate that milk teeth were considered unimportant since they are lost naturally? An anxious note creeps in a week later: 'Attendance Officer called and mentioned the possibility of this school being closed. Managers informed.' As average attendance was still 99.3%, (possibly assisted by closure during epidemics,) the rationale must have been the lack of local school-aged children. Another incidental holiday was given on Princess Mary's wedding day.

How frustrating it must have been under the new pressures that 'school work [was] hampered by shortage of exercise books.' A Managers' meeting was held and 'Resolution passed deprecating closing of school.' Two days later, on April 1st. the new school year started. From 1923 school years were to run from 1st. August to 31st. July, but it was looking increasingly unlikely that Alvediston School would be affected by this. Numbers were down to thirteen, ranging from the 'super-normally bright' Jack Hull, who went on to get a first class honours degree in Mathematics at Oxford and whose memories are included in the next chapter, to some whom she found 'very difficult to classify' due to their needs for help. Miss Cooper's struggle to justify keeping the school open was not helped by the regular appearance of 'unclean heads' which had to be excluded for a week. Even the standards of cleaning, so recently praised, came under fire when the H.M.I. 'pointed out that the room was insufficiently dusted, and [he] made suggestions for more 'recognition' in Reading.' Mercifully, 'Otherwise he expressed satisfaction with the work.' He noted an improvement since the older children had moved to Ebbesbourne. 'Order is good and a pleasing relationship exists between the teacher and scholars. The children are natural and readily communicative, . . . pleasingly responsive . . . They take a living interest in the common things of the countryside' and the 3 Rs were generally good. Not a bad epitaph for the establishment, as it turned out. Incidentally, the written work on display in the school room at Tyneham, Dorset, gives an indication of the familiarity with nature of rural children at this time.

Although Miss Cooper could take comfort from this report, she must have known that soon she would lose her charges, her home and the school which had almost certainly been her life. She had to close the school for a few days in July when she lost her voice, and then the dreaded day came on the 13th. of that month. 'The Correspondent visited the school bringing a letter from the Board of Education, saying that this school 'cannot be considered necessary.' It will be closed on Aug. 31st.' The following day she noted bravely: 'Usual work this week.' The stock was to be transferred to Ebbesbourne Wake School, which lasted for another sixty-three years. On 22nd. July 1922, 'School assembled for the last time today. With the consent of the managers, worn out dilapidated books given to the children', whose names were: Jack and Arthur Hull, Edward and Frank Dalton, Edith and Dorothy Carter, Joe Collis, Frank and Douglas Compton, Edmund Roberts, Stuart and Molly Marks and the youngest, the five year-old Reginald Marks. Nearly eighty years later, Reg dictated his memories, which are included in this book.

The following day, stocktaking was completed and arrangements made for the school to be 'well cleaned' for one last time. With a dignity and economy of words which gave no indication of her feelings after fourteen years at the heart of the community, years which had seen unprecedented change and great hardship, the mistress ended with: 'This Log Book closed and sent to Trowbridge. D.W. Cooper, Head Teacher 1908 – 1922.'

Presumably Miss Cooper left to teach elsewhere, but she returned to Alvediston, probably on retirement. She lived at the Old Vicarage with Miss Wynne. From 1903-9 the vicar was the Rev. G.

Wynne, and he would have been at Alvediston when Miss Cooper arrived, but it is not clear whether Miss Wynne was a relation. When Miss Wynne moved to Salisbury, Miss Cooper went to Pimperne. In St. Mary's churchyard there is a stone marking the grave of 'Mary Cooper, my dear mother', who died in November 1916. Perhaps, among all the stress of running the school during the First World War, Dorothy Cooper also lost her mother. She herself is not buried here, but she is still fondly remembered by Pat Scrivens, the daughter of one of her pupils, Dolly Lodge, nee Compton, who worked for Miss Wynne and Miss Cooper at the Old Vicarage.

❋ Alvediston ❋

The Manor

A Time Line to demonstrate Ownership and leases ~ The Early Centuries ~ The Lawes and Rogers Families ~ The Sims Family ~ The Grant Family at Church Farm and the Marks Family at Elcombe and Bigly Farms ~ Manor House and Farm after 1938 ~ The Earl and Countess of Avon ~ 1980s – 2010 ~ Other Manor Properties, Past and Present ~ More About Bigly

A Time Line to demonstrate Ownership and leases

King Edwy granted the Manor to Wilton Abbey, which retained ownership until the Dissolution of the Monasteries

955	King Edwy granted the manor to Wilton Abbey
1066	Wilton Abbey held all Alvediston
1086	Wilton Abbey held all except Trow
1216	Wilton Abbey granted a lease to the Berenger family
1330	Ingram Berenger forfeited his lands for one year
1350	The Manor passed from the Berengers to the Pinnock family
1356	Nicholas Pinnock conveyed it to John Everard and Walter Godmanstone
1359	Everard passed it to Wilton Abbey. The Pinnocks probably rented it under new arrangements
1536	Wilton Abbey was dissolved by Henry VIII

1541   Sir William Herbert was given the estate

1551   He became 1st Earl of Pembroke, the family retained the Manor of Alvediston until 1918

Some possible tenants:

1485   William Taylor

1505   Thomas Tylden

mid 16th. C. onwards King / Kyng family (not Samways Kings)

Definite tenants:

1632-3   From the survey of Pembroke manors, William Gould was a freeholder and Thomas Toomer a tenant by indenture

mid 17th. C. the Lawes family, passing to a nephew, Joseph W. G. Rogers

1818   the Rogers family

by 1873 Frederick Gray of Samways rented the Manor and put his farm bailiff into the Manor House. First Henry Henly / Henley, later

1883   Josiah Sims

1918   the Manor was sold as 2 farms: Church (350 acres) and Elcombe (400 acres) to Thomas Henry Sims (Josiah's cousin) and Alfred Gladstone Hull (Josiah's son-in-law). The Hull family continued to live in the house

1923   the Manor was owned by Sims and Son (T.H. Sims and son Tom), Thomas Henry lived in the Manor House and Tom at Church Farmhouse

1938   Lady Glanusk bought the Manor House and farmstead, T.H. Sims moved into the former Police House, Elcombe Farmhouse

1940s   Bigly / Bigley and Elcombe farms, (by then 300 a.) were sold to William Marks, who sold 100 a. to J.M. Wort and farmed the rest himself. W. Marks continued to live at Shortsmead

1948   Mr. and Mrs. Mason bought the Manor House and farmstead

1954   Mr. and Mrs. Beckingham moved in, the property having been bought on their behalf by London trustees

1956   Trunnions, sold by Mrs. Gillam two years previously, was sold again, and became part of the manor estate

1959   George Grant bought Church Farm, the farmhouse was sold to Gen. and Mrs. Dewing

1966   The Earl and Countess of Avon bought the Manor House and farmstead

1975   the farm was sold to Lord Congleton, Trunnions was sold out of the estate

1977-8 3 properties in Elcombe Lane were sold, and became known as: Elcombe House, Elcombe Cottage, (formerly 2 homes), and Little Elcombe

1984   Rodney and Sue Heath bought the Manor House and 2 remaining cottages, Cross Cottage (gardener's cottage, formerly Post Office) and the Old School House, later adding the Old School Hall. The last two, like Trunnions, had passed in and out of ownership with the Manor for four decades

1988   Andrew Wardall bought the farmstead, which had already been converted into stables. He ran a bloodstock shipping company from there, later concentrating on breeding bloodstock

2000   Andrew and Rachel Wardall built a new house at Manor Farm Stud

The Early Centuries

WHATEVER THE ORIGINS of the name Alvediston, the manor itself had a remarkably low profile for much of its history, eclipsed by Norrington and Samways, as is obvious by the memorials in the church: the south aisle being dominated by the former and the north by the latter, with just two smaller plaques tucked away in a corner commemorating inhabitants of the manor house. In the vast acreage of the Wilton Estate, whether under the Abbey or the Pembrokes, a small manor towards the west of 'the vale of Chalke, the most sequestered and unfrequented district of the county', (Bowles), could easily be overlooked. However, there are a few details available for the earlier years and more from the mid-nineteenth century onwards.

In 955 King Edwy granted the hundred 'mansiunculae' or small dwellings in Chalke to Wilton Abbey, and this would have included the area covered by Alvediston, although it is not recorded by name. According to the *V.C.H.* the abbey probably owned all Alvediston in 1066, and all except Trow in 1086. 'Alfweiteston' appears in 1165, (Peter Meers' research) and 'Alfetheston' in 1197, (*V.C.H.*), but details are sketchy. However, from 1216, the Berengers were ensconced in the manor holding it 'at fee-farm' which reduced the control of the abbey.

The first Berenger was known as 'the butler'. Perhaps he served in court, where his kinsman, Walter Gifford, was a favourite of King William I, the Conqueror. Gifford's name is immortalised in Fonthill Gifford, where he held the manor. A few generations later Ingram, or Ingleram, Berenger inherited Alvediston manor in 1272, when he was very young, so his mother, Christine, acted as his guardian. She seems to have entrusted it to John of Grimstead and then his son. This John of Grimstead had considerable authority in Alvediston, as he 'held the advowson' of the village, which means that he had the right to present clergy to the living; he had what is now known as the patronage of a benefice. This, too, passed to his son. All went well for some years after Ingram achieved his majority; he gained free warren, i.e. hunting rights over his land, in 1304, but then somehow blotted his copybook, forfeiting his estate for a year from 1330. A writ of 1331 required the valuation of his lands and those of three others 'attainted as adherents to Edmund, late Earl of Kent', so his loyalty to King Edward III was under scrutiny. These inquisitions provide a convenient survey of his land in Ebbesbourne Wake and Alvediston. Henry le Frye, perhaps an ancestor of the Fry family still living in the area, was one of the jurors.

Berenger's manor of Alvediston had a 'capital messuage' or house and outbuildings, a garden, a dovecot, a windmill, two hundred and twenty acres of arable land, three and a half of meadow and ten of woodland. Rural society was undergoing change at this time, illustrated by the levels of tenant: 'free' tenants brought in twenty shillings of rent while 'customary' tenants produced twenty-six shillings and eight pence. The latter owed their lord, Berenger, goods and labour as well as money. Finally, there were 'cottars' who were essentially labourers, renting their cottage homes. Berenger, meanwhile, was a tenant himself, of the Abbess of Wilton, owing her money and goods. His other manor of Ebbesbourne was held from the king. By 1332 he was sufficiently restored for another inquisition to agree to the abbess of Wilton granting him for life two 'messuages' and eighteen acres in Alvediston, 'held of the King in chief'. He died in 1336 and was succeeded by his son, John, who died seven years later. John's son, Ingram was a minor and in 1350 John's nephew granted the manor to Nicholas Pinnock. In 1356 it was conveyed to John Everard and Walter de Godmanston, who may have been agents for the Abbess of Wilton because just three years later another inquisition agreed that Everard could pass Alvediston manor to the abbey in return for 'two tapers burning at the altar of Saint Edith in the Abbey church every day during the celebration of divine service.' Everard retained his land at Stratford-sub-Castle in Salisbury. In twenty-three years the rent paid for the manor had fallen from £8 10/- to £6 10/8d. This, like the flurry of conveyances, and perhaps the tapers at the altar, reflect the depredations of the Black Death. However, some names persisted: in 1752 Anne

Wyndham, an only child whose father owned Norrington and who also inherited the Ashcombe estate from her grandfather, Robert Barber, married the Hon. James Everard Arundell; John and Richard de Perham appeared as witnesses in some of the inquisitions and the Parham family returned as tenants of Norrington five hundred years later, while the surname Ingram appears in the parish registers in the eighteenth and nineteenth centuries, and there are still Ingrams in the valley today. Are the descended from Ingram Berenger?

The Pinnock family continued to rent the property from the abbey, possibly until the Dissolution of the Monasteries in the 1540s. Early in the fifteenth century, Alice, a daughter of John of Trow, married Geoffrey Pinnock, uniting two local families, although Trow, too, had passed to Wilton Abbey in 1345.

Little is known about those who farmed the manor under either the Abbey or the Pembrokes, until the later years. Adam Nicolson, in 'Arcadia' gives a fascinating account of the Wilton Estate, especially in the sixteenth and seventeenth centuries, from which one can imagine life in the far south-west of the estate. From 1485-1505, there was a William Taylor, 'farmer of Alvediston' in the estate records, and Thomas Tylden takes over, with a William Kyng who was a bailiff also mentioned, presumably an ancestor of the King family who feature large in local agriculture later. There are wills and other legal documents for members of the King family from the sixteenth century, (e.g. Nicholas in 1555, John in 1559, Matthew in 1594 and 'William Husbandman' in 1635).

However, in a *Survey of manors in co. Wilts, 1632-3*, there is a list of tenants and the value of their lands and buildings, giving both surnames and field names which are familiar today. William Goulde, gentleman was a freeholder, and Thomas Toomore a tenant by indenture, i.e. a sealed document or contract for property to be held, in this case, for the lives of his three sons, which included:

A dwelling house of 5 ground rooms lofted over and well repaired, 2 barns of 11 rooms, 2 stables, a cart house and cowhouse . . . a backside [yard], garden and orchard (in all 1 acre)', and meadows: Church Mead (8 acres), Long Mead (3½ acres), Fiddle Pit Mead (1¼ acre) and Green Way (2 acres). He had 140 acres of arable land among 7 fields (West, Middle and probably East Fields, and in the Peked, the Long and the Wood Closes, lastly 'in the Himphaid'); 8 acres 'of underwood and common pasture for 500 sheep'. The rent was 50s. 8d., and specified quantities of wheat, barley and oats, 12 capons, 12 geese, 160 pigeons and 45 wethers (castrated rams), or 11s. 5d. 'at the lord's discretion.

The V.C.H. notes that this part of Alvediston formed the manor's demesne farmstead, i.e. it provided food for the lord of the manor, Lord Pembroke, and that part of what is now known as Church House is late sixteenth or early seventeenth century: 'it had a three-room plan with a passage leading to a central rear wing'.

William Gould and his third daughter, 'Averen' or Averill, who was only fourteen, were among the copyhold tenants. Meadow land was held in Sheet and Tapps Closes, arable in Long and Upper Perham Fields, in Great and Little Sands, in Shap Close, Great Gaston, Broad Lease and in North Field. He also had access to common land and he held 'pastures and lands in Alvediston, called Perham Lands, sometime in the tenure of Robert Samwayes, gentleman, and now of the tenant' ~ more familiar field names and an indication of the intricacies of land tenure.

The 'dwelling house of 3 ground rooms, 2 lofted over, well timbered and sufficiently repaired' which Robert Toomer and Thomas Tilden held may have been the forerunner of the Manor House, surrounded by small paddocks: Home Close, Well Close and Upper Close and Wet Meadow (one field behind the house had a pond until the mid-twentieth century). They, like most of the other copyholders, had plots in the three large arable areas: South, Middle and Home Fields. There were several Toomers, and the names Morgan, Bannister, Poulden, Combe, Kinge, Bound and Hiscokes also appear. It is strange, today, to imagine so many, scattered, busy smallholders providing a livelihood, of sorts, for so many families in just a part of the current village.

The Lawes and Rogers Families

FROM THE MID seventeenth century records are clearer. The *V.C.H.* says that the land was leased to the Lawes family from that time. In the 1630s, a fifteen year-old William Lawes was named as a 'life' on a copyhold agreement in Broad Chalke. Copyhold tenancies were common from c. 1450 to 1650, allowing land to be held for usually three lives in a family, thus giving security of tenure at a cost of conservatism and close scrutiny by neighbours to ensure that no-one stepped out of long-accepted line. However, from the Restoration in 1660, as copyhold began to decline in favour of leasehold and rack-rent, custom and self-sufficiency were outsmarted by the lure of money, creating a class of agricultural labourer from less well-off yeomen farmers, while a few tenant farmers became more powerful. By the early nineteenth century, William Cobbett was both entranced by the beauty and fertility of the landscape in this area and scandalised by the exploitation of the poor. The diary of Charlotte Grove of Ferne, later wife of the rector of Berwick St. John, catalogues their misery in the post-Napoleonic war depression.

There is a lease from Lord Pembroke to William Lawes and his wife Anne dated 1693 and their daughter, recorded as 'Rebeck' in the register, was baptized at Alvediston two years earlier, when their eldest son, William, was eighteen. Mrs. Anne Lawes outlived her husband

and eldest son, reaching the grand age of ninety-nine in 1748, by which time another son John had the manor farm. He was probably the builder of the house as we know it today, upon the remains of one or more previous houses, about which there is frustratingly little information except, as Rodney Heath, the present owner, writes: 'The cellars seem to date from a much earlier period and are primarily built with large stone or chalk blocks', while the red bricks may have come from the kilns of Downton, that material being rare in the Chalke valley. The *V.C.H.* believes that the west front, (facing the road), dates from the early eighteenth century, confirming the style as Queen Anne; her reign was 1702-14. The east front 'was added or altered in the mid 18th century.' The story concerning a John Lawes adduced by the hunting parson of Chettle, William Chafin, in his 'Anecdotes and History of Cranborne Chase' as somewhat spurious evidence of the gentlemanly agreement between Lord Rivers and local farmers over deer-hunting is quoted in the chapter on Samways, as it was written at the time of Thomas King's 'Chase Cause'.

Bowles records a 'brass tablet against the north pillar of the chancel aisle': 'In memory of Katherine Lawes, who died 25th. December, 1758, aged 63.'

This Katherine, (spelt with a 'C' in the registers, where there is also confusion about 'Laws' with or without an 'e'), was married to the elder John Lawes, and they had five children: Elizabeth, John, Ann, Susanna and William, who died aged four. Unfortunately, during the Victorian church restoration the tablet was placed high on the north wall of the north transept, where it has discoloured and 'run', making it almost unreadable.

To return to the inhabitants of the manor, when the last Lawes, Thomas, died in 1818, at a great age, the lease passed to his young nephew, Joseph Walter Goddard Rogers. He and his wife, Mary, had seven children and, in 1827, Bowles described Mr. Rogers as 'the owner, and partly the occupier of the premises, under Lord Pembroke's lease'. As his widow died in Notting Hill, perhaps they spent the rest of their time in London. Rodney Heath, the present owner, learnt the sad story of how the Rogers family came to leave the manor:

During the summer of 1999, I had an unannounced visit from a Diana Maynard, an English lady, accompanied by her cousin, a young American called Edward Rogers, whose ancestors had lived in Alvediston. I was delighted to show them around the property. Subsequently, I was sent some notes by Diana Maynard containing the following information:

'Joseph Rogers, who had assumed the lease in 1819, died in Alvediston in 1852. His eldest son, John Rogers, who had been born in Alvediston on 21st. November, 1824, (died in Dendron, Virginia, U.S.A. on 20th. May, 1904) inherited the lease but under terms of his father's will, the lease was charged with annuities in favour of his mother, sister and brothers. Presumably John Rogers was able to pay these annuities out of profit from the sale of sheep and cattle raised on the three farms of Church, Elcombe and Bigley. All apparently went well until the advent of competitively priced beef from Argentina which made the payment of the requisite annuities impossible.

'Instead of trying to negotiate a moratorium or reduction in the annuities, John Rogers took out a mortgage on all that he owned in order to purchase from an insurance company annuities in the amounts to which other members of his family were entitled. Unfortunately for him, Argentine beef continued to flood the English market. Frustrated and bitter, he sold his equity in the property in 1873, using the proceeds to purchase through a London banker, a farm in Virginia. He left immediately for his new home which he called Elcombe. He was shortly followed by his wife and five sons and had no further contact or communication with any of his brothers, sister or Alvediston.'

In 1939 Miss Alice Rogers collected $100 from relatives towards a bell restoration fund, but sadly her initiative and their generosity came to naught with the onset of the Second World War the same year.

Joseph and Mary Rogers' deaths are recorded on a handsome tablet of white marble on a charcoal-grey marble background, just below Katherine Lawes', and rather dwarfed by the two King monuments nearby, certainly by those of the Wyndhams opposite:

In memory of
Joseph Walter Goddard Rogers
who died December 4th. 1852
aged 63 years
Also of Mary his wife,
who died at Notting-Hill, London
Jan. 7th. 1858, aged 62 years.

Both Joseph and John Rogers were active in the life of the church and village at a time when a Parham, Rogers, Day triumvirate relished sharing responsibility after the dominance of the King family. Indeed, just a year before John Rogers' unhappy departure from his birthplace, a note in the Church Log Book reads: '1872 It was agreed by Mr. Day, Mr. Rogers and Mr. Parham to pay £4 each towards defraying the expenses of the church. P.S. Desprez, chairman.'

This was before collections were a regular feature of services, so the goodwill of the locally well-heeled was essential, but the church was usually still dependent upon spontaneous donations. It is particularly poignant that John Rogers' precipitate and resentful departure occurred at a time when the community was flourishing, with a newly refurbished church, a school about to be opened and a pub recently established in the village. However, as Peter Meers points out in his book on Ebbesbourne, the 1870s marked the beginning of the decline of agriculture which had shattering effects on the rural economy. Although farming continued to dominate village life for another eighty years or so, in the twenty-first century very few inhabitants are involved. 'The first signs of this major revolution appeared between the censuses of 1871 and 1881 and were the result of rapidly rising demand compounded by a series of wet summers and poor harvests. The rising price of grain forced Gladstone to allow the importation by steamship across the Atlantic of cheap prairie-grown corn from North America, and meat and cheese were imported from elsewhere. In the 1830s about 2% of the grain consumed in England had been imported. In the decade beginning 1880 the figure was 45%, and for wheat, 60%. Between 1870 and 1890 chalk-land production of wheat and barley fell by over 25%, the number of sheep fell by 20%, and water meadows went out of use.' John Rogers' personal tragedy and its effect on three of the five farms in Alvediston bring these figures into sharp focus.

Next, the Manor house declined in prestige. Confusingly, in the 1851 census, Samways is described as 'Alvediston House', inhabited by the last Thomas King, while Josiah and Mary Rogers, their son John and five daughters lived in 'New Buildings' with three female servants. Since we know that they lived at the manor, the novelty of the eighteenth century construction clearly had not worn off even after over a hundred years. This is hardly surprising. Dwellings appeared and decayed without causing much stir, but, apart from Norrington, Samways and the house at Church Farm, which had been established for centuries, all the others were basically cottages, some insubstantial, in which working families were crowded in alarming density. By 1881, even the Manor house had sunk into anonymity, only distinguished from other homes in the 'Street' by being inhabited by the farm bailiff, Henry Henly, (elsewhere spelt Henley), his daughter and one servant.

Rear of Manor Farm, with Josiah Sims (in doorway) and his cousin Thomas Henry
Sims. Note the cottage (right) on the opposite side of the road. (Jean Heaney)

The Sims Family

HOWEVER, TWO YEARS later the Manor House came into its own again with the arrival of Josiah Sims as farm bailiff to Frederick Gray of Samways, who rented the manor land from Lord Pembroke. Josiah's descendents have contributed useful family information. The 1891 census may still have counted the manor as just another home in the Street, but Josiah's grandchildren referred to their childhood home as 'Manor Farm' or 'the Manor'. His mother was a Benjafield, from the farming family in Ebbesbourne Wake, and Josiah was a farm bailiff in Tollard Royal before moving to Alvediston. It is not quite clear when he became a tenant farmer in his own right, but at some stage he began renting the Elcombe part of Manor Farm, while his cousin, Thomas Henry, had the Church Farm part. In 1872 he had married Emma Roberts, whose family ran 'The Rose and Thistle' inn in Rockbourne, and their elder daughter,

Amy Sims (a cousin from Yeovil) pushing Peggy and Dick Hull outside the front of Manor Farm, c. 1910. (Rosalyn Barnes)

Evlyn, was born in August 1877, May (or Maisie) arriving almost exactly six years later, at about the same time as the family moved to Alvediston. As Josiah and Emma were staunch nonconformists they were not involved with the church. However, they were influential and clearly popular in the village, so much so that, in accordance with the Parish Councils Act of 1895, Josiah was chosen as the first District Councillor, gaining twenty-two votes to the vicar's fourteen, which must have been a blow for democracy since the village had been ruled by the church and landowners since time immemorial. The previous year had seen the opening of the Primitive Methodist Chapel in East or Ice Lane. Initially it had sixty 'sittings', but these were increased to a hundred and eight just nine years later. In view of the chapel's short active life it is good to know that it was at maximum accommodation in time for both Josiah's daughters' weddings, and it is extraordinary to imagine the need for such a commodious place of worship in addition to a church, in such a small village, even allowing for the fact that non-conformists travel to worship more readily than Anglicans.

May was the first to marry, in 1906, aged twenty-three. Edgar John Hull was a Primitive Methodist minister who came to take the chapel service once a quarter. They were only married for eight years as May died of T.B. in 1914. Edgar's best man was his brother, Alfred Gladstone, who had emigrated to South Africa and was working in the Post Office there. He and Evlyn decided to follow their brother and sister's lead, and married, also in the chapel, in 1908. Both wedding parties were photographed outside the then main entrance, on the east side of the house. One of Evlyn's young bridesmaids was Doris Sims, daughter of Josiah's cousin Tom Henry and his wife Blanche.

The wedding of Evlyn Sims and Alfred Gladstone Hull, June 1908. The wedding took place at the Methodist Chapel, and the photograph was taken in the Manor House grounds. Doris Sims was the small bridesmaid on the right. (Jean Heaney)

After starting married life at Lower Bridmore Farm, Berwick St. John, Alfred and Evlyn moved back to Alvediston, living with her parents. Alfred valiantly 'learnt' farming from his father-in-law and from books. They had five children, Dick, Margaret, (Peggy), Alfred John, (Jack), Arthur and Wilfred. When they were very young the children had lessons in the attic; Jack's memories of doing long division on a slate up there may show his early aptitude for maths. Years later he got a first class degree in the subject at Oxford, probably the only pupil of Alvediston School to scale such academic heights. The family's first teacher was Ella Benjafield, wife of Percy at the manor in Ebbesbourne Wake. In another part of that manor lived Percy's sister, Mabel Buchanan and her daughter, (Elizabeth) Geraldine.

Geraldine, or Gerry, as she became known, had an interesting history which came to light in her birthplace after her death in 2008, (having celebrated her centenary the previous November.) Her family asked for her ashes to be buried with her Benjafield relations in Ebbesbourne Wake churchyard, left money to the church and provided a 'Book of Record' for contributions about the lives of others who may donate in this way, including a page about her life, with photographs. Almost immediately their hope that the album will help people to connect family stories bore fruit.

When Josiah and Emma Sims moved to Alvediston, George Benjafield and his significantly younger second wife, Sarah, lived at the manor in Ebbesbourne with their six children. Mabel, the second, was fourteen. In 1901 she was working as housekeeper to Wilfred Benjafield at 'The Close' nearby. She married Gerald Buchanan and they made a new life on a ranch in Saskatchewan, Canada. However, only months before his first child's birth, Gerald contracted lock-jaw and died. Mabel's return across prairie and ocean must have been harrowing, but she made it back to her childhood home in time to give birth to Geraldine. By then her youngest brother, Percy, was living at the manor with his wife Ellen, 'Aunt Ella' to Geraldine and her Hull cousins. An abiding memory which has been passed down through both families is that, when Geraldine walked over to Alvediston with her aunt for lessons in the Manor attic with the Hull children, she had to steel herself to pass squawking and hissing geese in a farm, probably West End, along the way. In 1919, she and her mother moved to Salisbury so that she could pursue her education at the Godolphin. Any schooling beyond that provided in the village presented problems hard to imagine today, when parents have a choice of state schools in both directions, accessed by bus, and there is a further dizzying selection of private establishments within range of the school run. Less than a hundred years ago the options for secondary education, if parents could afford to consider them, necessitated boarding in Shaftesbury or Salisbury, staying with convenient relations, the whole family moving into town, or, for the very few, public school. The vast majority of children, of course, started work on the land or in service at thirteen or fourteen with little expectation of moving far beyond local villages, as work dictated, until the young men were hurled into the melée of the First World War.

Until her last years, Geraldine remained in Salisbury, marrying Robert Potter, a young architect who arrived in the city and became well-known there in the Brandt, Potter and Hare (later the Sarum) Partnership which had a high reputation in ecclesiastical circles. During the war, Robert was mostly in India so Geraldine and her two sons went to live with her mother and Aunt Ella in Meyrick Avenue. Her daughter was born several years later. Her elder son, John, lives in Salisbury.

To return to the Sims / Hull family: as Josiah's health failed, Alfred took on more and more responsibility for the farm. The year after Josiah's death in 1917 must have been momentous for the growing family in many ways: the reality of the end of the war would have taken a while to permeate through to Alvediston as conditions at home were still grim and servicemen returned only gradually; influenza struck viciously at this time, but the family at the manor came through all this. However, the Wilton Estate, with its need for a huge workforce, inevitably had to make changes and Alvediston manor was one of the estates which came up for sale. Alfred Hull joined forces with Thomas Henry Sims to buy the two separate farms, Elcombe and Church, jointly but, within a few years, the combination of financial and educational problems, led to further changes. By 1923, Alfred had to relinquish his holding in the Alvediston farms in favour of Sims and Son, Thomas Henry and Tom.

Some years before his death in 2001, Jack Hull wrote down his memories, and had this to say about his childhood:

I was born on the 13th. of April in 1913 in the Manor House in Alvediston which is a tiny village in the south of Wiltshire. I know it was a Sunday morning and a message was sent down to the Chapel where a service was being held. I don't know what I weighed but I think I was quite heavy.

My mother was 35 years old and my father was 33. I already had a brother called Dick who was nearly four and Margaret was nearly 3. I was named Alfred John but it would have been confusing to call me Alfred because that was my father's first name. So eventually, apart from a few nicknames, I was known as Jack.

Manor House was a big house with big gardens and an orchard with lots of fruit trees. There were five bedrooms as well as more rooms in the attic, and two more brothers, Arthur and Wilfred arrived, so then there were five children altogether. One of my Grandmas lived with us. She had come to the house in 1883 when my mother was six years old.

My father was a farmer, so I saw cows and horses and sheep and pigs. He had a tiny car called a Swift. There was room for only one grown-up person or two little ones perhaps.

In the next village there was a cousin named Geraldine and she came over to our house with her aunt, named Ella, who gave us all lessons. When I was six, I started going to the village school and I could read a bit and do little sums. Children were aged up to thirteen but there was only one teacher for all of us.

In the evenings, we often played games together. Of course, there was no television or wireless and no electricity, so we had some oil lamps downstairs but we had candles when we went up to bed.

I don't think we had any pocket money because there weren't any shops anyway, but there was a little post office and the postman came twice a day to the village on his bicycle. Two bakers' vans called and a butcher and a fish man. We had milk from the farm.

Quite soon, the children aged ten and upwards had to go to the school in the next village, called Ebbesbourne Wake, and there were only about twelve of us left. After a year like that, somebody decided our school must be closed, and we all had to go to the next village. I think I was a bit scared at the thought of that, because we had to walk about a mile on a country road ~ there were practically no cars at that time. We took sandwiches and a bottle of drink, and I think I must have had some pocket-money because in Ebbesbourne there was a village shop and I can remember buying a half-pennyworth of sweets there. I seem to remember that I enjoyed most of the lessons and we had a good lady teacher.

One day at school I wasn't well and they managed to arrange for the fish-man who was on his rounds to take me home in his van pulled by a horse. There weren't any telephones, so my mother was surprised when I arrived.

By 1924, Dick was at a boarding school in Shaftesbury, and Margaret, (who by then was usually called Peggy) went to a school in Salisbury and came home, often on a bicycle, for the weekends. There were no buses. In the village there was another farmer called Uncle Tom and he had a Ford car and sometimes he would drive to the market in Shaftesbury and he would give my mother and me a lift, so I got to know Shaftesbury fairly well, and mother did some useful shopping there.

My parents decided it would be better for their children's

schooling if we lived in a town, so in April 1924 we moved to Salisbury, but my father still had a farm. Grandma moved with us of course, but gradually became house-bound until she died in 1931.

They had bought a three-storey detached house which was pleasantly situated. The three younger boys started at new schools. Wilf and I went to St. Mark's and Arthur to St. Thomas's School. (While at St. Mark's I had gone on a day trip to the Exhibition at Wembley). After one term I moved on to the Bishop's School. The others followed four or five years later. I walked about 1½ miles to school and home for dinner, so that was about six miles a day. I think I must have enjoyed school life as I have scarcely any unpleasant memories.

From here, Jean Heaney, Peggy's daughter, takes up the story.

When Lord Pembroke decided to sell the land the local farmers were renting in the Alvediston area, this caused many of them financial problems. Alfred Hull took out a mortgage to buy a farm at Prescombe on the Salisbury side of Ebbesbourne Wake, but there was no farmhouse attached. Thinking of his children's education he bought a house in Hulse Road, Salisbury in 1924, and drove out to Prescombe every day, where he had a small office built. Dick continued as a boarder at Shaftesbury Grammar School for a little longer, and the others started at local schools in Salisbury. Peggy had already moved to the High School there, lodging with an aunt, and travelling out to Alvediston at weekends, often on a bicycle, so she continued there. The three younger boys finished up at Bishop Wordsworth School. When Dick left school he took lodgings at Ebbesbourne and started work with his father at Prescombe farm, perhaps in the expectation that he would become an 'under-foreman'. Emma continued to live with the family after Josiah's death, so she moved to Salisbury with them until she died in 1931.

In 1932 Alfred decided to sell the house in Hulse Road, and get a house built at Prescombe farm, so the family moved there. This made it easier for Alfred and Dick to work. In September 1932 Peggy was married at the Methodist chapel in Alvediston to Geoffrey Buxton, a young airman she had met in Victoria Park, Salisbury, some six years earlier, and they sailed together for Egypt where Geoffrey was stationed. Jack started at Oxford University. Arthur started a job with Dunn's farm Seeds in Salisbury and lodged there, and only Wilfred was still at school, and travelled to Salisbury daily.

By 1936 farming had become very unprofitable, so with a mortgage still in place Alfred was forced to sell Prescombe farm and its land at a very low price, and he and Evlyn moved back to Salisbury to a rented house in Campbell Road. At 57, and with 2-3 million unemployed it was difficult for Alfred to find a job, and it was not until 1939 that he got a clerical position with the Wilts and Dorset Bus Company. By this time Dick had married Rachel Henstridge and settled in Breamore, near Fordingbridge, where he worked in farming for the rest of his life, but he was never to have his own farm. Arthur and Wilfred still lived at home.

When war broke out the four brothers all 'joined up'. Dick and Wilfred joined the army, Arthur became a pilot in the RAF, and Jack, having obtained a first class honours degree in Maths at St John's College, Oxford, also joined the RAF, but mainly as a civilian for them in rather 'hush-hush' work in meteorology, spending almost three years in Lisbon. Peggy moved into Campbell Road with her parents and her two children for several years while her husband, Geoffrey, was fighting in Malta.

Arthur married his childhood sweetheart, Peggy Lampard, early in the war, but tragically he was killed returning from a bombing raid when he was only 26. After the war Jack returned to a career as a maths teacher at Hereford Grammar School. He married Moya Wadie, and finished his career as Head of Maths at Hereford

Sixth Form College. Wilfred's career was with the General Accident Insurance Company in Salisbury. He married Mary Whitlock, and later they moved to London when he was promoted. Peggy spent her life as the wife of a regular serviceman, moving all over the country.

Alfred died in 1952, and Evlyn lived with Wilfred and Mary, spending time with all her children and grandchildren until she died in 1965.

These accounts give a fascinating insight into the limited horizons balanced by the importance of deliveries, the development of self-reliance in the young and the wonder of the slightly wider world opened up by car travel, within a few decades extending to flights across the world in aircraft and life in different countries and cultures. The move to Salisbury might have been traumatic for a boy who, less than two years earlier, was daunted by walking to school in the next village, but the family's fortunes reflect the massive upheavals felt in the country as a whole through two world wars and a crippling economic depression. Many other families were dispersed to seek a life and employment in towns; some spread out to neighbouring villages, but only two remain in Alvediston to this day. The number of descendents who visit, seeking to re-establish family links with the village shows how valuable a family archive like the Sims'/ Hull's is. More information can be found in 'Footprints through a Century', written by Peggy's daughter, Jean Heaney, about her family from the 1880s to the 1980s, starting in Alvediston and especially following her father's career as a photographer in the RAF, where, among other fascinating experiences, he met and worked with Lawrence of Arabia. After her marriage, Peggy's life as a service wife whether abroad, moving around this country or in Salisbury with her parents and children for long wartime years would have been impossible to anticipate during her Alvediston childhood but probably resonates with the experience of many other women of the time.

What of the other branches of the family? 'Uncle Percy Benjafield' of Ebbesbourne Wake Manor was also approached by Lord Pembroke with a request that he buy the property, in 1920/21. However, as he could not afford the asking price he moved to a farm in Farnham which he passed to his son Guy and then to his grandson John, who was still there in 2000. Doris Sims, Evlyn's child bridesmaid, and daughter of Thomas Henry and Blanche, became a music teacher but died unexpectedly during a minor operation in about 1935. In her memories recorded for this book Joan Reeves recalls the shock felt by the entire village. Tom Henry Sims sold the three hundred acres of Elcombe and Bigly Farms to William Marks of Shortsmead, and lived at Church Farm but, after Alfred Hull had to sell up his part of the manor estate, he moved up to the Manor and stayed there until he sold it to Lady Glanusk in 1938. He then went to the former Police House, which was known as Elcombe Farmhouse.

In 1918, this house had been sold by the Pembroke Estate as let to the Wilts. County Council and occupied as THE POLICE STATION.

> The House, the Front Portion Brick and Slate and the Back Portion Stone and Thatched contains Front Entrance Passage, Sitting Room, Kitchen at Back with Range and Dresser; Back Kitchen with Grate and Copper; Pantry, Three bedrooms ~ Two Attic Rooms, with Lean-to Slated Wood and Coal House.
>
> Large Garden, with Stone and Tiled Piggery, E.C.' (earth closet) and Draw-well. The Property is let to the Wiltshire County Council at an Annual Rent of £6. 0s. 0d. Outgoings ~ Tithe, commuted amount, 3s. 0d. Land Tax, 5s. 9d.

Thomas Henry Sims' younger son, Ben, lived next door, in what is now Elcombe Cottage, farming 'Long Ground', now Manor Farm Stud, incorporating most of the original Manor Farm. Meanwhile the elder son, Tom, and his wife, Ivy, farmed Church Farm, living in the current Church House until Tom became very ill with a brain tumour. Ivy kept the farm going for a time with advice from Bill Marks. Tom and Ivy had two children, Faith and Keith. Faith was a G.I. bride, so emigrated to America. She died in 1998. As Keith joined the Navy, the house was sold to General and Mrs. Dewing.

The Grant family at Church Farm and the Marks family at Elcombe and Bigly Farms

CHURCH FARM WAS sold to George Grant, in 1959. Roy Marks recalls working for George and his aunt when they lived at Glebe Farm, Fifield Bavant. George specialised in

James (Jim) Kelly Topp (1904-62) and his son Peter Douglas Topp (1927-95) by the dairy at Church Farm, 1950s or earlier. (Mildred Read) [Church Farm dairy]

sheep with his wife, Pay. They brought up their family in the new farmhouse at the top of the hill. Pay used to breed Jacob's sheep, with their distinctive black and white fleeces, Soays, small, goat-like sheep, and Mouflons, one of the earliest breeds of domesticated sheep, in addition to the main flocks. Church Farm remains in the Grant family, farmed by Pay and her son, Joe who built Little Aston in 2005.

Tom Henry's other daughter, Gwendoline, became Mrs. Gillam. In the 1940s, when her father retired, they joined forces to build the bungalow 'Trunnions', just to the east of the old chapel, on land which was part of the manor farm. Thomas Henry died in 1949, his wife having pre-deceased him by five years.

The Marks family has continued at Elcombe Farm to this day, and it has been worked by succeeding generations: Bill's son Roy, and Bella, Roy's nephew Trevor, and Sue; now their daughter, Christina, has joined them. The actual acreage has fluctuated; Bill marks sold Bigly, (over a hundred acres), to Mr. Wort and rented it back. This farm now belongs to Perin Dineley, but Trevor still has the shooting rights. Elcombe Farm comprised one hundred and fifty acres in 2009, since, in recent years, nineteen were sold to Perin Dineley to join Bigly and ten to Les Kail when he built Hunter's Lodge next to the farm buildings. However, the Marks family now farms a thousand acres in all, much of it rented outside the village. The dairy has long gone and is now converted into a house; there is no arable land, where recently there were fields of corn. Today, sheep and cattle are reared, and the shoot is an important source of income, while, in the summer, two teepees provide holiday accommodation and party venues. In late Spring 2011, Elcombe Farm was put on the open market, and a new chapter is about to begin.

Manor House and Farm after 1938

THE MANOR HOUSE changed hands several times during the middle years of the twentieth century. Victoria Bailey, Baroness Glanusk, (a place famous for its whisky), who bought the house and immediate farmland in 1938, carried out major renovations in her ten-year ownership, transforming it from a manor farmhouse into something altogether grander with the aid of panelling, doors, mantels, pediments and ornaments from other residences. Reg Marks was one of the builders involved and other workmen lodged next to the 'shop', presumably the small one run in conjunction with the Post Office in the Street. Lady Glanusk later married Mr. P.B. Frere, and the next owners were the Masons, whose fortunes stemmed from Mason's Sauce. They were only there for five or six years. The sales brochure of 1953 describes the Manor House, a thatched and brick cottage, (now Cross Cottage, formerly the Post Office), another cottage west of the Ansty road, visible from the Sims' photographs but since demolished, the farm house, (now Elcombe House), three farm cottages along Elcombe Lane, 170 acres and the farm steading, (now Manor Farm Stud). The steading consisted of a range of farm buildings adapted for the use of the Alvediston Pedigree Jersey Herd. They comprised a cow house, divided into eight loose boxes to tie sixteen, (but up to twenty-six,) another loose box, garage, dairy, boiler house, implement shed, a four bay Dutch barn, a barn converted into three covered yards for young stock, feed and root houses and a workshop. There were also three further loose boxes including a bull pen, and standing for ten cows. The former Primitive Methodist chapel, which had closed and been sold in 1951 to Mr. Sims, (under covenant that liquor should never be sold there, and that it should never be used as a dance hall), had already degenerated into a corn store. The sales particulars describe the land as having rich pastures and leys giving healthy grazing; 'great root yields and the custom and corn crops are prolific. With its high-yielding pedigree Jersey herd the farm is self supporting and produces in addition handsome 'cash crops'. It could well maintain a dairy or beef herd of 50/60 and followers.'

Deeds for Elcombe Farmhouse note that the Masons sold in 1954 to trustees for Mrs. Beckingham, who owned it until 1966. The Beckinghams added a further one hundred and fifty acres, post and railed most of the paddocks with oak fencing and devoted much of their farming interests to the breeding of thoroughbred horses, as well as pigs and Jersey cattle. They moved to Berwick St. John, having sold the property and approximately three hundred acres to the former Prime Minister, Anthony Eden, First Earl of Avon.

The Earl and Countess of Avon

ANUMBER OF BIOGRAPHIES have charted Anthony Eden's life and achievements in great detail, so only a brief sketch will be given here. He was born in 1897 and brought up in County Durham, at Windlestone, a great country house, but in the middle of mining country, and he was very conscious of the needs of working men. Early in his political career he concentrated on social and economic policy. He had an elder sister and was the third of four sons, so always knew he would have to find a career. At ten he was sent south to a preparatory school in Cobham, Surrey called Sandroyd, which years later moved to its present site, the Pitt-Rivers' former home, Rushmore, just a few miles from Alvediston. While he was still at Eton, his eldest brother, Jack, was killed during the early weeks of the First World War, and in 1915 he joined the King's Royal Rifle

Sir Anthony Eden, Lord Avon, with Hereford bull. (Clarissa, Countess of Avon)

Corps, as an officer with recruits from his home county of Durham. He won the Military Cross and became the youngest Brigade Major in the army, but he also lost his beloved younger brother, Nicholas, in the Battle of Jutland in May 1916. Nicholas had joined the navy only a few months earlier, before his sixteenth birthday. At the end of the Second World War his elder son, Simon, was killed in Burma. His second son had died soon after birth and only Nicholas outlived him, by eight years: his ashes are buried by his father's grave in Alvediston churchyard.

After the First World War he went to Christ Church, Oxford where, already fluent in French and German, both of which proved useful in his future career, he studied oriental languages, gaining a first. He was able to pursue his lifelong interests in art, the theatre and literature, but also became increasingly interested in politics. In December 1923, a month after his marriage to Beatrice Beckett, he was elected Conservative M.P. for Warwick and Leamington as Captain Eden, at a time of political confusion, initially in opposition, but the Conservatives led in the election of the following October. After Eden's death, Lord Carr said of his domestic politics:

> His great concern was with thoughts of joint consultation, the sharing of information, of decision-taking, of partnership. He kept using the phrase 'a property-owning democracy'. Although that was largely thought of in terms of home ownership, in his mind the really important part of it was the ownership of responsibility, the sense of ownership of one's job, of proper dignity and satisfaction in one's work. That was what he meant to be the domestic theme of his premiership.

Also in January 1977 Edward Heath, by then a former Prime Minister himself, told the House of Commons:

> For my generation at university, in the second half of the 1930s, Anthony Eden personified the struggle against tyranny in Europe. He had a deep and passionate belief in the maintenance of the rule of law. I do not believe it possible to understand any period of his life or any aspect of his career without recognising how deep that belief went.

His experiences of war, as a soldier, a politician and a bereaved relative, informed his actions as Foreign Secretary, (a post he held three times, 1935-38, 1940-44 and 1950-55), and as Prime Minister, (1955-57). He wrote: 'War promoted working together into something good and true and rare, the like of which was never to be found in civil life.' Famously, he opposed appeasement with Hitler, initially an unpopular move, but, as his biographer Thorpe writes:

> Eden's stance . . . during the Munich period, illustrated his deep belief in the sanctity of diplomatic agreements as a means of underpinning international stability. He showed himself to be an optimistic idealist in these matters . . . Eden's belief in upholding a regulated structure in the conduct of foreign relations was to underpin his actions in the post-war era also, particularly at Geneva in 1954', (the conference on Korea and Indo-China,) 'but also in his detailed work on the Western European Union and the European Defence Community. Even Nasser, who eventually broke the 1954 Suez Base Treaty, was a man with whom Eden at first negotiated in good faith.'

In 1956 the Suez crisis was complicated by the anti-colonial attitude of America's President Eisenhower and his Secretary of State, John Foster Dulles. Anthony Eden was born just ten days before Queen Victoria's Diamond Jubilee, when the might of the British Empire was fervently celebrated. However, its influence was beginning to wane already, and continued to do so, but Eden and his contemporaries in Britain grew up valuing it enormously. Likewise, as a decorated veteran of the First World War and as Foreign Secretary for much of the Second, he believed that there was no contradiction in fighting for peace when necessary. When the Suez crisis was at its worst he maintained, in a national broadcast:

> All my life I have been a man of peace, working for peace, striving for peace, negotiating for peace. I have been a League of Nations man

and a United Nations man and I'm still the same man, with the same convictions. I couldn't be other, even if I wished.'

Eden's marriage to Beatrice was not easy, especially as she had no interest in politics. After their son Simon's death in June 1945, it became harder still for them both, and in 1950 they were divorced.

His second wife, Clarissa Churchill, niece of Sir Winston, was born in 1920, and she maintains an interest in Alvediston to this day. She was significantly younger than her two brothers, and, her father Jack being close to his more colourful brother, the two families saw a great deal of each other. Through her mother, the young Clarissa met many liberals and intellectuals, and grew up to be far more independent than many of her peers. She spent time in Paris and Oxford, pursuing her interests in art, literature, travel and philosophy, and worked for 'Vogue' magazine, in film publicity, and for a publisher, after experience in the Foreign Office during the war. Despite limited formal education, she was extremely well-read and well-informed so was able to fulfil her intention to support her husband, who, just months after their marriage in August 1952, became extremely ill with a gall-bladder problem which, due to bungled treatment, led to complications for the rest of his life. His wife's nursing care was crucial to his survival, and her country cottage became a vital retreat. Rose Bower is situated at the west end of Broad Chalke, in the incongruously named Little London. To the south is Mount Sorrel, owned for many years by the Gawen family and to the north, a property which has been incorporated into Knapp Farm but which once belonged to the Parhams, all of Norrington. Clarissa Churchill had bought it in the late 1940s, after a tip-off from her old friend Cecil Beaton, who had moved to Reddish House in Broad Chalke. In her memoirs she describes her 'Gainsborough view down the valley with a wych-elm in the foreground.' Thus began an enduring relationship with the area, such that when, after Eden's retirement from politics, they needed a permanent home away from the stresses of London, it was no surprise that, after eight years in a manor near Pewsey, they fixed upon 'a smaller red-brick Queen Anne manor in ~ to my joy and Anthony's ruefulness ~ the very same Wiltshire valley where my cottage was.'

Although written a few months before their arrival in Alvediston, an extract from Anthony Eden's diary in August 1966, (quoted by Robert Rhodes James in his biography), sums up the attraction for them of rural life:

> A lovely day. C. and I spent it happily in the garden. Alone all day which we much enjoy. Nobody is better company than C. whatever she is doing or not doing. A first walk over newly harvested stubble with C. and a talk to the Wiltshire boy driving the tractor and trailer. Delightful contrast to press and politics.

Another 'Wiltshire boy', Christopher Lodge, great-grandson of George Compton, has his own recollections of his neighbour.

> When I was about six or seven I 'borrowed' my father's broom handle to knock down conkers by the Manor House gardens. I had managed to get it stuck up a tree. Panicking about what my father would do when he discovered I had lost his broom handle, I was circling the tree wondering how I could get it down. Just then Lady Avon spotted me and chased me away.
>
>   Next day I was walking along the road with some friends when a big, black car drew up beside us. Lord Avon slowly climbed out and I thought, 'I'm in a terrible hole here.' He pulled out the broom handle and handed it to me, saying, 'Yours, I believe.' I was so relieved!'

In April 2000, Lady Avon contributed some memories of her time at the manor to a local history exhibition:

The Manor House was clearly a very pretty unpretentious farm manor until a relation of my husband's, who lived there previously, [Lady Glanusk], put in elaborate mantlepieces and overdoors, which we thought rather too much. We unfortunately had to remove the elaborate iron gates to the road (made by . . . [Lucien Varwell], a blacksmith in Ebbesbourne Wake, who was, I believe, renowned for his wrought ironwork) because in those days trippers would stand and stare in to catch a glimpse of my husband. It is true that I was very keen on the garden, though maddeningly the strip of greensand was across the road on the farm, and the garden was on chalk. My especial love were the old-fashioned roses, of which there were over 70. There was also an interesting collection of crabtrees where, I am told, there is now a swimming pool. The fig-tree was never prolific, but the alpine strawberries flourished. Mr. Nichols managed the kitchen garden so that we never bought fruit or vegetables the whole year round. There were doves in the dovecote and hens and bees in the orchard, and pheasants to hang in the outhouse.

My husband had a marvellous eye for quality in pictures and furniture, and this he carried over to his Hereford herd. He could spot a good bull's potential by looking at it, although he had only known about horses previously. The Avon Herd was a great source of pleasure to him and he exported his young bulls all over the world and had plans with a Normandy breeder to start crossing Hereford with Simmenthals. He was president of the Hereford Herd Book Society.

The unwooded portion of the Downs, on the other side of the road, in May was a sheet of cowslips and orchids ~ alas, no more. Our time at Alvediston was a very happy one. As you know, I had a cottage at Broadchalke since 1947, and the Ebble Valley would be my favourite place to live in the world.

Mr. Kenneth Nichols and his wife Louie, had worked in several great houses and gardens, she as a housemaid and he as a gardener, both rising to significant responsibility, which is hardly surprising as they worked incredibly hard right into old age. When his wife became frail, Mr. Nichols quietly took on all the cooking and housework, keeping the Old School House where they lived in retirement as spick and span as she had done. When she died he was recovering from broken bones in his back after a fall from an apple tree, which he insisted on pruning, but he returned home and maintained his high standards, rising early to get through his chores before cooking a lunch which always included home grown fruit and vegetables. He kept himself well-informed on current affairs, and loved to entertain visitors on his dauntingly complex electronic organ. When he died on a sunny Good Friday afternoon in 2004, he was mowing his lawn. He was one whose war-time experiences, (he was born in 1915 and lost an uncle in the First World War, then saw little of his wife and son while he served during the Second), made him adamant that he wished to keep his remembrance private.

In the last two years of his life Lord Avon's health failed even more alarmingly, although his wife wrote later: 'He fought his last illness with doggedness and optimism.' The farmstead and much of the land was sold to his neighbour at West End, Lord Congleton. In January 1977 the Edens were abroad as usual in the winter, trying to benefit from Florida sunshine. He was flown back on 9th. January and died in Alvediston five days later. On the 17th., he was buried very quietly in front of St. Mary's church, in a service conducted by the vicar of Ebbesbourne and Alvediston, the Rev. John Williams and the former Bishop of Sherborne, the Right Rev. Victor Pike. His grave has attracted many visitors over the years; it is a simple tombstone, engraved by Reynolds Stone, who, Astrid Garran writes, was considered the finest lettering engraver of his generation. Largely self taught except for a fortnight at Eric Gill's workshop, he arrived at his particular gifts after spending two years as an apprentice at the Cambridge University Press, under the influence of the scholar and typographer, Stanley Morrison, who became his mentor . . . [He] was also celebrated for his incomparable wood engravings, bookplates with lettering inspired by the Italian renaissance italic script and book illustrations. He carried out many public commissions, including the coat of arms on your passport, the £5 and £10 notes, discontinued with decimalisation, *The Times* masthead in the 1950s, stamps, and logos for publishers and companies like Dolcis.

He designed over 100 memorial inscriptions, including Winston Churchill's in Westminster Abbey. He painted watercolours of his beloved Dorset all his life, living in the Old Rectory, Litton Cheney, whose wild garden was his inspiration. Unassuming, scholarly and a superb craftsman, he was above all an artist with an artist's vision. He died in 1979, aged 70.

On 30th. September, 2008, the Countess of Avon unveiled a memorial to her husband in St. Mary's church. A striking bas relief of her husband was carved in Portland stone above her chosen inscription:

ANTHONY

EDEN

1897-1977

Unshaken, unseduced,

unterrified,

His loyalty he kept,

his love, his zeal.

MILTON – Paradise Lost

The sculptor was Martin Jennings, who set up his workshop in

Oxfordshire in 1984, from where he has worked in stone, slate, marble and bronze. His bronze portraits, figure and abstract sculptures may be found in collections in many parts of the world and some of his more personal works are illustrated in 'The Art of Remembrance'. One of his latest important sculptures is the statue of Sir John Betjeman at the new Eurostar terminal at St. Pancras station. After the unveiling, both Lady Avon and Sir Peter Tapsell, M.P., (who had worked with Sir Anthony Eden), addressed guests at a lunch in the Samways barn which has been adapted for functions. The commissioning of this memorial came about as part of a great effort to raise £100,000 to restore the church. To have two modern works of such beauty and simplicity as well as the more elaborate Rysbrach and other seventeenth and eighteenth century Wyndham memorials is a rare privilege.

In 1984, Lady Avon sold the Manor House quietly to Rodney and Sue Heath, who have lived there since. Their children grew up there and, in October 2006, a hundred years after the first Sims wedding, their daughter Emma married Simon Cameron at St. Mary's church and there was another reception on the lawn.

1980s to 2010

AFTER LORD AVON's death, the three houses at the bottom of Elcombe Lane were sold. Elcombe House, formerly the Police House, went to Ken and June Jenkins, who had previously run the shop in Ebbesbourne. Elcombe Cottage, which had been two homes, was sold to Mrs. Annabel Hillary, whose son and his wife already lived in Fifield Bavant. Mrs. Hillary, who had a PhD. in horticulture, devised a cottage garden which was admired for miles around. She was very active in the church and village, a great cook and a stalwart of the Wilton W. I., a very kind and memorable character: the sort who, when the great gale of January 1990 was blowing its worst, unable to venture too far due to massive beech trees straddling the lane, availed herself of the kindling raining down onto her lawns, while a pan of marmalade simmered on her Aga! She was already well over eighty. She died in 2002, aged ninety-four.

For six years from 1986, Mrs. Rosamund Russ lived at Elcombe House. She, too, created a beautiful garden with the aid of George Kellow, whose wife helped in the house. She had great experience of house renovation, employing a variety of unlikely characters whom she tended to 'find' and feed generously. Despite having some interests in common, she and Mrs. Hillary were essentially two unique characters. The frisson hovering over their boundary wall was generally entertaining to those who loved them both. 3 Elcombe Lane had been rented to Mr. Fishlock. His son Michael was an eminent architect, responsible for the restoration of Hampton Court after the fire there. Reg Marks remembered doing up this cottage many years ago, after it had found an alternative use and livestock were bedded down in the sitting room. Trunnions, which had been built by the Sims family, was still part of the manor estate when the Avons owned it, and was used by Lord Avon's farm manager. It was sold in 1975, when Lord Avon gave up the farm.

Elcombe Farm now has a house, built by Trevor and Sue Marks. There are two other homes sited on part of the earlier farmstead: a small-holding called Hunter's Lodge, and the former dairy was recently converted into Elcombe Barn.

Other Manor Properties, Past and Present

AT THE OTHER end of the Manor estate, is the farmhouse for the manor estate, the old Church Farmhouse, later known as Church Cottage, and now Church House. The main part of it dates from the late sixteenth or early seventeenth century, when the

Lawes family was at the Manor. After the Sims' time, it passed from the Dewings to Anthony and Jill Bullen in 1966, and Jill continued to nurture the garden which they had established, bringing to it her own special skills. Anthony's death in 1994 was felt deeply by everyone in the village. Jill moved to Bowerchalke in 2000. In about 1990 the barn below, which had been the Grants' lambing shed, and previously a dairy was restored and became known as Church Barn. The old School House and School Hall are separate dwellings: Salisbury Diocese had sold the house to Len Frampton and the hall to the village as a 'reading room' in the nineteen-fifties. In 1960, Dolly Lodge, Len Frampton's sister-in-law, sold the house to the Beckinghams, and the old hall was sold when its use, essentially as a village hall, came to an end. In 1979, while Lord Congleton owned the manor farmstead, a barn was converted into living accommodation. This has continued to be used in conjunction with the stables.

These stables are now Manor Farm Stud, owned by Andrew and Rachel Wardall, who built a new house there at the turn of the century. For many years, Andrew ran a bloodstock shipping company from there, but he now concentrates on breeding bloodstock, and exquisite mares and foals graze the fields in the spring.

More About Bigly

ELCOMBE LANE LEADS up to the Ox Drove where, at 758 feet, (according to Desmond Hawkins), the buildings at Bigly, (sometimes spelt Bigley) have been converted into a house for Perin and Sonya Dineley, and their family. Others have been restored or built, to provide shelter for the sheep, and Sonya has this story to tell:

There is a ghost at Bigly. He appropriately appears to be a shepherd and takes a keen interest in new developments particularly on the ovine front. He wears a floppy, we think felt hat and a smock placing him possibly somewhere in the eighteen hundreds. It is difficult to be more specific as a shepherd's attire remained relatively unchanged for many years.

He was first sighted in the initial few days of the building project by one of the builders. He was covering up the old root cellar and got a distinct feeling he was being watched. Indeed he was. Some months later four of us saw him walking up the farm lane to the old yards. He stopped briefly to watch us training our New Zealand huntaway puppy. Perhaps it was something of a novelty for him, such a dog not having existed in his era.

It wasn't until some years later that I saw him again, the day after we had artificially inseminated the first of our Suffolk ewes. The procedure is minor surgery and must have seemed profoundly unnatural to him. I rushed out the next morning to check they were okay and as I got closer I could see him standing amongst them. The sheep were oblivious. It sounds rather a cliché but it was a very foggy morning and as I got closer he simply turned and walked away into the mist. One gets a terrible lurch in the stomach when you see something you know not to be real but as he walked away my fear was replaced by a great sense of peace. He seemed to have been checking them too.

Despite this, being a God-fearing Catholic, I saw it fit to have him blessed just in case he was seeking release from some torment from the past. He appeared on the very day of the blessing. In the modern world where everything is supposed to have a rational, scientific explanation we rather like the idea that there are still things that are inexplicable. That there is still some mystery. He seems content to be here with us so despite the occasional lurch in our stomachs we are now quite content to have him too.

It is easy to become confused by the buildings and names at Bigly. The 1851 census has George Bradley (63) as innkeeper of the 'Bentinck Arms', which he ran with his French-born wife, (56, 'Adline', from 'Toluse'), surely an exotic rarity in these parts, and their sixteen-year old son. Remembering Charlotte Grove's diary note in February 1833: 'Bradley from Alvedistone (sic) bought eight of our pigs. He was in the Battle of Waterloo', all becomes clear. The 1841 census records George Bradley as an 'ag'. lab'. His wife and four children are noted without detail. Perhaps he brought her home with him when his soldiering days ended, and prospered.

Alexander and Jane Pole were bringing up a growing family in 'Bentinck Buildings', from where he worked as a carter and labourer. William Hill, a keeper, and his wife Susannah lived at 'Bentinck Cottage', and their married daughter, a house servant, was with them at the time. Finally, Henry and Mary Pole, aged 83 and 73 respectively, lived in 'Bigly'. Their status of 'pauper' denotes the plight of former farm labourers such as Henry. Even with family nearby, it must have been hard for them up there. Thus there was a little cluster of nine adults and five children on the hill, passed by flocks and herds being driven to Salisbury, and possibly Shaftesbury, markets. The inn at Bigly, (temporarily known as the 'Bentinck Arms') was later run by William Mullins and the licence was brought down to the new village pub, the 'Crown', some time between 1851 and '67, most likely when the new railways transported flocks which had previously trudged to market on foot, although the droves continued to be used for local animal movement. William Mullins rented the 'Crown' from the Wilton estate. The land and other buildings have also belonged at various times to the Manor, Samways, the Compton and Marks families.

Land which at one time or another has belonged to the manor has been divided and regrouped ~ owned, leased or rented in numerous patterns over the centuries, rather like some primitive organism, yet the fields, coombes and downland slopes which have been grazed or cultivated or coppiced or hunted over have probably changed little under man's temporary and changing activities.

✳ *Alvediston* ✳

Norrington or Northington and Trow

Early History

NIKOLAUS PEVSNER, WRITING in 1963, described the manor house of Norrington as 'a lucky survival'. Another 'lucky survival' in the form of archaeological remains of a medieval village lies in a field immediately to the south-west of the house, but although Norrington was already listed as a medieval village, it was not surveyed until October 1989. Today, the house, farm buildings and earthworks are screened from view from roads by folds in the hills but they can be seen from ancient roads, droves and some footpaths. The house has been owned by only three families in over six hundred and thirty years: the Gawens, the Wyndhams and the Sykes. John Aubrey, (1625 – 1697) who lived in Broad Chalke for much of his life, (during some of Norrington's more turbulent years and when others were still fresh in local memory), quoted, in

Norrington Manor. (Biddy Trahair, thanks to Jonathan Sykes)

his 'Natural History of Wiltshire': 'Omnium rerum est vicissitudo', which he translated as, 'Families, and also places, have their fatalities.' He went on: 'This verse puts me in mind of several places in this countie that are or have been fortunate to their owners, or e` contra.' He elaborated this theory in discussion of the Gawens, to be quoted later. In Bowles' words: 'Perhaps there is no place in this or any other county, which has higher pretensions to be noticed, as well for its antiquity, as from the persons who in succession, from time to time, have been owners of it.' The tension of its seclusion and its historical importance, locally at least, has run like a thread through its story.

Norrington and Alvediston seem to have been separate entities until the mid- fourteenth century, but exactly when the settlement there began is rather hazy. Tradition holds that Danewort or Dwarf Elder, which can be found along the track north of the medieval village, only grows 'from the blood of Danes', who invaded Briton during the ninth to eleventh centuries. In 1640, however, Parkinson rather spoilt this by insisting that the name derives from 'danes', meaning 'diarrhoea' caused by ingesting the black berries which, although valuable as food for birds, can poison humans.

Bowles maintained that in 955, when King Edwy granted the manor of Alvediston to the nuns at Wilton, lands belonging to 'one Aelfegus, which I interpret Aiulfus' were on the boundary. He believed that Aiulfus was a Saxon who managed to gain such favour with the Norman William the Conqueror that he became both sheriff (responsible for justice and keeping the peace locally) and chamberlain with responsibilities in the royal household. Interestingly, several subsequent owners of Norrington have followed suit. Indeed, his descendents assumed the name Chamberlain from holding that office, while Tristram Sykes was the latest to become High Sheriff of Wiltshire in 1987, over a thousand years after Aiulfus. The *Victoria County History* does not make the connection with Aiulfus but does mention five Chamberlains from 1210 to 1304. Bowles makes another connection:

> We find that the proprietors of the manor and estate at Compton, in this county, were also proprietors of the estate at Norrington, and that the manor of Compton is still distinguished by the addition of Chamberlain [now Compton Chamberlayne].

As will become clear later, by the seventeenth century the owners of Norrington had one small property in Compton Chamberlayne. In the custom of the day, there was another layer of ownership: the overlordship, which was held by the king in the early thirteenth century and also in 1304, but had passed to the prior of Wallingford by 1361, in contrast to the manor of Alvediston, which was under the control of the abbess of Wilton and later, the earls of Pembroke.

John of Berwick bought it next and, in 1307, was granted free warren, i.e. the right to keep and hunt game. There is also evidence of a warren, or area designated for the breeding of smaller game, e.g. rabbits. From him via his sister, it passed to the Hussey family, prominent in Berwick St. John, and thence to John Gawen seventy years later. Bowles believed that the recumbent figure in the south aisle of St. Mary's church is most likely in memory of Roger Hussey, John of Berwick's grandson, as he took part in military expeditions into Scotland and France and also defended the Sussex coast between 1338 and 1346, thus meriting 'the dress of a warrior... and the absence of a sword and dagger is accounted for, that death had rendered each of them of no use.' Popular opinion today favours Sir Richard Hoare's suggestion that John Gawen is commemorated as builder of both Norrington and the south aisle (see page 57).

Bowles quotes from the deed of sale between 'John Huse' and 'John Goweyn the younger, and . . . Petronilla (or Parnell) his wife,' which he found to be 'in excellent preservation, and written in the hand of the day; it has two seals appendant to it, one of this John Huse, and the other the official one of John Shoune, then mayor of New Sarum.'

The Medieval Village

THE MEDIEVAL VILLAGE, first recorded in 1198, is thought to have been subsidiary to Alvediston, itself recorded in 1165. However, as R.W. Southern points out in 'The Making of the Middle Ages', very little about village life was recorded until the thirteenth century. 'The annals of village life are short, yet no more substantial work was accomplished in our period', (the Middle Ages), 'than the building up of a village life which, though full of hardships and shortages, was not without dignity, colour, and the independence which comes from a well-established routine. So much depended on the establishment of this routine, and so little can be said about it.' Walking along the streets and paths of this ancient settlement, between the clearly defined boundaries of peasant properties, the twenty-first century visitor is frustrated by the lack of detail: when did the first families arrive? The record of 1198 probably referred to an already well-established village. When was the village deserted? Notes on the 1989 survey suggest that the houses to the west may have been deliberately planned in the mid seventeenth century, when Wadham Wyndham extended the manor house and laid out formal gardens, so the 'medieval' village may have been inhabited for centuries after that period, but there does not seem to be any record of a final clearance. Perhaps it just fell into ruin when the Wyndhams moved away and rented out the farm, leaving the house to be used as labourers' homes; or had the village already begun to decay? How did the village change? Was it originally to the south-east of the present manor? A survey of 1640 by Walter Cantloe, referred to below, would seem to support this idea. Was the village ever decimated by plague, and did disease contribute to its final demise? The village of Fifield Bavant was reduced by plague, while Bishopstone moved some distance west of the surviving church for the same reason. What effect did changing patterns of agriculture have? Sheep and arable farming have predominated throughout its known history but, while Alvediston had a two-field rotation system in the twelfth century and three-field by the mid sixteenth, the number of open fields, (cultivated by individuals in strips) in Norrington is uncertain. The warren granted to John of Berwick in 1307 was to the north-west of the village; nearly five hundred years later, the enclosure map of 1792 showed that Norrington, unlike Alvediston, was already enclosed, so the ancient method of open-field agriculture had been replaced by a more efficient arrangement which had far-reaching effects on villagers, making them labourers for the landowner, and this could have spelt the end of the village.

There are so many questions, but the fact that there are so few definite answers need not detract from the sense of connection with our predecessors in this area. If the detail is still shrouded in mystery, as the dwellings are covered in grass, there is no doubt that many lives were lived there in a routine that was much closer to nature than ours can ever be. R.W. Southern again:

> Materially, there was probably remarkably little difference between the life of the peasant in the thirteenth century and in the village before it was transformed by modern mechanisms: the produce of the land had increased six fold or ten fold during these centuries, but very little of this increase went into the pocket or stomach of the individual peasant. Compared with the rest of the community, he remained immune from new wants, or the means of satisfying them. Everywhere the peasant kept himself alive on a diet whose scarcity and monotony was broken only by intermittent feastings, at harvest time, at pig-killing time, and when people got married or died. There were great differences in the fortunes of individual peasants: families rose and fell, holdings grew and withered away again, following laws similar to those which governed the rise and fall of kingdoms. Over the fortunes of all, high and low, there presided the unpredictable factors of marriage and childbirth. The rules of succession, infinitely various and complicated, often modified, but with the general authority of centuries of growth behind them, were the framework within which the pattern of village ~ as of national ~ life was woven.' Records before 1200 are sparse and erratic, 'scattered documents: the passing remarks of chroniclers on famines, murrains [cattle diseases], droughts, storms and years of plenty; charters which throw light on the most deceptive of all standards of people's well-being ~ their legal status; miracle stories and crime stories which show that there was plenty of ready violence . . . men maimed, blinded or emasculated judicially for small offences. The village, from these accounts, seems to have had for its narrow means a strange capacity for supporting men cruelly afflicted in the course of either nature or of law.

It is possible to pick up something of the unwritten history of the peasantry of England from this peaceful meadow. Perhaps 'virtual experiences' today leave too little to the imagination.

There is evidence of eighteen to twenty properties with gardens behind them, built along streets which are clearly visible as lumps and dips in the fields to the south-west and south of the house so it was a significant and close-knit settlement which developed over a period of time. By 1312 there were twelve 'half-yardlanders' but these records stop in the mid-fourteenth century, when Norrington was combined with Alvediston for taxation purposes. A yardland was about thirty acres, so a half-yardlander rented about fifteen, just about enough to live on, but each tenant had a number of duties and dues to pay to the lord of the manor at every time and season of the year, which could be onerous. All this coincided with John Gawen building the oldest part of the present manor house, so this was clearly a time of change. Those living in the manor house would have had carte blanche to move dwellings or even whole streets or villages and the survey clearly shows the site of the manor house cutting into the north-east corner of the settlement. While the creation of formal gardens and ponds in the seventeenth century wreaked further damage, Gawen's plans three hundred years earlier were clearly much grander than those of his predecessors. The village church was one feature which became more common from the thirteenth century onwards, so it is significant that the site was in Alvediston and not in the village of Norrington. If the theory that John Gawen was responsible for the building of the south transept of St. Mary's is correct, it would indicate that he was prepared to put substantial sums of money towards ensuring that the vital spiritual centre of the community remained in Alvediston, rather than building one on his doorstep. One account from the early seventeenth century indicates that there was a church with bells at Norrington, but it was a 'record' of a highly contentious court case, written in

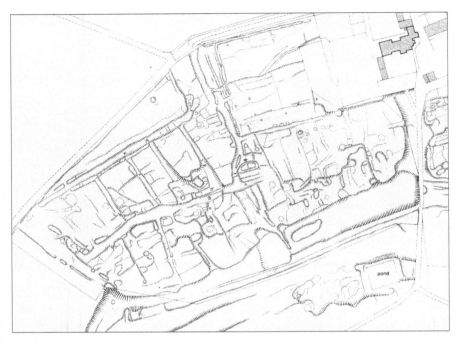

A plot of part of the earthworks of Norrington deserted village . (English Heritage)

contemporary tabloid style, and riven with risible inaccuracies, so it is not very reliable. There is some conjecture that there was once a chapel over the undercroft, and that it was swept away in the major changes made by Wadham Wyndham. However, Charlotte Grove, writing in 1837, mentions seeing the chapel when she was shown over the house, so an area must have been recognised as such then. If there was a chapel, it would have been used for private, family devotions only. Presumably, the recusant Gawens had some means of celebrating Mass when they were persecuted for not attending their parish church in the late sixteenth and the early seventeenth centuries, but it must have been discreet.

However, the remains of cottages, gardens, streets, ponds, water-meadows, (still visible in the field to the south-west of the house, now traversed by the footpath), and a stone quarry are documented by the 1989 Royal Commission on the Historical Monuments of England,

(RCHME) survey. Unfortunately, the accompanying notes refer to letters which do not appear on the plan, and no-one seems to have a complete set. This makes plotting the remains on the map or in the fields slightly haphazard and open to dispute.

The main 'street', which goes west from the house end of the settlement ends in a turn north, but does not appear to lead anywhere, so was probably only used for access to the properties. Another 'holloway' goes north from the eastern end of the street to join the main farm track. It appears that the cottages faced onto the street, with gardens behind; those to the north having a path, like a back alley, running along at the ends of the gardens. Originally, this probably continued east towards the manor house, perhaps joining the farm track at the present junction of the drive with the north farm track. This may have disappeared when John Gawen started building, or when Wadham Wyndham extended and landscaped the property, necessitating the development of the stretch of farm track which runs behind the house and garden. The earthworks closest to the house on both east and west sides of the drive are probably the oldest, but are also the most damaged by landscaping and by the siting of drains and other works carried out for the house and farm. It looks as if the 'street' originally continued for some distance to the east of the drive, with at least two or three properties adjoining it. Indeed, Walter Cantloe's 'True and perfect Survey and Plat [plot of ground] of the manor of Norenton', drawn in 1640 for William Gawen in the last, contentious years of the family's ownership, shows only one building to the west and three to the north and east. Allowing for these to be representative rather than entirely accurate, the survey would indicate that there was more development to the east than to the west, until Wyndham landscaped the area around the house.

In *The Time Traveller's Guide to Medieval England*, Ian Mortimer describes every aspect of life in the fourteenth century in fascinating detail. A village house would have low walls of limewashed cob and narrow windows with external shutters. A broad thatched roof rises from about chest height to twenty-five feet or more, with smoke coming from one of the crude triangular openings ~ makeshift louvres ~ built into either end of the ridge. The thatch itself, which probably is laden with moss and lichen, extends over the walls by a good eighteen inches, giving the whole building the aspect of a frown. The cobbles of the toft (the area on which the house is built) are uneven and have partially sunk into the mud. A small fence runs around the whole house and garden. Adjacent to the house are water butts and piles of firewood. Nearby are a hut containing a privy, a working cart, the remains of a broken cart, a haywain, a thatched stable, a goose house, a hen house, a barn and perhaps a brew house and bake house.

Mortimer explains that, however random this picture may seem today, everything was placed and arranged for a purpose. The plots in Norrington's village look small for all the above, but the overall impression is not unlike the inspiration for rustic art in the nineteenth century.

The original pond complex was to the north of the present ornamental pond, which is passed as the drive turns north towards the house. This later pond has an island and still dries out when the Ebble runs dry. Of the earlier ponds, the western one began where the Ebble turns east from its north-easterly course and the other two followed lengthwise just north of the stream. In 1640, Cantloe showed one long pond extending from the turn in the Ebble to just east of the house, which would probably have passed under the approach drive. In medieval times, the ponds would have been stocked with fish, which formed a vital part of the diet for many centuries. On either side of the drive as it approached the 'new' pond, there is evidence of strip lynchets. As G.M. Trevelyan explains in his *English Social*

History, the later fourteenth century, (incidentally, also the time of Chaucer), saw changes in land-ownership and use which had long-lasting effects on the countryside. Since Saxon times, the land had been owned by feudal lords of manors. They had their own 'demesne', (estate), farmed by peasants or 'villeins' on certain days in payment for the strips of land in huge, unenclosed fields which the villeins could work for themselves and their families.

Characteristically, there were three of these open, arable fields in a manor farm, but numbers varied. The strips were marked out by the turn of the plough, a pattern that can be seen in ploughed fields today. The furrow between each ridge of land served as a drain for surplus water as well as the boundary of each strip. Villeins would farm several strips in each huge field, thus the good and bad land could be shared out fairly, and it behoved the village to work well as a community, another advantage of the system. Mortimer refutes the usual idea that whole fields were either cultivated or fallow (and grazed by animals) saying that it was the individual strips which varied in use year by year. Meadows for hay were cultivated on the same basis and, after harvest, each was thrown open for grazing, which helped to fertilise the land for the next crop. Other grazing was on common land and, indeed, sheep farming was a vital part of the agrarian economy throughout the land. The feudal system depended on the peasant farmer being content to look no further than the provision of his individual needs, and to conform to the feudal laws which bound him to his lord and to the local soil: he had to work on the lord's land on certain days of the year, regardless of his own priorities; his corn had to be ground at the lord's mill, (in the case of Norrington, Windmill Hill was to the south of the farm); his family would see their best beast seized on his death, a tax known as 'heriot'; he could not even give his children in marriage without his lord's consent, and 'merchet' was a fine levied on marriage.

During the fourteenth century, a crucial time in Norrington's history, changes came, initially due to the growing population in the first half of the century putting pressure on the number of strips of land available. This meant that the lords and their bailiffs were in a strong position to make ever greater demands on the peasantry and to reverse earlier moves to commute field service dues to money payment, which had given the villeins a little more independence and had led to the growth in the number of hired workers. However, another great swing in agrarian fortunes arose through the Black Death of 1348-9, and subsequent, lesser plagues. The population was decimated by somewhere between a third and a half, so land was once more readily available and peasant farmers built up such significant holdings that they were in a position to hire labour themselves, and the labourers could demand higher wages. A middle class of yeoman farmers became a feature and this, of course, produced new pressures on the village community. No longer was it incumbent upon them to work co-operatively as equals; as labour costs rose beyond the lord's economic power, he was forced to rent out land to the burgeoning yeomen. Sometimes the money rent was commuted to produce, thus arose the relationship of the home farm providing for the needs of the local landowner. G.M. Trevelyan writes of these yeomen: 'The increase in their numbers and prosperity set the tone of the new England for centuries to come. The motive of the English yeoman ~ his independence, his hearty good nature, his skill in archery ~ fills the ballads from the time of the Hundred Years War' (1337-1453) 'to the Stuart era' (1603-1714). This is the agricultural background to the years of the Gawen family at Norrington. John Gawen arrived just three years before the now landless labourers rose against the farmers, who were supported by Parliament and the law, in strikes, riots and even unions. Although, by virtue of their scarcity, the peasants retained the upper hand, the new class system kept them subservient and dependent on the romantic vision portrayed above expressing 'his hearty good nature' in the labourers' favour.

The Gawen Family, 1377-1658

THE GAWEN FAMILY may be able to trace their origins back to the fifth century and the legends of King Arthur and the Knights of the Round Table. Arthur himself is generally believed to have lived in fact but Norman Davies (in *The Isles, a History*) maintains that his 'role in history is less important than his role in creative fiction.' Christopher Snyder, in his *Exploring the World of King Arthur* believes that Arthur may not even have been a king but rather a '*dux bellorum*' or 'leader of battles', whose importance as a mythological and folk hero led to, and was greatly enhanced by, the literature of succeeding centuries and by his usefulness to succeeding kings. Before the fifth century, the Celts and Romans dominated culture during the Iron Age, with Christianity adding a whole new dimension from the late fourth century, beginning with the missionary St. Patrick. Each of these influences can be found in the Arthurian legends, but, with Huns, Goths and 'barbarians' from Scotland and Ireland flooding into the land, the Britons became uneasy so they actually invited Germanic mercenaries from Europe to come to their aid. Predictably, these groups of Anglo-Saxons soon became a threat to their hosts and Arthur personifies the British struggle against them. The racial and cultural ingredients of the marinade of the blood flowing through our veins have been more potent and in action for longer than one might be led to believe today.

The Anglo-Saxons eventually won the struggle, but as the Britons fell from political prominence they took heart in a heroic national past which came to feature Arthur as a 'once and future' redeemer. The Arthurian myth then passed into early medieval literature, which is a mixed bag of Latin chronicles, bardic poetry and Christian hagiography. The elusive Arthur appears in one account as a Christian warrior, in the next as a tyrannical monarch. Annals record his victories and his death, yet magic surrounds his martial feats and mystery envelops his grave. By the twelfth century the details of Arthur's career were filled in by an inventive clerk named Geoffrey of Monmouth, and soon after that French and German writers began producing chivalric romances centring around the famous monarch and his court, called Camelot.'(Christopher Snyder.)

The monks of Glastonbury, (thought to be the 'Isle of Avalon' standing up in the marshlands of the Somerset Levels, to which the mortally wounded Arthur was conveyed after the battle of Camlann, and where he is believed to have been buried,) may well have seized the opportunity to develop their Abbey as a lucrative shrine. Thus we find the elements of racial disharmony, the manipulation of 'history' for particular ends, romantic fantasy and even the growth of tourism, albeit in the form of pilgrimage, all of which have resonances today. It is interesting to ponder what Arthur and his knights would make of current laments for 'true Anglo-Saxons'.

From the Romans, the British had inherited and learnt the use of horses, so, when Arthur and his men fought on horseback they became known as 'knights'. This army repelled the foot soldier Saxons in the battle of Badon, traditionally on Salisbury Plain, and King Arthur ruled from 'Camelot', (probably in Cornwall, perhaps Camelford.) However, Arthur's rule and dominance of the Saxons disintegrated after forty years, due to infighting and romantic intrigue and he was killed in battle. In spite of all the conflict and conflicting stories, or perhaps because uncertainty left the stories open to interpretation, first the Normans used Arthur to justify their antagonism to the Anglo-Saxons, (English), then the Angevin-Norman Plantagenets exploited his memory to increase their power and began to develop the Arthurian myth as a symbol of the new

Englishness. The Tudors traced their Welsh ancestry back to Arthur and Henry VIII had his own face painted as Arthur's when he had the Round Table of Winchester restored. In literature, the poem 'Sir Gawain and the Green Knight' was one of the earliest, in 1400, while Sir Thomas Malory wrote the most famous 'account' of Arthur's life in 'Le Morte d'Arthur' later in that century. The Elizabethan Spenser continued the fascination with his stories and, of course, the Victorian age saw a huge burgeoning of interest with Tennyson, Sir Walter Scott and the Pre-Raphaelites. More recently, both books and films have examined the subject from just about every point of view.

One of his knights was his nephew, Sir Gawain (also known as Gawain, Gauvain, Gawein and even the Welsh Gwalchunei), about whom legends with both classical and Celtic roots abound. Like some sort of sun god, his great strength was supposed to wax and wane with the sun, so he was at his most dangerous and exciting in the mornings. While the French favoured Sir Lancelot, Gawain appealed to the English and Welsh. Indeed, some would even credit him with being the St. Govan of the hermit's cell on the Pembrokeshire cliffs, but his character seems to have been more courtly than saintly. His courtesy and chivalry were a potent mix for the ladies, which led to numerous adventures and near-disasters, especially after noon when his strength waned, or when his temper got the better of him. After his innocent brothers were killed during Lancelot's rescue of Guinevere, Gawain challenged his former friend to a dual, during which he received a blow which was ultimately fatal, but not before he had been reconciled to Lancelot and persuaded him to go to Arthur's aid against Mordred in what proved to be Arthur's final battle.

There are two famous legends about Gawain. *Sir Gawain and the Green Knight* was written in c. 1400. This ghastly and troublesome knight appeared at Arthur's court one New Year's Day and, after vitriolic outbursts, challenged Arthur to deal him a blow which he would return at his own court a year later. Gawain leapt to his

king's defence, offering to take on the challenge and beheading the
Green Knight, who promptly retrieved his head, reminded Gawain
of his turn a year hence and galloped away. On his way to this grisly
assignation Gawain was detained at a castle, got embroiled with the
lady, (who gave him a few kisses and a green girdle as a token of good-
luck, later adopted by other knights of the round Table as a reminder
of Gawain's courage) and ultimately discovered that the 'lord' of the
castle was the Green Knight, who had set the trap to discredit Arthur
and his knights. Having achieved this, he was content just to give
Gawain a very slight wound.

The Wedding of Sir Gawain and Dame Ragnell, was written as
an anonymous poem, circa 1450, and one version was adapted from
the Middle English by Dr. David Breedon. A version also appears
in Chaucer's 'Wife of Bath'. The poem of 1450 illustrates the lengths
to which Sir Gawain went to prove his loyalty to his king. Arthur
pursued a deer into a thicket alone, where he was accosted by 'a quaynt
grome', (strange man) delightfully named Sir Gromer Somer Joure
who accused him of giving his land to Sir Gawain. Sir Gromer shared
some characteristics with the 'Green Knight'. After some bargaining,
he agreed not to kill Arthur on condition that he return alone to that
place after a twelve-month with the answer to the question of what
women love best, and that he did not share this secret with anyone.
Sir Gawain, however, concerned for his king, persuaded him to tell
why he was so heavy-hearted and immediately volunteered to help
him in his quest. They set out in different directions and, on their
return, they each compiled a book of their researches. A year after
his first encounter, Arthur duly set off for the woods again, clutching
the books. This time he was met by 'a Lady…as ungodly a creature
as evere man sawe', (and indeed, the description bears this out.)
However, she rode a richly accoutred palfrey with unexpected grace.
To Arthur's consternation, she dismissed the labours of the past
year and demanded marriage to Sir Gawain on pain of the king's

death. Arthur made no attempt to spare her his horror at this but she was adamant, so he made his miserable way back to his court in Carlisle. Sir Gawain came out to meet him and, in true knightly style, determined to show his loyalty to King Arthur by marrying this Dame Ragnelle 'thowghe she were a fend (fiend); thowghe she were as foulle as Belsabub', (Beelzebub, or the devil), for which, indeed, the wretched king had done his best to prepare him. On the appointed day the two set out. Arthur left Gawain while he met Dame Ragnelle. On hearing that Gawain would marry her, she gave Arthur the answer to the riddle: what women want most is sovereignty. Not surprisingly, neither seeker had thought of this one, but Arthur duly dashed off to find Sir Gromer Somer Joure and triumphantly reported the answer. The knight was furious that Dame Ragnelle, ('that old scott', or nag who was in fact his sister,) had enlightened the king, but the spell had been broken and he could not kill Arthur or regain his land as he had intended. Back Arthur went to the dame who, to his distress, insisted that she and Gawain be married publicly, with full ceremony. When the king introduced her to his court there was general consternation and much weeping by thwarted ladies. At the wedding breakfast she disgusted the company with her greed and foul manners. In the bedchamber, poor Sir Gawain turned aside, bracing himself to kiss her, to find to his joy and amazement that she had been transformed into 'the fairest creature that evere he sawe.' However, his trials were not over: he had to choose whether to have her fair at night and foul by day or the other way round. Naturally, this was a dilemma, but he struck gold when he handed the choice back to her, giving her sovereignty probably more in shock than intention. 'Garamercy' (many thanks) she said, as well she might, because the spell which had been cast by her stepmother was finally broken. The night passed far better than Gawain had expected and they had five years of marital bliss and fidelity, which was the more remarkable as Gawain had a dreadful reputation with women.

Keith Gawen has researched his family history and believes that the family dates back to the time of King Arthur. 'The evidence after so long can only be circumstantial, but when all the details are put together, the case becomes nearly overwhelming.' This, of course, presupposes more certainty about King Arthur himself than Norman Davies would allow, but there are other authors, e.g. Elizabeth Jenkins, ('The Mystery of King Arthur', 1974), to whom Keith Gawen refers, who have no doubt about his historical authenticity. The name Gawain also occurs as Gawaine, which could easily be shortened to Gawen. Norrington, he feels, is near enough to Salisbury Plain, where the battle of Badon probably took place, and to Glastonbury, Arthur's base, for it to be a logical place for Gawain's descendents to settle; it is reasonable to assume that the monument of a recumbent knight in the Norrington aisle is a Gawen. The fact that the John Gawen who was granted Norrington by Richard II was known as 'the Younger' and that he became a sheriff indicates that the family was established locally. 'One further small piece of information,' concludes Keith Gawen, 'notes the physical description of Sir Gareth, Gawaine's brother as being a very large man. Large physical size was relatively uncommon in those times.' Gareth also had 'huge hands. This is an attribute throughout the family even today. Many of the male line are well over six feet in height and huge men. Temperament is another attribute they have in common. There is a picture . . . of Sir Gawain seducing the North Wales princess. They were a lively family in the 17th century, with strong views and principles, and many are still that way inclined today. Generally, the Gawen family throughout time has been a rebellious and hot bloodied clan. Bohemian in outlook, and a law unto themselves. Altogether very like the Sir Gawain of legend.' He also quotes Aubrey, who noted in 1721 that the house was 450 years old and that it was not known if the Gawens were descended from King Arthur, so theories were current then, too.

Views differ about Gawain's death. According to Christopher Snyder, he challenged a reluctant Lancelot to a dual in France and died shortly after returning to England with Arthur, to take on the usurper, Modred. (King Arthur and Modred managed to inflict mortal wounds upon each other at the battle of Camlann.) Some believe that he died at Sandwich; that his skull was put on view in Dover castle; William of Malmesbury in 1125 thought that his tomb was found 'on the sea shore'. In 'Some Old Wiltshire Homes' Hoare is quoted as saying that 'old tradition' claimed that he was killed in a battle against Modred near Sandwich and that his body was carried 'into his own countrey in Scotland to be enterred' (sic.) Bowles wrote: 'In the year 1082, in a province of Wales, called Rose, was his sepulchre found.' As mentioned earlier a claim was made connecting St. Govan's Head with Gawain, ousting the more likely claim to fame of the sixth century Irish monk, Govan. In the history of Broad Chalke (2000), we read: 'With the departure of the Romans the Christian myth persists with the historical legend of the Arthurian hero, Sir Gwain, lying buried just to the west and near the summit of the Howgare road,' (running parallel to South Street and on up towards Hut and Lodge Farm) 'a mile or so from the present church. Sir Gwain was a perfect knight whose story is of the protection given him against the Green Knight by – "a girdle of green silk with a golden hem".' One thing is clear: the stories surrounding Sir Gawain were felt to be sufficiently important for claims as his place of death or burial to have been made throughout the land.

In spite of all this, the Gawen family appears to have lived quietly and respectably at Norrington. Bowles records a John Gawen as a knight of the shire in 1395, while the name appears in 1392, 1402 and 1504 as sheriff of Wilts. Among other properties, they owned a house and small farm called Old Mount Sorrel Farm in Broad Chalke, previously owned by Henry Montsorel. Aubrey wrote: 'The Gawens of Norrington, in the parish of Alvediston, continued in this place four hundred fifty and odd yeares. They had also an estate in Broad Chalke, which was, perhaps, of as great antiquity. On the south downs of the farme of Broad Chalke is a little barrow called Gawen's –barrow, which must bee before ecclesiastical lawes were established.' The farmhouse burnt down in 1827 and the barns have been converted to houses, but can be seen on the opposite side of the road to the more modern 'Mount Sorrel Farm' which is set back from the road as you leave Broad Chalke, going westwards.

There was also a manor called Trow Crawley, associated with Trow, to the south of Norrington and held of Shaftesbury Abbey, which members of the Gawen family rented from the late fourteenth century, and which was merged with Norrington by1606. They owned Hurdcott Manor, near Barford St. Martin and more estates in Semley, where they contributed towards restoration of the church. Bowles, in 1830, recorded their arms in the church. A family historian, Heather Lewis, has discovered that there was a ship called 'Gawen' in Francis Drake's fleet which defeated the Armada, captained by a man of that name. As this occurred in 1588, this Gawen must have come from a more conforming branch of the family, perhaps one that lived on the south coast, (she found them in Rye, Brighton and Portsmouth, among other places.) By that time, Thomas Gawen of Norrington, a recusant Catholic, was falling foul of Elizabeth I's increasingly zealous Protestant practices. In 1592, he lost two thirds of his lands and nine years later was fined a total of £1,500, a staggering amount, (£1,380 for not attending church for sixty-nine months at £20 per month and £120 for refusing to submit and conform to the law.)

Meanwhile, the Pembrokes, whose manor of Alvediston was at the far south-west of their massive estate, owed their power to their Protestant tendencies. They gained Wilton at the Dissolution of the Monasteries and not only maintained but consolidated their power throughout the swings and changes of subsequent decades. Adam Nicolson describes how the first earl, ('tough, powerful and cynical') and his wife, ('serious and high-minded') together 'embodied the two streams of Tudor life: the untrammelled broking of power through violence, threat and political inflexibility; and the cleansing of the mind through education and integrity.' Two generations later, with the influence of Philip Sidney and his Arcadian ideals through his sister's marriage to the second earl, the brothers William and Philip Herbert became the third and fourth earls respectively, spanning the first half of the seventeenth century. William espoused 'courtly Protestantism' which became increasingly militant against Spanish and Catholic influences, and he looked back on Elizabeth's reign with nostalgia. While as involved at court as on their country estate, the brothers, who had gained vast wealth and prestige from James I, gradually moved into opposition to the court policies and even to the king himself. As the Gawens were neighbours of the Pembrokes both in Alvediston and in most of their other properties, it is intriguing to wonder how much their lives overlapped, if at all; and what it must have been like to exist and to hold firm to unpopular principles when living cheek-by-jowl with such powerful interests.

Bowles records Thomas Gawen's original estates, which may be of interest:

> The Manor of Norrington and Trow
> Lands called Browning's, a coppice and a 'messuage', (a dwelling with outbuildings) and land in Semley
> Six 'messuages' and land in Barford St. Martin
> Six 'messuages' and land in Broad Chalke
> One 'messuage' and two cottages with land in 'Burgh Chalke' (Bowerchalke)
> One 'messuage' with land and three cottages in Fovant
> 'One place of land and thirty acres of ditto', a cottage, a further seventeen acres and rent from one hundred and fifty acres in Ebbesbourne Wake

One 'messuage' with land and a cottage in Compton Chamberlain

Two 'messuages' with land and 'a close of pasture containing fifty acres, and sixty acres of arable land called Clowd Hills' in Baverstock

The Manor of Hurdcot, with the appurtenances and seventeen acres.

The total rental value was computed at £389. 7/4d., a 'very considerable estate in those days', according to Bowles. However, he reckons that the jury deciding this chose to account for only one-fifth of the true amount 'in mercy to the delinquents'. Bowles then goes completely off course by affirming that this Thomas Gawen survived not only Elizabeth, but James I too, and into the reign of Charles I. He is confusing him with his son, another Thomas. This mistake would deprive Alvediston of its most gruesome story and make Thomas' age as extraordinary as his demise. At the end of Elizabeth's reign Norrington was granted to Sir John Fortescue, who let it to Richard Kennell who, according to tradition at least, was a particularly unsavoury character. The Gawen family retained Hurdcott Manor where his wife Catherine remained while Thomas was imprisoned in London, possibly in the Tower, for refusing to pay his fine in 1601. They also kept properties in Broad Chalke and Ebbesbourne. In 1603, Queen Elizabeth was succeeded by James I, upon which Thomas Gawen was released, but he only enjoyed a month of freedom at Hurdcott before he died, in the August.

Star Chamber records about what happened next, quoted by Keith Gawen and by William Young of Ebbesbourne, inevitably vary but the strength of feeling aroused and Catherine Gawen's courage and forthrightness are undisputed.

One case, (Mrs. Gawen vs. Kennell), from 1606, describes Gawen as 'fat and corpulent', (therefore needing speedy burial) and 'a stiff and rough recusant'. The incumbent refused to bury him, as he had been excommunicated, and the Bishop of Sarum confirmed this, upon which Mrs. Gawen took the law into her own hands and buried him herself. A riot ensued, with a woman who spat in the constable's face being put in the stocks, so the constable, tithingman, (the collector of church taxes who, in other records was on the other side,) and minister forced their way into the church by a 'lytel private door'. Kennell then tried every calumny he could think of. Having failed to convince the assembled company that 'the brute Gawen' had fled overseas or had been seen riding through Blandford the previous day and was hiding, he took a man to the church at night and they dug open the grave. He now suggested that Gawen had been strangled or that his wife had been responsible for his death. Kennell asked that two coroners view the body, but they put this off for a fortnight for fear of the plague. When the tithingman refused to remove the body from the grave, Kennell hired someone else to drag the body some distance into a meadow. By this time the smell overpowered the assembled crowd of almost two hundred and only one member of the jury dared to approach the corpse. Kennell, possibly getting a bit desperate, ordered the shroud to be cut and still maintained that there was evidence of strangulation. The jury, however, decided that he had died in natural circumstances and the coroner demanded that the body be reburied. No-one would oblige so Kennell, determined to the last, had the body dragged back up to the church porch and left in there; then he hid the key, which infuriated the parishioners and prevented them from attending services. Finally, he had his enemy buried north to south instead of east to west 'as he was an overtoworthy neighbour, whilst he lived, so shall he be buried overtoworthy. If you dislike it I will have him dragged at a horse's tail and laid upon the downs.' The clergy and officers of the law were acquitted and commended. Kennell was fined £200, later reduced to £100 and imprisonment. Some parts of this account, such as that Mrs. Gawen buried her husband at 'Turves church, (Norrington)' and that bells were rung both there and in Alvediston church are distinctly suspect as there is no evidence of a church at Norrington. However, the details have become part of local lore; perhaps this is the tabloid version, although all of them are rather vivid.

A William Yonge of Ebbesbourne Wake, a husbandman of 37 or thereabouts, gave evidence in a Star Chamber case the previous year. He had known Thomas Gawen for twenty years as a near neighbour. In this version, Richard Kennell got Thomas Banester and William Fanstone to help him remove Gawen's coffin from the family vault six weeks after his death. It was then dragged through the churchyard and about twenty yards down a hill into a meadow, where Kennell's son Xopfer 'fetched hammer and pincers . . . broke open the coffin and tumbled the body out on its face and bellie upon the ground.' When Fanstone ripped the shroud 'from the lower breast to the crowne of the head', Kennell pronounced suicide by strangulation, but this idea was thrown out by the coroner, Hurst. Yonge, (or Young) said that the body was left on the ground for four or five days, during which time the church was kept locked to prevent reburial in the vault, until Kennell buried him 'overthwartly'.

Another Star Chamber case three years later was brought by Kennell against Thomas Gawen (presumably the son), Catherine, the widow, Sir Edmund Ludlowe and Thomas Tooman, Tithingman, who were 'charged with riot in Wiltshire.' In this version, on the Sunday after her husband's death, 'during divine service', (i.e. while Kennell and his supporters were at St. Mary's church), Catherine broke into Norrington with two servants and barred the doors. Next day she obtained reinforcements in weapons and manpower, including Tooman the tithingman, who incited the 'rioters' with his 'white rodde' and Ludlow, the nearest J.P. They are said to have held on for several days, 'shooting at the Kennells with bows and arrows'. The intemperate wording of Catherine's plea probably did not help her cause. She is recorded as claiming that she 'had suffered great waste at the hands of the Plaintiff and that she being a recusant did upon the King's coming report that times were changed for Catholics, and they should have better days. The bloody Queen was dead under which the Lord Chief Justice did rule the roost and Sir John Fortescue and his bloodsucker Sir Walter Raleigh. For the Lord Chief Justice was a disgrace . . . ' She was fined £500, Ludlow, £300 and Tooman, £100, both the latter being discharged from office. Others were fined lesser amounts and Mrs. Gawen was to pay on behalf of her servants if they could not afford their fines. These huge fines, coming so soon after that for £1,500, must have been a severe financial blow.

Whatever actually happened in those tumultuous years, a terrible legacy of unresolved discord was left, so on 6th. May, 2000, almost four hundred years later, the team vicar, Rev. Roger Redding, arranged with Father Joe Duggan, (priest at Tisbury and Wardour) and Tristram Sykes, (church warden and owner of Norrington) to hold a Requiem Mass and act of reconciliation in the church. This was attended by both Roman Catholics and Protestants from the local area and by Mr. and Mrs. Keith Gawen, representing the family, and was followed by a reception at Norrington Manor. Interestingly, in 1600, a Tristram Gawen is recorded. He, like Thomas and Walter, may have been a son of the famous Thomas Gawen. Three hundred and sixty years later another Tristram lived at Norrington.

Although Norrington was restored to the Gawens, the next Thomas once more forfeited it in 1653, during the Commonwealth, because as a Catholic and a monarchist he maintained that 'kings were the Lord's anointed,' (Bowles.) Almost all his estates were sold and when a Walter or William Barnes of Shaftesbury tried to buy Norrington secretly, in trust for Thomas and his son William, this ruse was spotted and it was sold to Wadham Wyndham in 1658. There are different versions about what happened to the family next, perhaps referring to different branches. The family tree quoted by Bowles records that Thomas moved to Horsington, Somerset, but died a few years later, in 1656. Deeds held by the Wiltshire and Swindon Record Office suggest that, by 1604, he was at North Cheriton, Somerset. In *Some Old Wiltshire Homes*, 1894, we read:

> In spite of his troubles, Thomas Gawen [the younger] survived to take an active part in the civil war, through which, like other rich Roman Catholics of that day, he followed the fortunes of his ill-fated monarch. In consequence, on the subsequent triumph of the Parliamentary party, all his estates were sold as the property of a delinquent who had been guilty of treason against the nation. A friendly neighbour endeavoured to defeat the ends of Parliamentary oppression by purchasing the property for Thomas Gawen and his son; but the kindly subterfuge was discovered, and a special Act dealing with the Gawen estates promulgated, declaring 'all secret trusts to be void', and fining the tenants £166. Thomas Gawen, who had suffered so much in the cause of religion and his king, was not fated to see the Restoration, but died four years before, on the 1st. of June 1656, almost in penury. His first wife was buried at St Mary's Church, commemorated by a stone in the floor, now partially obscured by a pew: 'Here lieth intombed the body of Gertrude Gawen, wife of Thomas Gawen of Norrington, Esq. and daughter of Richard Bluet of Holcum Rogus, Esq. who was buried the 29th. of January, 1637.'
>
> It is very uncertain if his son ever obtained the Norrington estates, for although William Gawen's name appears in a contract for the sale of the property, this contract was afterwards set aside, and he himself disappeared from the county. Subsequently the name is found no more in Wilts.

Bowles gives his date of birth as 1608, but he and his six siblings are absent from the registers, which suggests that his father kept clear of Norrington for some years after the traumas of the turn of the century. William's wife was another Catherine and at least two of his children were baptised in St Mary's, Thomas in 1635 and Mary in 1643. William's father, Thomas, appears in the burial register a day after his death, and his second wife, Ann, in 1678; (Bowles must be wrong here, as he gives the second wife as Elizabeth, later married to Benjamin Drew of Baverstock).

The extended family of the Gawens did not disappear from Wiltshire or even Alvediston immediately. According to Bowles, a memorandum about Norrington and Trow tithes 'in the hand-writing of Mr. Wyndham, the grand-father of Mrs. Arundell' (i.e. Wadham's grandson John), dated 1746, mentions Henry Gawen as tenant of part of the farm. Four generations of Gawens, believed by Keith Gawen to be from a younger branch of the family lived in Ebbesbourne Wake from 1654 until the death of the last member on the 3rd. February, 1771, although tantalisingly, not in the cottage in Duck Street called 'Gawens', with the date 1602. Peter Meers, in his book on Ebbesbourne, points out that William Young, the local historian who converted to Catholicism and championed the family, lived in this cottage for most of his life, so that may have something to do with the confusion and with the name. The enclosure map of 1792 shows two plots on the north side of Pound Street, below the old school house, with another stretching from Pound Street to the Ebble and a larger one covering land between the Ebble and the top road, to the north. These were known as 'Gawen's', 'Gawen's Ground', 'Gawen's Moor' and 'Gilven's Close' respectively, 'Gilven' being a corruption of 'Gawen', (hence 'Gylvern Garage', where the Booth family provided a vital service until the end of 2004, in premises built on 'Gilven's Close'.) Notes on Wardour, the Roman Catholic stronghold near Tisbury, refer to a 'Henry, Lord Arundell, who was one of the five Roman Catholic peers arrested over the Titus Oates plot in 1678. Also affected by the Titus Oates plot was John Garwen (sic) from Norrington Manor in Alvediston who was sent to St. Omers to study for the priesthood.

Eight years after his return as a Jesuit priest, he was arrested in the anti-Catholic uproar that resulted in Titus Oates's accusations and he was finally hanged, drawn and quartered at Tyburn on 20 June 1679. All this occurred twenty years after the Gawens lost Norrington so, whether he ever actually lived there prior to its sale or whether he was from another branch of the family that hailed from there, or was a younger son, it appears that the family's zeal and courage were unabated.

Keith Gawen's researches come up with this outcome for the Gawen family:

> As a result of the continuing persecution of Catholics, the family having sold Norrington, moved to Ireland where their faith would be totally accepted. When they moved they changed their name to 'Norrington' and remained in Ireland for about 150 years. No details of their life or history in Ireland can be found, but it is known that they returned to England using their original name about 1770.

He has intriguing information from a former rector of Berwick St. John and his daughter.

> My mother when she lived at Pett, came to know a neighbour Mrs. Fowke, whose son is related to the Norringtons, and she said that the Norringtons resided permanently in Ireland, and that at least one member of the family remained in England, changing their faith, and it is from this branch that our present day family is descended. Apparently the younger branch of the Gawens continued to live obscurely, and in poverty, for several generations in and around Alvediston. . . . [Trevor Gawen] was helped in his enquiries by the Rector of Berwick St. John. (N.B. Roger Henry Sparrow Fowke was rector from 1946 to 1955; in 1947 Alvediston parish came under his care as well, see *The Biography of a Country Church, Berwick St. John*

by Hazel Giffard.)

Whatever the later history of the family may be, the loss of Norrington must have been a great wrench, because it was fiercely contended. Finally however, the young heir, William Gawen, was outsmarted by the widow of the very Walter Barnes who had tried to rescue Norrington for him, and by her new husband. Wadham Wyndham, 'at this time a serjeant (sic) at law' and from November 1660 'one of his majesty's justices of the bench' (Bowles), was at a legal advantage. With the Gould descendents feeling cheated of Samways two centuries later, and the Gawen descendents feeling likewise about Norrington, Ebbesbourne seems to have been a haven for the dispossessed of its smaller but wealthier neighbouring village.

In Adam Nicolson's *Arcadia* a there is description of farming practices in the early seventeenth century, at a time when Norrington's fortunes were in a delicate state. John Norden's influential 'Surveior's Dialogue' was published in 1607. He described the origins of the manor as a voluntary arrangement for the mutual benefit of the lord, (who provided the tenant with land and security), and the tenant, (who in turn gave the lord his labour and loyalty), but soon this benign compact had hardened into the expectations of the 'custom of the manor'. Norden, a devout Christian, had a Pauline vision of community as a body whose every part should be nurtured for the good of the whole, a vision whose basis was love, not personal gain, but he described it in terms which soon had political overtones: 'And is not euery Mannor a little common wealth, whereof the Tenants are the members, the land the body, and the Lord the head?' he asked.

Nicolson explains:

This idea of organic health, and of balance as the source of that health, runs unbroken from the farming of the fields to the management of the country. It is an undivided conceptual ecology which can take in the workings of the physical body, the court at Whitehall, the family, the village, the land itself, the growing of crops, the transmission of wellbeing to the future, the inheritance of understanding from the past, and above all the interlocking roles of nobility, gentry and commonalty. It is the ideology of an establishment which is concerned to keep itself in the position of wealth and power. There is not a hint of democracy, let alone radicalism, about it, but it is a frame of mind which also sets itself against any form of authoritarianism.

Yet the 'custom of the manor' was enforced with Big Brother-like vigilance because that was the only way for the fragile balance of rural community to be held. This explains how members of the aristocracy such as the Pembrokes, influenced by essentially conservative, Arcadian ideals, found themselves ranged against the very court where they had enjoyed such lucrative and powerful patronage for so long, when the king was perceived to have broken his side of an almost sacred bargain by becoming authoritarian, and setting an example of narrow, uncompromising self-interest which seeped down to fracture a society already threatened by modern technology and which was making the 'custom of the manor' and all that it stood for obsolete. Descriptions of royal masques in Charles I's time prefigure the excesses of Marie Antoinette in her shepherdess phase, and the discrepancy between the expenditure on one 'pastoral' masque and the wages of even the relatively highly-paid shepherd on chalk downlands was outrageous. The Gawens, as Roman Catholics, found themselves aligned with the increasingly Catholic Crown. However, the whole breakdown of the manorial society of which they had been so much a part locally may have been as much of a shock to them as to anyone else in the drastic upheavals which culminated in the Civil War and its aftermath. As ever, unravelling the motives and principles of opposing forces in civil unrest is a deeply disturbing and unsatisfactory process.

The Wyndham Family, 1658-1952

THE HISTORY OF the vast and far-reaching Wyndham family is lovingly told by the last owner of their original home near the north Norfolk coast, Robert Wyndham Ketton-Cremer, in 'Felbrigg, the Story of a House', published by Century in association with the National Trust which has owned Felbrigg since his death in 1969. Bowles follows the family fortunes from their Norfolk origins, but the Wyndham family influence extends over huge areas of the country; the Norrington connection came via the Somerset branch, see below, but first, a brief summary of the earlier ancestors will be given.

John Wyndham bought the Felbrigg estate in 1450 from a family which had taken the name of 'Felbrigg', but he rented the house from the widowed Lady Felbrigg during her lifetime. Norfolk was in a state of disarray at this time, with two groups of powerful families competing with each other; the Wyndhams were in the ultimately dominant group, unlike the Felbriggs. Ketton-Cremer agrees with Bowles that the family name was probably derived from Wymondham, near Norwich, but dismisses as 'fanciful' the idea of descent from 'Ailwardus de Wymondham, an eminent Saxon', favoured earlier and quoted by Bowles. John Wyndham I (there were many more) appears to have been aggressively ambitious, enabling him to establish a powerful and wealthy dynasty from virtually nothing. After judicious purchases of manors and marriage to a rich widow, he joined a lethal triumvirate and 'together the three succeeded in establishing a kind of legal racket... . . . Their chief weapon was the illegal practice of 'maintenance', that is to say supporting litigants in whom they had no personal interest in order to damage others whom they desired to embarrass. Their secondary armament was to corrupt and overawe jurors and judges, threatening them with reprisals and attending court sittings with armed escorts of sometimes as many as four hundred men,' (from 'The Wyndhams of Somerset', by H.A. Wyndham). While most information about him is coloured by the fact that Paston, whose 'Letters' recorded life in that time and place, was one of his enemies he was, in the words of Ketton-Cremer, 'an exceptionally turbulent and unpopular figure.' Both Felbriggs and local people were dismayed by his arrival, and one member of the family took the house back by force after Lady Felbrigg's death, ousting Wyndham's second wife who was there alone at the time. Finally, the Wyndham claim was legally ratified.

The second John Wyndham consolidated the family by marrying women with powerful connections. There are two stories about this Wyndham. Ketton-Cremer maintained that, although his first father-in-law supported Richard III and became the Duke of Norfolk when Richard came to the throne, John still managed to retain royal favour when Henry VII defeated Richard at Bosworth in 1485, (where the Duke of Norfolk met his death at the head of Richard's army) even gaining a knighthood. However, when both he and his son Thomas married into the Scrope family, they became linked with the Earls of Suffolk, which proved disastrous, since Suffolk was a pretender to the throne. In 1502, Sir John was beheaded at the Tower for his sympathies and his widow retired to a nunnery. However, the tradition passed down through the Somerset family is that Sir John was a friend of Sir Walter Tyrell, who organised the murder of the princes in the Tower. Henry VII claimed that this was ordered by Richard III and used it as a pretext for his challenge to Richard's claim to the throne. Sir Walter died in Calais, with Sir John at his side, so Henry ordered that Sir John be arrested before he could disembark on his return to England. He was taken straight to the Tower, executed for high treason, and all his lands were confiscated. Although Henry VIII's mother was the sister of the dead princes, he restored all the Wyndham land to Sir John's son Thomas, who managed to exploit his Norfolk connections to further his glittering naval career. Interestingly, Bowles quotes Thomas Wyndham's will, admittedly getting the date of death a whole century wrong, at 1622 not 1522. In this he orders a thousand masses to be said for his soul. Bowles was in favour of Catholic Emancipation, a hot topic in the 1830s, when he was writing, so he takes the opportunity 'to shew a descendant of this Sir Thomas, now one of the worthy representatives of the city of Salisbury, "that the sacrifice of the mass, and the invocations of the saints, at any rate, were not always considered as superstitious and idolatrous, though in these our latter days they may have been so"'. This was a swipe at Mr. Wadham Wyndham, M.P. for Salisbury, 1818-33 and 1835-43. If Bowles' source was correct, the family managed several judicious religious changes of heart because Sir Thomas' heir, Edmund, benefitted from the dissolution of the monasteries, when the nearby Priory of Beeston came up for sale.

On Henry VIII's marriage to Jane Seymour Edmund was knighted, but, in a typical Tudor switchback of fortunes, narrowly escaped having his hand cut off for hitting a member of the Norfolk family in an argument on the royal tennis courts. After being pardoned he became High Sheriff of Norfolk and had to dispense justice himself. His sister, Margaret, married Sir Andrew Luttrell of Dunster Castle in Somerset, where the Luttrell family continued to live until it was left to the National Trust in the last century. The younger brother, John, met Elizabeth Sydenham, the heiress of Orchard, near Watchet, at his sister's home. When he married her in 1528 Orchard Sydenham became Orchard Wyndham, and this house remains in the Wyndham family to this day. Indeed, Orchard Wyndham, has been in the same family since the thirteenth century or earlier, passing through the female line three times: the Orchards or de Horcherds were first recorded in 1287; in 1420 Joan inherited. She was married to Richard Popham, and their daughter, also Joan, married John Sydenham, hence Orchard Sydenham.

This brings the family to the Eizabethan era, when the Gawens of Norrington were beginning to feel pressure as Roman Catholics. Sir Edmund had three sons, who changed their name to Windham with an 'i' which makes the distinction between the Norfolk and Somerset families easier. While the Orchard Wyndhams were prospering, Sir Edmund's eldest son, Roger set about bringing everyone in sight to court, with disastrous financial results. Ketton-Cremer describes him as a 'local tyrant' who was 'litigious to the point of mania'. Unfortunately for all but himself he had Felbrigg for thirty years. By the time he died, childless, some of the estate was mortgaged to Sir John Wyndham of Orchard, and Roger's brother, Francis, was also dead, without issue. The youngest brother and heir, Thomas, only had a year to try to reverse the family fortunes and to restore the confidence of the local community before he too expired, in 1599, perhaps unsurprisingly given the magnitude of his task.

Meanwhile the Somer-set branch was flourishing, so Thomas could rest easy in the knowledge that the whole estate was passed to Sir John Wyndham (1558-1645), grandson of the first John of Orchard Wyndham, on the understanding that 'the house of Felbrigg be dwelt upon, either by himself, or by some of his children of the name.' Since Sir John had nine sons and six daughters a nest egg would be welcome. He had married Joan Portman of

Lady Barbara Wyndham. (Sylvana Chandler, Orchard Wyndham)

Orchard Portman, also in Somerset, prompting Margaret Gifford's couplet:

> Two orchards had a several right to thee,
> A Portman graft to a Wyndham's fruitful tree.

Orchard Wyndham being, as it was to remain, the primary home of this branch of the family, it passed to the eldest son, another John, but it is a reflection of the father's wealth that he could not only settle his second surviving son at Felbrigg, but encourage him to rebuild the house. This Thomas also built up the estate and, like most Norfolk landowners, supported Parliament in the Civil War. At this point we leave Norfolk and the Felbrigg line to return to Thomas' father.

Sir John's mother was Florence Wadham, whose brother Nicholas founded Wadham College, Oxford, and whose name was given to the first Wyndham of Norrington. John and Florence Wyndham donated the precious linenfold panelling from the Orchard Wyndham solar chamber to Wadham College, and the family connection with the college remains strong. Indeed, the present William Wadham Wyndham went there. The Wadhams were an extremely wealthy family so Florence's marriage was very propitious for the

Sir Wadham Wyndham. (Sylvana Chandler, Orchard Wyndham)

Orchard Wyndhams. However, a bizarre near-tragedy remains her greatest claim to fame.

When Florence was heavily pregnant with her first and only child, she became ill and went into such a severe coma that it was assumed that she had died. She was buried in the family vault in St. Decumen's church at nearby Watchet. That night Atkins the sexton, planning to steal her rings, returned to the vault and prised open the coffin. However he was thwarted: the rings would not come off and in his panic he cut one of her swollen fingers. The pain revived her, at which point the guilty sexton rushed out into the night forgetting his lantern. With great presence of mind, Florence retrieved it, managed to get herself home, and soon afterwards gave birth to the John 'from whom' as Ketton-Cremer wrote, 'every living member of the Wyndham family is descended, apart from a branch in the United States whose progenitor was Thomas, the tough and enterprising sailor.'

Extraordinary as this tale seems, it was well documented at the time and other unfortunate women suffered similar experiences, most notably Mary Queen of Scots, who went into such a deep coma after falling from her horse when pregnant with the future James I of England and IV of Scotland that her half-brother, assuming that she was dead, proclaimed himself king. Conjecture about those who did not escape is awful, but Florence's revival and courage were celebrated in a ballad. Remarkably, not only did this son survive to father fifteen children and to live to eighty-six, but his mother long outlived his father, who died when the young John was only twelve. On his parents' elaborate memorial in St. Decumen's Church, Sir John inscribed:

Maritus.~ When changeless fate to death did change my life,
I pray'd it to be gentle to my wife.

Uxor.~ But shee who hart and hand to thee did wed,

Desir'd nothing more than this thie bedd.

Fatum. ~ I bought your souls, that link'd were each in either,
To rest above, your bodies here together.

Wadham Wyndham was Sir John's seventh surviving son. Born
in 1609, he lived through turbulent times, both nationally and in the
history of Norrington. He inherited some land in Somerset and was
well-established as a barrister when he finally secured Norrington in
1658. Two years later, he bought St. Edmund's College in Salisbury.
Helen Wilcockson, in an article in Issue 7 of 'Sarum Chronicle'
describes how Bishop Walter de la Wyle founded both St. Edmund's
Church and the College in the 1260s. St. Edmund's was the largest
of Salisbury's three parishes at that time, and the College was run as
a small monastic community under a provost. It had an infirmary,
and the college members had duties in the church and parish, as well
as attending lectures in the Cathedral. These aims were not always
fulfilled, and the College met the same fate as all religious houses
at Henry VIII's dissolution of the monasteries in 1536-9. It passed
through various hands and a handsome Tudor mansion was built.
The property remained in the Wyndham family from 1660 until 1871,
and was the seat of the Salisbury branch.

The year 1660 was momentous nationally and for Wadham
Wyndham. His extended family had been bitterly divided during the
Civil War, although his immediate family kept their Parliamentarian
sympathies discreetly in check. When Charles II was restored to
the throne, Wadham was knighted and became a high court judge
whose duties included the prosecution of those responsible for the
death of Charles I, (which coincidentally means that he may have
been involved with the sentencing to death by hanging, drawing and
quartering of the author's ancestor, the Rev. Hugh Peters, a Pilgrim
Father who returned to England and became a chaplain to Oliver

Cromwell's Council of State.) Sir Wadham also helped to allocate land and property after the Great Fire of London. He died on Christmas Day 1668, two years after the fire, when disputes were probably still raging.

Sir Wadham and Lady Barbara, (who came from Northamptonshire and with whom he had six sons and five daughters, continuing the prolific family trend), spent as much time as possible at Norrington which Bowles describes as 'their favourite residence'. It is interesting to note that Norrington, although much smaller than Sir Wadham's childhood home of Orchard Wyndham, shares a characteristic in its seclusion within a bowl of hills. They altered the fourteenth century house considerably. Although some changes may have occurred during the sixteenth century, by the time Sir Wadham and Lady Barbara had finished with it, only the hall, porch, a small room which may have been part of an earlier chapel and a crypt or cellar beneath remained. The solar was replaced by a magnificent banquetting hall with a grand fireplace above the undercroft, and a new range of buildings was built to the west. An east wing provided service areas, (kitchens, pantries, dairies and larders). The land around the house was landscaped in the style of the times. Even in 1830, Bowles described 'the remains of a capital mansion house, gardens, stew ponds, traces of a bowling green, terraces, &c. the natural concomitants of baronial residences.'

A survey of 1664 makes scant mention of dwellings for the poor, but the families working on the estate probably still lived in the medieval village. The 'capital messuage', (manor house), stable, outhouses, ponds, 'Backsids' and gardens covered seven acres. There was a house with barns and stables at Trow, and one cottage near the road had recently built by 'one Adlam.' 'Mr. Gold's Farme in Alvediston', (Samways), paid an annual rent of ten shillings to Norrington Manor. Field names have changed remarkably little, e.g. Horsecraft, Crookhill, Whisley (Whistley), Bushie Gaston (Bushy Garson), 20 Acres, Prest Field (probably now Westfield and West Leigh), Crawley, Windmill

Hill and Gascombe (Goscombe). Marshwood is now Manwood and there were three copses called Gawen's Plot, Gawen's Higher and Lower Copses. There was free warren on North Down and a 'purlieu' or tract of land adjoining Cranborne Chase and 'plase for Deere' to the south.

Portraits of Sir Wadham and Lady Barbara, formerly kept at Dinton, are now at Orchard Wyndham, and succeeding generations have been rather awed by Lady Barbara's fierce countenance. Indeed, she must have been a force to be reckoned with, as she managed the estate very ably for the first year after her husband's death while her eldest son John, a barrister-at-law in London, organised his affairs. She survived Wadham for thirty-six years, moving to St. Edmund's College in Salisbury with her six year-old son, another Wadham, who inherited St. Edmund's and made great changes there. That part of Salisbury, like areas of many towns associated with the family, bears their name in, for example, Wyndham Park, Road and Terrace. Wadham was the fourth surviving son. Another, George, fathered the branch which settled in Salisbury Close. Lady Barbara was buried with her husband in St Mary's Church, and theirs are the two earliest Wyndham memorials in the Norrington aisle.

Translations of the Latin inscriptions read:

Sir WADHAM WYNDHAM, son of John Wyndham, of Orchard Wyndham in the county of Somerset, the ninth son of that knight, whose merits were among the finest, and who [Wadham] was born from his marriage to Joan, the daughter of the Baronet Henry Portman in the same county. After many births and numerous children, of those she gave birth to with parental care and her own, she begot [Wadham]. With genius in his nature, after first tasting the other streams of the Muses, at length he dedicated himself to the study of forensic law, in which (as he stood as a pillar of understanding) he distinguished himself with such trustworthiness and skill that he served as a judge on the King's Bench of King Charles II and maintained its functions. He made the partnership of marriage with BARBARA, whom Sir GEORGE CLARKE of WATFORD in the county of Northamptonshire had fathered. He [Wadham] lived most fortunately; he was blessed with children ~ eight sons and four daughters ~ with honour, wealth and piety, with a loyal wife and children, etc. He enjoys in Heaven the justice, which for a long time he employed on Earth. He who brought hope to all, brought this man to his kingdom on 25th December, 1668, aged 59 years.

Beneath are laid the remains of BARBARA, the widow of WADHAM WYNDHAM buried nearby. While ensuring that her six sons were liberally educated, she greatly enriched the affairs left by the father through her prudence. She gave three daughters happily in marriage, the other died a virgin. She passed away [gave] not only to her own children, but brought alleviation to the distressed and welcome help to all in need, bestowing these supreme gifts because of her great piety. John, her eldest son, grieving, dedicates this monument. She died on the 26th December A.D. 1704, at the age of 78.

Presumably two sons died in infancy, too young to be 'liberally educated', but that is not a bad tally out of twelve children. Perhaps others who take a long time to decide on a career might explain their tardiness as 'first tasting the other streams of the Muses'.

From May 1669 to July 1670, Luke Dyer, her steward, kept detailed accounts which provide a fascinating insight into life on Norrington and Trow farms. They have been preserved in the Wyndham archive at the Somerset record Office, together with the survey of 1664, above. Overall, income was £442, 11s. 7d. and expenditure was £365, 9s. 8d., giving a profit of £77, 1s. 11d. One of the most striking things is the familiarity of the names, which still crop up throughout the Valley, even if no longer in Alvediston. The Poor Rate had been collected since Elizabethan times and, as Norrington and Trow farms crept into Berwick St. John, both Poor Rate and tithes, (for the church) were due in both parishes. Mr. George Stillingfleet caught up with eight years' rent for 'Whishley mead', (Whistley mead was in Berwick), due to the Earl of Salisbury. Law-day, lady or lade silver was due to the lord of the manor. Alvediston being a chapel of Broad Chalke, tithes were paid to the church there.

Mr. Fry was collector for the poor of Alvediston, Thomas Scamel (Scammell) for those of Berwick.

Samuel Coomb was mentioned as 'tithingman' and later, church warden.

Robert, then George, Toomer were church wardens, later tithingmen. (It will be remembered that 'Thomas Toomer the Tithingman' featured in the tales of the burial of Thomas Gawen.)

Richard Mullens (Mullins) came over from Broad Chalke to collect tithes, some for the clergy and some for Sir Jo. Penruddock, lord of the manor there.

John Monk was church warden of Berwick.

Samuel Foot of Berwick was the local blacksmith.

Other surnames which occur in the survey and generally in the registers may be familiar today, but in a wide selection of spellings, including:

Abbott, Acten (?Ackland), Adlom (Adlem), Baster (?Bannister), Bradle (Bradley), Bright, Bundy (of Chalke), Burge (of Marnhull), Cool, Cooper, Croker (Crocker), Cox, Dyer, Evens (Evans), Foel (Foyle), Harris, Haylock, Hiscock, King, Long, (? Lane, Lond, Lowe), Markes, ~ were these forerunners of the Marks family who arrived in Alvediston in the early twentieth century?~ Pery (Perry), Pool (?Pole / Paul / Poor), Poleden, (Poulden), Read, Sanders, Sanger, Skinner, Small, Staples, Trowbroge (Trowbridge), Vinsent (Vincent), Whit (White), Young and the irresistibly named 'Hinery Warom', (Henry Wareham).

Pigeons were sold by the dozen; there were some pigs, presumably enough for domestic consumption, and about eight hundred sheep in two flocks, north and south, each with its own shepherd; most of the cattle were kept for dairy purposes ~ quantities of cheese and butter were produced ~ while oxen as well as horses were used to draw ploughs and carts. Arable crops included oats, beans, peas, barley and wheat. Lists of casual workers for the harvest of each of these crops as well as for hay demonstrate the interdependence of landowner and agricultural worker, both male and female. They are also a reminder that although many of these families were, and remained for centuries, living in poverty and with limited horizons unimaginable today, they gleaned a vast wealth of experience of farming practices, the cycle of the seasons, animals, plants, birds, soil, self-sufficiency and survival which gave them a wisdom and a toughness which can easily be overlooked, and agricultural work has only recently become the solitary occupation which we see today. 'Riding' or cleaning out the pond gave six men a total of sixty-seven days' work, others were paid to transport goods to Lady Wyndham in Salisbury; there were hedges to be laid and maintained and hurdles to be made, horses to be shod, sheep to be shorn and their fleeces to be prepared for sale.

'Nesecaries Bought', 'Houshold Expence' and 'Emplements' are totalled up for each month, but sometimes the sequence of months is confusing. They include: a bottle, an earthenware pot, sieves, cheesecloth, a 'huchmuck' (wicker strainer used in brewing), brooms, rakes, crooks, shovel, nails; harness for the horses and oxen, and the horse-hide to make them with; cloth for clothing, canvas, buttons, thread, sacking ties and twine, ropes and cartlines, a well-rope and a bed cord; brimstone, shot and powder; seeds and plants, soap, starch and candles; '3 dishes and a mouse trap'; barrels, planks of wood for the wheat barn, raddle and 'tobacko for Sheepe', (used, like pitch and tar, to treat their ailments), and, from Robert King at

Trow: '1 rick staddel, 1 mill, 2 troes [troughs], 1 bucket & Chaine & 13 rakes to serve bese [beasts]'. In the same month, June 1669, at the beginning of the account, a wagon was also bought from Donhead. Food under these headings includes: meat, suet, (a lot of suet), salt, pepper and ginger, malt, currants and raisins, oatmeal, carrots and turnips, 'Sallet Oyl', chicken ~ and really not much else. This places the traditional Christmas dinner of beef followed by a suet and dried fruit pudding at the heart of English fare, but most people would have got by on a bowl of porrigey gruel. It is also a reminder of the huge amount of food and number of items which could be produced on the estate. Thomas Haylock's role is not clear. Although his brother Steven, (who often bought cereals from the estate), seems to have been a regular worker, Thomas was only paid for two days' work in the entire record, admittedly at a higher rate than most. However, among the purchases are listed two pairs of shoes, stockings, coarse dowlais cloth, canvas and woollen cloth, and even 'draarsh' (drawers) for Thomas Haylock, although no-one else seems to have been so favoured.

Finally, the accounts note the local markets and the wide area of commercial dealings. Luke Dyer attended markets at Salisbury and Shaftesbury, and fairs at Hindon, Berwick, Chilmark, Gillingham and Mere. In addition to his 'half yeares wages' of £7, he was allowed expenses for markets and fairs: in February 1669 he received 13/4d. and in May 1670, 6/8d.

John Wyndham I of Norrington had an interesting career. Born in 1647, as well as his legal experience he was a commander of the local militia, the Foot Regiment of Salisbury. This was not just a 'Home Guard' role: in 1685 he fought at Sedgemoor, where James II's army defeated Monmouth. Again, unlike the archetype, he questioned army practices, being disgusted by the behaviour of the 'New Model Army' during and after the Civil War, and by the abuses he saw committed by an army on the rampage after Sedgemoor. That same year, as Tory

M.P. for Salisbury, he took advantage of the opportunity to protest against the dangers to society of unfettered militarism in the only Parliament held in James II's reign. He believed that Parliament should ensure that the army's size and influence were kept well under control. He cared deeply about Norrington.

He married Alice Fownes and had five sons and two daughters. The eldest son was another John but the youngest seems to have been a much more flamboyant character, judging from their choice of memorials. Bowles records a 'tomb . . . within iron rails,' to the memory of John Wyndham the elder. This must have been removed to make way for the new vestry in 1866. All that remains is a large, broken slab just outside the vestry door, upon which the words 'John Wyndham' are now scarcely visible. On the floor of the Norrington aisle is a stone slab, presumably once next to John's, which reads:

> Here Lyeth the Body of Mrs. Alice Wyndham, Daughter of Thomas Fownes late of Stepleton In the County of Dorsett Esq. A Lady Of Exemplary Virtue, Great Charity And Unaffected Piety She was The Happy Wife of Colonel John Wyndham Who Lyes under the Adjoining Tombstone For above fifty Years, And Departed This life, After a Short but Melancholy Widowhood On the 16th. of May 1725 Aged 70 Universally Lamented.

This is standard wording for the time, but the sons' characters emerge from the memorials on either side of the south window. On the right is a superb example of mid-eighteenth century sculpture, executed by Johannes Michel Rysbrack, (born 1694 in Antwerp, died 1770 in London), a Flemish master who established himself in London from 1720. His work includes a monument to Sir Isaac Newton in Westminster Abbey, a statue of Marlborough, and busts of Walpole, Bolingbroke and Pope. In Queen Square, Bristol, there is a bronze equestrian statue of William III by Rysbrack. Thomas, the youngest son, must have commissioned this memorial to his parents in his will, since it was sculpted a year after his death, (and about twenty-two years after his father's.) For all its beauty, it is but a pale reflection of the enormous edifice to his own memory by the west door in Salisbury Cathedral. Whatever the relations between the brothers, it is hard not to imagine a bit of one-upmanship by the youngest; his contribution reads:

> To the Memory of JOHN WYNDHAM of Norrington Esq.
> And of ALICE His Wife, Daughter of THOMAS FOWNES
> Of Stepleton in the County Of Dorset Esq, who are Both
> Buried near to this Wall, in the Church Yard
> belonging to this Church, this Monument was placed by
> the Order and at the Expence of The Right Honble
> THOMAS Lord WYNDHAM Baron WYNDHAM of Finglass
> And some time Lord High Chancellor of Ireland, their
> Son, as a Testimony of that Honour and Respect which
> He had for them. June 1746
> The said JOHN WYNDHAM Esq. departed this Life
> On the 29th. of February 1723/4; Aged 76
> The said ALICE, his Wife, departed this life
> On the 16th. of May 1726, aged 70.

It was a shame that Thomas had to hazard a guess about the year of his father's death, (an ambiguity which is quite common in the burial register), and that his mother's death is recorded a year late, a minor detail among the tributes to the benefactor. Thomas, being childless and unmarried, had no immediate heir to honour him. Unlike his Tory father, he was a Whig. Educated at a school in Salisbury Cathedral Close, then at the family's alma mater, Wadham College Oxford, he had progressed through Lincoln's Inn to become recorder of Salisbury when he was only twenty-four, in 1706. In 1724 he was appointed Chief Justice of the court of Common Pleas in Ireland and then Lord Chancellor there seven years later. This was a poisoned chalice, as Ireland was in religious turmoil. The Hon H.A. Wyndham, writing his family history, 1688-1837, explained that although the Anglican Church was dominant the considerably larger Catholic Church joined forces with Presbyterians and other Non-Conformists against them. As Chief Justice, his circuit extended from Cork to Carrickfergus. The poverty concerned him; he wrote: 'Some parts of the North are well cultivated, but the southern parts are very thinly inhabited, and scarce a tree or hedge to be seen for 20 miles together.' A great contrast to his native Alvediston.

As Lord Wyndham of Finglass he presided over the Irish House of Lords. The Hon. H.A. Wyndham related that he was recommended by the Archbishop as a 'native of England', who had 'undoubted Whiggish Character' and was 'always attached to the revolution and Hanoverian Succession'. He was genuinely concerned that only nine of twenty-two Irish Bishops were English-born, and kept 'busy against popery'. However, with the Archbishop he promoted laws to aid agriculture, politics, the linen industry and, in the Dublin workhouse, poor relief. 'His work and personality had helped to establish a tranquillity which in 1745 allayed the danger he had envisaged of Ireland embarrassing England', (in the Jacobite Rising). Thus the ill-health which enforced his retirement to Salisbury Close in 1739 was hardly surprising, especially as one of his final acts was to officiate at the trial of one of his fellow lords for murder and treason. Another difference between himself and his brother John was his refusal to invest in land, so he left a generous legacy to Wadham College. (It is interesting to note that his contemporary at Orchard Wyndham, the Tory Sir William Wyndham (1687-1740), third baronet and Queen Anne's Chancellor of the Exchequer, (1713-14), was one of the West Country's chief Jacobite leaders, a distinction which landed him in the Tower for a time and curtailed his illustrious parliamentary career. Apparently undeterred, he led the opposition to Walpole, and expended the rest of his energy on his home. In 1732, John Gay wrote to Pope: 'Sir William Wyndham is at present amusing himself with some real improvements and a great many visionary castles.')

Meanwhile, Sir Wadham and Lady Barbara's second son, William, was establishing another very important branch of the family in Dinton. When he bought the Dinton Estate in 1689, for £2,235, it had a fairly modest, seventeenth century, H-shaped brick house, which fulfilled the family's needs until his great-grandson's time. His eldest daughter, Henrietta, narrowly escaped the same trauma as her forebear, Florence. She appeared to have died but, her mother being convinced that there was still the slightest moisture on a mirror held to her mouth, wisely refused to allow her to be moved. Suddenly, Henrietta awoke. However, her fear of burial alive must have been acute as she ordered in her will that, after death, her corpse be kept unburied for a week unless she died of smallpox. In this case, rapid burial was essential to try to contain infection, but she still insisted that burial should be delayed for as long as possible. Seven other Williams followed the first, and the relevance of this branch of the family, many of whose memorials may be found in the church at Dinton, will soon become clear.

To return to Norrington: it is fascinating to speculate on the relationship between John II and Thomas, but it may be significant that Bowles noted of John that 'By his will, dated 4th. July, 1748, he desires to be buried in Alvediston church, and that his funeral expences (sic) should not exceed 320l. (£320) of which 200l. were to be laid out in erecting a monument over his burial place for his late wife and himself.' Although large, it is simplicity itself, and makes the sums which Thomas must have expended difficult to imagine.

To the Memory of

ANN
Late Wife of JOHN WYNDHAM Esq.
of NORRINGTON
and sole heiress of
ROB. BARBER Esq.
Of ASHCOMB
Who died June the 20th. 1748
Aged 51

And Also
To the Memory of
The said JOHN WYNDHAM Esq.
eldest son of JOHN WYNDHAM
of NORRINGTON Esq.
and ALICE his Wife
who died Dec. the 27th. 1750

In the same year that John died, a son, William, was born to the Felbrigg family of Windhams. He became a Whig M.P., a friend and colleague of the famous Rockingham, North, Fox and Burke, and, in 1782, confided in the great Dr. Johnson when he was uncertain whether to accept the responsible post of Chief Secretary to the Lord Lieutenant of Ireland. Johnson's advice is worth quoting:

I have no great timidity in my own disposition, and am no encourager of it in others. Never be afraid to think yourself fit for anything for which your friends think you fit. You will become an able negotiator; a very pretty rascal. No one in Ireland wears even the mask of incorruption. No one professes to do for sixpence what he can get a shilling for doing. Set sail; and see where the winds and the waves will carry you.

While some of this counsel may be questionable, the final sentence still encourages today. Windham went on to become Pitt's Secretary at War in 1794.

John II's wife Anne was local, Ashcombe (as it is now spelt) House being in Berwick St. John. John and Anne, however, were the last of the Wyndhams to live at Norrington, and they moved to Salisbury Close in 1718. They had only one child, a girl also named Anne, who married the Honorable James Everard Arundell about two years after her father's death. (Incidentally, the name Everard had already arisen in the history of this village, with John Everard of Stratford sub Castle, who granted the manor of Alvediston and a windmill to Wilton Abbey in 1306, presumably having himself held it of the king, so there must have been some connection already.) Beneath Thomas Wyndham's florid memorial in Salisbury Cathedral is a sad little stone slab inscribed:

> Here lieth the Body of
> James Everard Arundell
> Son of the Honble. James
> Everard & Ann Arundell.
> He died April the 18th.
> 1756 Aged 1 month.

However, they had other children, including another James Everard, who inherited from his parents.

In deference to Sir Wadham's will, John left the family home entailed to his now quite distant cousin William of Dinton, since Sir Wadham had stipulated that all his other properties must pass through the male line. Fortunately for her, Anne inherited plenty of other properties and she and her husband named the house in the Close 'Arundells', as it is still known today. More recently, Sir Edward Heath, late Prime Minister, lived there until his death in 2005. On

Anne Arundell's death in 1803, the fourth William Wyndham of Dinton inherited Norrington. He it was who rebuilt Dinton House.

Norrington Tenants until 1836

B Y THIS TIME, the focus of the family having been transferred to Dinton for almost a hundred years, the house at Norrington was beginning to suffer. The farm was let to a series of farmers; possibly one of the earliest was Francis Fry, whose memorial in the church has been something of an enigma. Some years ago, two brasses bearing inscriptions to Francis Fry, Gent., who died in 1710 and his wife Jane, who died seven years earlier were found behind the altar curtains. Bowles notes: 'This Francis Fry, it is believed, was tenant of the Norrington Farm; he was of the family of Fry of Ashgrove, who gave the ground in Chevicombe Bottom, in Donhead St. Mary parish, as a burial ground for the Quakers. Of the same family, is the husband of the philanthropic Mrs. Fry, who, like a second Howard, has visited most of the gaols in England and Ireland, instilling religious principles into those females who were found inmates.' Francis and Jane must have been living in Alvediston in 1672, as their daughter, Sarah was baptised here then. Theirs was a prolific union as Thomas, born in 1682/3, was their fourth son and Frances, (1684), their ninth daughter!

Whatever the true significance of these brasses, (recently beautifully restored by William Lack with the help and advice of Martin Stuchfield), it is intriguing to think that both the church and Norrington were associated with families who had fallen foul of the church of the day. In 1658 during the Commonwealth, when the latter Thomas Gawen finally lost Norrington to the Wyndhams, the Quaker William Fry, owner of nearby Higher Ashgrove Farm, was fined for not paying tithes. He then spent the first four years of the Restoration in Salisbury Gaol for the same offence, so he was persecuted by both sides. It is easy to confuse the Ashcombe estate in the parish of Berwick St. John (from where Anne Barber married John Wyndham) with the Frys' Higher Ashgrove farm in Donhead St. Mary, especially as the Quaker burial ground was in Ashcombe or Chevicombe Bottom, (and both may be found near Ashmore village!) In September 2009, the restored brasses were hung in the Victorian north chapel where the writing and decoration show up in natural light. The mystery of Quaker memorials originally being in the chancel of the church, and in Bowles' time 'over the communion table' is probably explained by the 'low church' Protestantism of the early eighteenth century. What is more surprising is that they remained there during the Victorian restoration, when the altar became more prominent. Perhaps the curtains were considered sufficient to hide them.

Bowles researched Norrington tenants in relation to tithes due to the church. He found, among the papers of 'the late Mr. Lawes', tenant of the Manor, an undated list of tithes due from the village, collated by a 'former inhabitant', John Fry. Edward Fricker may have followed the Fry family. Bowles quotes £370 as the rent paid by Mr. Fricker in 1729. That year, according to a memorandum by Mr. Wyndham, Mr. Fricker produced £360 worth of wheat, as well as barley and oats. He also 'kept 1800 sheep, wintered at home 1300, had 560 ewes, 350 lambs, and wintered out 400 hogs'. From this, Bowles deduced that 'Mr. Wyndham was a very considerate landlord.' In his will written in 1737, shortly before his death, it is clear that Edward Fricker hailed from Stockton and Wylye, a pleasing link with the Sykes family, who lived in Stockton two hundred years later, and bought Norrington in 1952. Presumably his son followed, because a new seven-year lease was taken out by a Mr. Fricker in 1744, 'at the trifling rise of £30 per annum,' (Bowles). In 1830, Mr. Fricker's tomb was noted by Bowles, but it may have been cleared for the church restoration, or it may be the unidentified tomb near the tower. Edward's daughter, Anne, married into the Lawes family, who lived at the manor for several generations. In 1746, Henry Gawen rented part of the farm and 'Farmer Fricker' the rest. The next tenant was Thomas Wardner, whose son, also Thomas, was baptised in 1759. When these tenants began living in the manor house is not clear, but they were residents of Alvediston. However, the King family who bought Samways in 1780, and took over the tenancy of Norrington from the Wardners in 1787, never lived there. Bowles records that 'Mr. Thomas Wardner, who had been a respectable yeoman, at one time living at Norrington Farm' had moved on to Ashmore, where he died, and so he was buried in Berwick St. John church. The Kings' tenancy continued until the final Thomas King, who, Charlotte Grove reported in March 1835, 'is going to give up the Norrington Farm.' Five years earlier she had written: 'We went to see Norrington House. Lady Gawen lived there at the Restoration, who left it to her lawyer and he sold it.' Thus was the history recorded at that time, and Catherine Gawen had gained a title. Charlotte did not elaborate on the state of the house after so many years' neglect, but Charles Bowles had no compunction about berating the landlord, William Wyndham:

> Mr. Wyndham has, within these last few years, built a stately and capacious mansion house at Dinton. He served the office of sheriff for Wiltshire in the year 1814, and . . . he is an active magistrate, a commissioner for the affairs of taxes, a good neighbour, and a most kind and considerate landlord . . . I regret, with all this, and more, which might be justly said in favour of Mr. Wyndham, that Norrington House, and the buildings belonging to it, endeared as they ought to be to Mr. Wyndham, from having been the residence of Sir Wadham Wyndham, his great benefactor, should have been so neglected, and if I might venture to offer three words of advice to one who, on every other occasion, appears not to be in want of any, it is this ~ that he

would restore Norrington house, and make it fit for the residence of a gentleman, or at all events, repair the house, and compel the tenant of the estate to reside in it. I have myself no predilection for field sports, but a few hundreds of pounds might make Norrington House a snug comfortable hunting box, fit for the reception of some one of Mr. Wyndham's younger sons.

The description in *Some Old Wiltshire Homes*, written sixty-four years later, ensures that the Wyndhams' neglect and Bowles' part in the revival of Norrington was rammed home:

> ... towards the close of the [eighteenth] century, the house became so ruinous that, after being first abandoned to labourers, it was finally deserted. Ivy grew on the walls, which here and there showed ominous fissures; the glass disappeared from the casements; grass grew up between stone flags in the hall; the storms of winter spent their fury against its time-worn walls, and winds whistled shrilly through its deserted chambers; the house was fast becoming a ruin.

The timely intervention of 'the Wiltshire historian' saved the house. The use of such a large house for the accommodation of labourers, who normally raised vast families in tiny cottages, may explain the final demise of the medieval village.

By September 1834, Charlotte Grove was writing: 'Went to Norrington. They have rebuilt part of it in the Gothick style.' So what of the successfully chastened Mr. Wyndham?

William Wyndham IV of Dinton, 1749-1841

FROM THE NATIONAL trust leaflet on Philipps, formerly Dinton, House we learn that this fourth William Wyndham of Dinton was born in 1769, the eldest son of an eccentric, energetic agricultural pioneer, and he inherited both energy and agricultural interests, together with great wealth, on reaching his majority. His father was considered perturbably rustic by a Mrs. Harris, who wrote to the first Earl of Malmesbury describing her visit to Dinton:

> At Dinton nothing is done, except disparking a pretty park which his father had made. The squire came into the court to survey our horses not us. The first salutation he gave us was ~ You have broke your splinter bars, fixed his eyes on the horses and left us to get out of the coach as we could. . . . Not a single person at dinner but we five; our conversation was chiefly of grass and dogs . . . So much for rural felicity.

His son, William IV of Dinton, was only seventeen when his father died. Three years after he came into his inheritance he married Laetitia Popham of Clavelshay who, although apparently the daughter of a wealthy lawyer, was reputed to have royal paternity which may explain her enormous dowry. Bowles discreetly describes her as 'the adopted daughter of Alexander Popham, Esq. deceased.' Sylvana Chandler (née Wyndham) reports that a visiting Australian historian informed the family that 'a dowry of £20,000 was the going rate for royal bastards'! They were as prolific as most Wyndham families seem to have been, producing six sons and six daughters. Soon their friends and neighbours, the Benetts of Pythouse and the Groves of Ferne

William Wyndham IV of Dinton. (Sylvana Chandler, Orchard Wyndham)

were building new homes on a grand scale and William and Laetitia may have felt inspired to follow suit. The old house was demolished and between 1812 and c. 1818 their new home was designed and built. Another Palladian-style mansion, this was designed by Jeffry Wyatt, later Sir Jeffry 'Wyatville', antecedent of the Thomas Wyatt who restored St. Mary's church in 1866, also related to James Wyatt, who left his inimitable and somewhat controversial mark on both Wilton House and Salisbury Cathedral. It is intriguing to speculate what may have happened to Norrington if the focus of the local branch of the family had not moved over the hill to Dinton. By 1825, it was described by John Britton in 'The Beauties of Wiltshire' as 'a modern and handsome edifice . . . recently finished from designs by Jeffry Wyatville Esq. It is arranged with every attention to domestic comfort and elegant accommodation.' In 1830, the Benett, Grove and Wyndham families were united against agricultural labourers who rose up against the reforms and new machinery which threatened their livelihood. Thus the time of elaborate development on the home front, (admittedly they had twelve children and an army of servants to house) was accompanied by great changes in the countryside about which he cared passionately. As well as being a keen and innovative farmer, he was an avid sportsman and horseman. However, he was assiduous in his duties, if Charlotte Grove's comments are anything to go by. On April 5th 1815: 'My father went to the Justices Meeting. Only Mr. Wyndham there. The rest of the gentlemen out foxhunting'! He entered into the fray of his tenant Thomas King's court case against Lord Rivers; as Charlotte wrote: 'He is very earnest about his Chace cause.' He became a lieutenant–colonel in the Local Militia of Wiltshire; when he was High Sheriff of Wiltshire the diarist mentioned seeing him during a visit to his daughter 'in his dressed coat and bag wig', and he supported John Benett's successful challenge of the Pembrokes for the parliamentary seat of Wilton. In 1828 he became Mayor of Wilton and three years later was causing Charlotte (Grove) anguish on behalf of her husband Rev. Richard Downes, rector of Berwick St. John, in a dispute over the boundary between Alvediston and Berwick at Norrington, which affected the tithes due to Downes.

In November 1831 she wrote: 'Mr. C. Bowles came here to settle the dispute of tythe (sic) between Mr. Wyndham and my husband.' As Mr. Bowles had written his 'advice' to Mr. Wyndham only a year previously there may have been a little extra tension. In 'A Hundred of Chalke', (1830) Bowles, who was also the recorder of Shaftesbury, explains that the Whistley Mead part of Trow, owned by Wyndham, 'formerly paid, and may still pay to the lord of the manor of Berwick, a fee-farm rent of 14s.' Presumably the rector thought he was entitled to commensurate tithes.

The Parham Family, 1836 – 1952

EIGHTEEN MONTHS AFTER Charlotte reported on Norrington's 'Gothick' facelift, she wrote: 'We walked to Norrington. They are getting it ready for Mrs. Parham,' and in April 1836 she walked over again, 'saw Mrs. Parham the farmer's wife there. Mr. Wyndham has quite done up the old house.' Such was the power of the written word of an acknowledged historian. On another visit Charlotte 'saw Mrs. Parham, her youngest child and governess; also saw the banqueting room, chapel etc.' These would not have been currently in use. The Parham family continued to farm Norrington and to take a leading role in village life until the Wyndhams had to sell up in the 1950s. Reg Marks' doleful experience as an indoor servant in 1930 was mainly due to the character of the current chatelaine. Joan Reeves, (nee Compton) recalls Mr. Parham's active concern when her brother fell down a well some twelve years earlier and both church and school records pay tribute to their involvement, albeit in a style which seems paternalistic today. The later Grove diaries, written with more exuberance than attention to grammar or spelling by Agnes wife of the last Mr. Grove of Ferne, record a visit in 1884:

I drove W' (Walter, her husband,) and Burt to play cricket at Alva Distan. Mrs. Parran who lives at Norrington where they were playing is a most beautiful old house showed us all over it & a curious old cellar with beautiful stone-work ceiling.

There are two diverting details about Agnes. She was the daughter of Lord Pitt-Rivers, a descendent of the Lord Rivers who brought the case against Thomas King, tenant of Norrington seventy years earlier. Also, notwithstanding the syntax of the above, she was a close friend of Thomas Hardy, who wrote a poem of lament on her death.

The copy of Bowles' *Hundred of Chalke* inscribed 'James N.(?) Parham 1870' has every mention of his family name marked in pencil, e.g.:

In the 9th year of the reign of King Edward the 3rd, [1336] he sent letters to the sheriffs of England, commanding them to make an exact return into the exchequer, of the names of the villages and the possessors thereof in every county, which was accordingly done. And these returns, called *Nomina Villarum*, are now remaining in the exchequer.

. . . the village of Alvediston belonged to Ingelram Berenger and John de Parham,' (page 33).

The burial of a Mr. George Parham in 1825 is noted in the Semley registers, (p. 82), and 'the mansion house built by the late Mr. George Parham' was near the common between Semley Hill and Pythouse, (p. 88).

In the Willoughby family tree in the chapter on Berwick St. John, is found reference to Christopher, 'from whom the Lords W.' (Willoughby) 'de Parham in the sixteenth century', (p.152).

Trow, which was later rented and then owned by the Gawens, was divided into three in the mid-thirteenth century, one third going to 'Richard Perham, clerk'. His son John, also a 'clerk', i.e. in holy orders, although neither name occurs in the lists of Alvediston or Berwick clergy, 'released' his part to John Gawen in 1402. Thus there was a link with Norrington centuries before the family farmed it for the Wyndhams ~ if Bowles' information is correct, (p. 211).

In 1830, 'The present owner' of Woodhouse Farm on the Bowerchalke boundary of Fifield Bavant, 'is Mr. Thomas Parham, and he has been for some years,' (p. 255).

Trying to unravel Bowles' account and to fit it into the recent research into Broad Chalke for the history published in 2000 is a bit of a challenge. It seems that James Parham rented Manor Farm, Broad Chalke, from the Pembrokes from 1820, and East Gerrardston, (now Knapp) Farm from 1828, from St. Nicholas Hospital in Salisbury. This included, but on a separate lease, a farmstead called Bennett's. Bowles, incidentally, affirms that Thomas Gawen earlier had Knapp as well as the adjoining Mouse-Hill or Mount-Sorrell Farm. He also believed that 'The family of Perham, or Parham, is one that has lived in this parish, or in some one of the adjoining parishes, from the time of Richard II if not antecedent to the reign of that monarch, to the present period...... Besides the above, Mr. Parham holds a small freehold, formerly Northover's', also in Broad Chalke. In 1835, he gave up all these properties to move to Norrington. It must have been most satisfactory to move to a place which had been connected with his family so many centuries before. There may have been a sadder reason. James married Charlotte and had a family in Broad Chalke. In 1822, his daughter, Sarah, died at a year old, two years later Charlotte died, and in 1831, twelve-year old Emily also died. He seems to have remarried and had children before his move, (in the 1841 census, Charles was 15, George, 10, Harry, 8 and Ann 6; Harry took on the farm. Thomas, missing from this census, came between Charles and George.) On James' death in 1873, at the ripe old age of eighty-three, he was buried alongside his first wife and daughters near the door of All Saints' Church, Broad Chalke in a grave marked by a substantial tombstone. By that time, he must have handed the tenancy of Norrington to his son and retired to Ebbesbourne Wake, as there is a memorial window to him on the south side of the chancel. Tactfully, his second wife, Eliza, who predeceased him by eight years, is also remembered there.

Charles Parham rented Knighton Manor Farm and lived in the house there from 1875, maintaining the Parham link with Broad Chalke at least for some years; by then the farm covered thirteen hundred and forty acres, requiring the labour of thirty men and ten boys. Peter Meers found Parhams in the Ebbesbourne census returns for 1841 and '51. A James Parham, born in 1811, was an agricultural labourer living in Prescombe Cottage, (the farmhouse was not yet built), while the widow Elizabeth Parham lived with her brother, a shoemaker, so their fortunes evidently varied. There were other Parhams in Alvediston too: in 1800 and 1803 respectively, Joseph and James were baptised, sons of Joseph and Sarah Parham, but that is all we know about them.

From the Church Log Book we can learn a little about the Norrington dynasty. When James arrived, the church was firmly under the control of the last Thomas King, as it had been with his predecessors. Thomas King also retired to Ebbesbourne Wake, but the dates of both moves are unclear. In 1848 James Parham, Joseph Rogers (tenant of the Manor,) and Thomas King were all on the 'list of persons qualified to serve as church wardens for the year ensuing' and by 1855 the latter was off the list, having not actually served for at least five years, which indicates that it took some time for Parham to be able to wield much influence. However from then on until the book closed in 1943 his family was very much to the fore. George qualified as church warden in 1858, while James was still in office with Mr. Rogers of the Manor. Henry's name appears, with George's, five years later, when plans for the church restoration began to be drawn up, and Bernard (from the next generation) was appointed in 1892. Three years later the Parish Councils Act separated ecclesiastical and non-ecclesiastical affairs. Bernard chaired the first Parish Council Meeting and also a meeting two years later at the Vicarage to discuss plans for Queen Victoria's Diamond Jubilee celebrations, sardonically reported by the Rev. Charles Ousby Trew:

> Suggestions for a general feast, and a bonfire were well received ~ and a suggestion by the vicar for a supply of the village with water was heartily approved. On minor points much discord was manifested and the meeting finally broke up without any settled plan.

It would appear that Bernard was selected for potentially awkward gatherings and, even if his diplomacy was not able to smooth all feathers he remained church warden at least until 1943. When his sister was married in 1898 the school closed early, while the following year a Mrs. Parham of Streatham donated the eagle lectern which is still used today. Perhaps the local Mrs. P. felt spurred to emulate this generosity: she donated £1 to the cassock fund. The Parham influence on the school was less marked as the vicar was in charge. In 1884 a visit by Mrs. and Miss Parham, bearing oranges for the children, was noted. A Committee of Managers was only set up in 1892, but Bernard was chosen as one of them and in 1903, at the start of an inter-regnum, he took over as school correspondent, a role normally always filled by the vicar. During the Second World War, a 'Home and beacon' searchlight, which had first been placed on Samways land, at Crockerton, was moved to the field to the north-east of the house, and is called Searchlight to this day.

Bernard Parham's long life began twelve years after the Crimean War, (1868), and spanned the Boer War, two World Wars, major agricultural depressions in the 1870s and 1930s, the life of Alvediston School and almost all the years of the later phase of resident clergy.

He died in 1956 and is buried with his wife in the churchyard at Alvediston. His second Christian name was Norrington. Bernard and Mabel Parham had two children: Jack joined the army in 1914, at eighteen, was awarded the Croix de Guerre and is recorded on the memorial cross, among those from Alvediston who served in World War I. He had a distinguished career in the Royal Artillery, both as a regular soldier and in World War II, rising to Major General. His sister Mildred was often known as 'Jill', but is also still referred to locally as Miss Parham. She held the fort at the farm as her father grew older. About once a year, she used to drive a team of horses across from Norrington into the old lane behind the former Church Farmhouse and over to West End to ensure that it remained open. Clearly the whole family remained devoted to Norrington and would have loved to have taken up the offer of buying it, had they been in a position to do so. However, Miss Parham moved out of the area in 1957.

The End of the Wyndham Era

I N 1876, WILLIAM Wyndham VI of Dinton inherited Orchard Wyndham in Somerset from his relation, the 4th. Earl of Egremont. Unfortunately, this gentleman had not only restored Orchard Wyndham, which sorely needed attention, but had gone on to build a massive new house at Silverton in Devon, sufficient to rival another Wyndham home at Petworth. This meant that William VI gained a triple mortgage with the old family home, and a terrible dilemma. Sylvana Chandler writes, 'However, no-one ever doubted that the 'Old House' had to be saved', even though the debt took a hundred years to be cleared. Thus, for most of the time that the Parhams were tenants, their landlords were struggling financially. Visiting Orchard Wyndham, the sense of family loyalty and commitment remains palpable to this day. William VII of Dinton died in 1917 and his son, the eighth William, moved to Orchard Wyndham, having had to sell the estate at Dinton. Bertram Philipps bought it and renamed the house Philipps House. Norrington remained in the family until William VIII died in 1950. His heir was his nephew, George, but he was hit by huge death duties. George's daughter, Sylvana Chandler, writes that he 'often spoke of Norrington with affection but took the line that the old house, Orchard Wyndham, had to be protected and maintained . . . [He] sold Norrington with great reluctance.' Shortly before the sale, he took his son, another William, to see it. 'He fell in love with the place and has regretted the sale ever since.' The family returned to Sir Wadham's birthplace, but kept his favourite residence for as long as possible.

The reluctance of each owner and of at least some of the tenants to part with Norrington is heart-rending, and the same emotion is palpable in many of the changes of ownership and tenancy of the Manor and Samways. Norrington is unusual in that family ownership has spanned centuries, although the Wyndhams moved out of the house in the third generation. In other cases, three or four generations seem to be the limit before constraints, usually financial, force a family out. However, this sense of 'rootedness' and loyalty is not confined to the big houses: when talking to and corresponding with the descendents of many other Alvediston families similarly intense emotions are soon uncovered.

The Sykes Family, 1952 to Today

IN 1952 Mr. Frank Sykes, a well-known Wiltshire agriculturalist bought it. (He was the son of Brigadier-General Sir Percy Molesworth Sykes KCIE, CB, CMG, who led a fascinating and eventful life as a soldier, diplomat, scholar and author, with especial expertise and experience in Persia). Frank's son, Tristram, moved there with his wife Sheila five years later, so Norrington was at last occupied by its owner and his family once more. Tristram built up the farm again and was very active in the church and community generally. He was High Sheriff of Wiltshire in 1987-8, Deputy Lord Lieutenant from 1985-2006, president of the Wiltshire National Farmers' Union and, for many years, chairman of 'Taste of the West', which promoted locally produced food. Locally, he was a long-standing church warden, parish councillor, a founder and the chairman of the Chalke Valley Link Scheme and both founder and prime mover of a choir, the Ebble Chorale. But above all he was a Wiltshireman who, in the words of a local obituary, 'was an unfailing friend and ally, a true Christian, and an ambassador for all that is best in parish and people.' The gap left in the village is still sorely felt.

Members of the Sykes family still own Norrington manor house and farm.

The Architecture of the House

IT ONLY REMAINS to describe the architecture of the house. The National Monuments office holds a number of photographs and a Country Life article, featured on 26th. June, 1958, shortly after Tristram and Sheila Sykes took up residence there. There are no traces of the house or houses which stood on the site prior to John Gawen's time, but a substantial portion of his building remains intact, notably the hall and undercroft, joined by a tiny room to the north-west of the hall, and possibly the porch, which followed soon after, all described in 'The English Medieval House' by Margaret Wood. Inevitably, there is dissension about the dating of the hall and porch. 'Some Old Wiltshire Homes', (1894), refers to this: J.H. Parker in his 'Domestic Architecture of the Middle Ages', (1852-9) favoured the fifteenth century for both, (also offered by the *V.C.H.*); Sir Richard Hoare attributed them to the first John Gawen in the reign of Richard

II, (1377-1399), while 'Murray, quoting from both Hoare and Parker, adopts both opinions' in his *Handbook to Wilts, Dorset and Somerset*. Over a hundred years later, anyone attempting to research the history of this village must have some sympathy for the hedging of Murray's bets. Margaret Wood whose book, first published in 1965, was considered a classic, will be followed here.

The hall is 38 foot 6 inches by 23 foot, and has four bays or compartments, divided by roof arches. Windows are set in these bays, three showing at the front of the house. They are of the design characteristic of the fourteenth century: tall, with two lights and a transom (a horizontal stone bar used to fix shutters, so that glass, which was very expensive, could be kept for upper lights). The tops of the windows are trefoiled, i.e. three rounded shapes are fitted into an arch, and the space between them is filled with a slightly flattened quatrefoil, all contained in a larger arch.

This design points to notable architects Henry Yevele or William of Wynford. Fragments of medieval glass remain in the windows to this day, notably John Gawen's coat of arms with fleur de lys d'or incorporated into one. 'Some Old Wiltshire Homes' describes the dais, which remained in spite of nineteenth century sub-division of the hall: 'The steps of the dais in the hall remain, extending across the present drawing room, so that the stone flooring of that apartment is higher at one end than the other.' When the Sykes restored the hall to one room, removing the passage on the north side, they levelled the floor, no longer requiring a dais on which to sit at high table. Originally, a service passage would have been screened off at the east end. A notable relic is a moulded bracket with two of the iron spikes for candles still in place. This is on a wall between windows.

From the west end, the Gawen family would have been able to pass into the solar, or private sitting room. This was replaced in the seventeenth century, but there is a minute room to the north-west off the hall, leading down to a crypt, undercroft or cellar under the solar.

This was an area for storage, and the stone, vaulted roof is typical, providing protection against fire. Being directly under the master's apartments made it extra secure. Interestingly, the use of divining rods clearly indicates a spring beneath the floor. Households were almost self-supporting, relying on fairs which were sometimes annual to stock up on locally unobtainable materials, fabrics and spices etc. The northern third of the undercroft has a complex form of vaulting called 'tierceron', which Margaret Wood believes may indicate, with its east-west orientation, a 'chapel subdivision' to the solar. The existence of a chapel is mentioned in several documents and would make sense in view of later generations' recusancy. A Green Man appears in the roof.

The face of the Green Man occurs in various guises from medieval times, most of the oldest ones are to be found in churches, probably because the carvings there have been least disturbed. The generic term 'Green Man' is used for convenience rather than from certitude, since very little is known about these carvings, but they bring together two favourite themes in stonemasonry: the face and leaves, in an image that can portray many moods. The earliest in England are twelfth century, although they can be found elsewhere from Roman times, and in Britain they are often found at crossing places, especially on the doorways to churches, following Celtic tradition. The leaves often twine around the head or seem to issue from the mouth, so may look like a tongue even when that is not the case, especially as they were often stylised. However, in some cases the faces are carved roughly in comparison with exquisite leaves. Sometimes masons portrayed the faces of well-known people, sometimes they used ordinary young men as models or they created a visage to which no-one would wish to lay claim. Those whose tongues were hanging out were supposed to ward off evil. After the Black Death in the fourteenth century, more frightening faces appear, reflecting the horror of that period. Whatever the purpose, at a time when few people could read, carved faces and the choice and design of leaves could illustrate emotions and tell stories with which anyone could identify.

Like many houses of that time, Norrington has two entrances at the opposite end of the hall from the dais. This meant that there was access to courts to the north, (to more service areas), and to the south, the main entrance. Margaret Wood believes that the porch was added in the early fifteenth century, and this is one of Norrington's most interesting features. The porch doorway is not central, being slightly to the east, and its pointed arch is within a square frame. Within the 'lierne' or stellar roof vaulting can be seen, in one corner, the carved head of Henry IV, who reigned from 1399 to 1413. The other corners feature a bishop, a lawyer and a face whose profession cannot be identified. They all commemorate the king's visit during one of his sojourns at Clarendon Palace near Salisbury, and provide a wonderful dating process. At the centre, is a strange face with his tongue appearing to hang out; probably another Green Man. The association with the warding off of evil was especially appropriate at a house entrance. In 'Some Old Wiltshire Homes', 1894, the mouldings are described as 'equal, if not superior, to any in the country'.

The dating of the next phase of development is open to discussion as some authorities refer to Elizabethan changes. Whether the Thomas Gawen of that era had the time, inclination or money for home improvements, especially in the latter years of that queen's reign remains open to question, but certainly Wadham Wyndham, having finally got his hands on the place, determined to leave his mark upon it. To the left of the crypt are his kitchens, now abandoned, with a massive banqueting room above. This has a splendid fireplace and chimney piece, but it, too, is deserted. To construct these rooms, Wyndham had to demolish the ancient solar wing, where the family's private apartments had been. To the west, a new wing was built, which was only joined at a corner. The purpose of this wing is not certain, especially as the service wing to the east was rebuilt and extended northwards, providing kitchens, pantries, dairies and larders. A photograph from 1944 shows a clock tower on the roof of the west wing. When this appeared is not known, but perhaps this wing was used for stabling or as servants' quarters at some stage. At any event, it is now converted into two cottages, and the clock tower is no more. The V.C.H. reports that the house was re-roofed in the eighteenth century, but was in bad repair by the end of that century. The 'Gothick' improvements reported by Charlotte Grove in 1834 fortunately did not impinge too drastically upon the main fabric of the old house, and at least it was saved from almost certain total decay. A hundred and twenty years later, more renovation was undertaken by Tristram and Sheila Sykes.

Trow

TROW IS NOW part of Norrington Farm but it has a significant history of its own. It lies south of the Berwick to Alvediston road, and farm buildings with two cottages can be seen shortly before the road runs down into the centre of the village. Opposite Crook Hill Cottages and the drive to Norrington is a track, called Trow Hollow, which leads up to Trow Down and joins the Ox Drove. Trow Down is one of the highest points in this area, reaching 243 metres (798 feet), and tumuli known as Trow Down Round Barrows are found in that area. The down is also a Site of Special Scientific Interest and was immortalised locally as the location of Thomas King's fracas with Lord Rivers' keeper, (see Samways chapter.) As explained in the chapters on the Features of Alvediston and Alvediston Manor, Trow appeared in the Domesday Book, when Aileva held 2 of the 7 ½ hides of land, but by 1086, Richard Poingiant held it. The woodland recorded in the Domesday Book possibly later contracted into Elcombe Copse, (recorded in 1567) and Goscombe and Manwood Copses, (recorded in 1664.)

Many Roman coins have been found on Trow land. The land adjoining Trow was thoroughly excavated by the eminent nineteenth century archaeologist, General Pitt-Rivers of Rushmore. Recently, a silver spoon and a thirteenth century copper alloy seal matrix were discovered. The matrix is a pointed oval shape with a loop for hanging. This style was popular with women at that time. The outer face is inscribed with words around the edge thought to read: '+S'AL–ANDE D'TROWE', which may mean: 'The seal of Alexander of Trow', with a central motif of the Lamb of God with a standard, and a cross. This is typical of the personalised seals which were superceded by anonymous ones towards the end of the century. It is probably the earliest personal artifact held in the village, and it is fitting that the land is currently farmed by Alexander Sykes.

Disentangling the estate of Trow, Trough, Trojan, Trogan or Troi from that of Trow Crawley, which seems to have been part of it, and discerning the lines of ownership from the various options on offer is a challenge beyond the remit of this book. The *V.C.H.* goes into it in some detail. It appears that Alexander de Trow's land went to Wilton Abbey in the mid-fourteenth century, while a manor later called Trow Crawley went to Shaftesbury Abbey. Three fields north of Trow farm buildings called Crawley Knapp, South and North Crawley keep the name in circulation.

By the fourteenth century, there is a link with the Bavant family, which points to the relationship with Fifield Bavant. The *V.C.H.* quotes records of the Trow estate in 1362 comprising fifty-seven acres of arable land and pasture for two hundred sheep, while in 1425 the Trow Crawley estate seemed to cover two hundred and forty acres of arable to only ten acres of pasture. In comparison, in 1312 the demesne (or 'home farm') of Norrington included a hundred and forty acres of arable, and in 1361 there was pasture for three hundred sheep. Bowles maintains that John Gawen had all the lands of Trow by 1402, while the *V.C.H.* says that he rented Trow Crawley from the late fourteenth century, but that the estate of Trow was not in Gawen hands until the latter half of the sixteenth. It seems safe to say that Trow and Norrington were fully merged by 1606, that the Gawen family continued to farm at least part of Trow after two-thirds of their estates were confiscated, that Henry Gawen was renting part of Trow in 1746 and that part, known as Whistley Mead, remained in the parish of Berwick St. John. Whatever the permutations of tenancy, Norrington and Trow have been jointly owned for at least four hundred years, unlike the rest of Alvediston, which has been swapped around and regrouped with dizzying regularity.

Samways (or Parhams, or The Tower)

Early History from the 12th century ~ John Samwaye and the Building of Samways, c. 1530 ~ The Gould Family, 1610 – 91, Extension of Samways ~ The Frekes and Pitts, 1691 – 1780 ~ The King Family, 1780 – 1850s, Earlier History ~ 'The Chase Case', 1816 ~ Henry King and Chilmark Descendents ~ 'Wicked Tom King' (?) ~ William Day, 185? – c.1875, The Stud, The Clock Tower and Victorian Changes to the House ~ Frederick Gray, c. 1875 – 1904, Sale Particulars 1904 ~ Frederick Benjafield, 1904 – 11 ~ The Hoole Family, 1911 – 86 ~ Claire Farrow, 1986 – 2009 ~ Description of the Property in 2009

Early History from the 12th Century

T HE ORIGINS OF the land and house now known as Samways are not entirely clear, but the *Victoria County History* (V.C.H.) suggests a history beginning before 1200, and closely related to the land of the manor, which it adjoins. The Parham family feature for about a hundred and fifty years from this time and reappear in the history of Alvediston in the nineteenth and twentieth centuries, when they farmed Norrington as tenants of the Wyndhams.

As so often happens, the V.C.H. account differs from that of Charles Bowles. The former maintains that a 'messuage' (or dwelling house with outbuildings to serve the adjoining land,) called

Samways Farm. (Claire Morris)

'Staenihalle' may have belonged originally to John of Trow and passed via his son, Richard White, and another owner to Wilton Abbey, probably with the land as well. In about 1192, Wilton Abbey granted more land which had come its way from White to John of Parham for life. There seems to have been a series of John Parhams, one of whom married Alice de Bayeux, through whose inheritance in 1252, the family gained a 'hide' in Alvediston, (a hide being considered enough to support a family, depending on the type of land.) While this land originally may have been part of Alvediston manor, it probably became what was known as 'Parhams' and ultimately Samways. In the fourteenth century an Edmund Parham was succeeded by his son Richard, who was living in 1359. (Richard 'de Perham' seems to have had massive money problems. Chancery records of 1350 show him appearing before the Mayor of London because he owed Thomas atte Green, a London wine merchant, £100. It was a troublesome year for him because he also appeared before the Mayor of Oxford, owing John atte Ruyssh of Wallingford £40. It is interesting to speculate how and why he travelled so widely, let alone managed to run up such considerable debts.)

At this point, the V.C.H. has a gap of about two hundred years. Perhaps Richard Parham had to sell Samways c.1343 to pay debts, but the new owner seems to have got on the wrong side of the law too. Charles Bowles has a typically colourful account which may have led innocently to misunderstandings in later years:

> The earliest proprietor of the estate which I have been able to discover, is John de Upton, who was also owner of the estate at Upton, in Berwick St. John, although I have omitted to describe him as such. This John de Upton obtained leave in the year 1343, from Robert Bingham, bishop of Salisbury, to erect an oratory or chapel in his house at Upton in Berwick, and also in this his mansion house in Alvediston. He appears to have been, if not a deer stealer, one at least who used deer hunting as an amusement, to a large extent; for in the year 1346, proceedings were had at law against him, at the suit of Elizabeth de Burgh, the then owner of Cranborne Chase, for entering her free chase of Cranborne at Ashmore, and other places, *without licence,* and for taking *several deer,* which offence he repeated *for eleven years in succession,* to her damage of forty marks [£26 3s. 4d.]; which sum not being paid according to an adjudication of the Court of King's Bench, he was, in the year 1359, taken into custody, and there detained until he paid the penalty.

Bowles' 'omission' to mention John de Upton as owner of the Upton estate is confusing enough, but the unravelling of the ownerships of Upton and Samways may lead to an explanation of another puzzle in the history of Alvediston. It appears that there was a family in Berwick St. John which took the name Upton from their lands in the thirteenth and fourteenth centuries, but some of the land passed to the Lucy family, (thus the estate became known as Upton Lucy), and on to the Fitzherberts. Alice Fitzherbert married Sir Thomas West, who died in 1386. Their son, also Thomas, married Joan de la Warre, and ended up with huge estates in five counties. He became Baron West and later the barony of West was amalgamated with that of de la Warre but the 'truly ancient and honourable families of West and De la Warr' died out in the mid sixteenth century. Somehow, Bowles became convinced that 'a single stone in the wall' of the north transept of the church, 'having on it a cheveron between three roses, the arms of Gold or Gould,' was 'empaling a fesse dansette, the arms of West de la War', and that beneath it there was 'a flat stone, having on it a shield, the arms of West; but the inscription is hid by a pew erected over it.' This, written in 1830, five years after the last, unpopular Thomas King inherited Samways, may have unwittingly set off several wild goose chases which are discussed later in this chapter. The stone believed to be referred to was probably disfigured by age and difficult to decipher. It was found abandoned in Ebbesbourne Wake churchyard a hundred years later, but it actually commemorates the marriage of William Gould with Eleanor Chadwell of Ebbesbourne in 1603, fifty years after the demise of the West and de la Warre family. The claim in the late nineteenth century that the Goulds were the rightful owners of Samways and the legal battles which Josiah Gould was encouraged to fight seem to have got mixed up with Bowles' conviction that the Goulds were connected with the Wests and de la Warres. It may be that a previous Thomas King's random placing of new pews, partially obscuring ancient grave slabs, contributed to exploitable confusion which pertains to this day. This saga shows the dangers and credibility of unbridled righteous indignation, a not uncommon village affliction.

As for John of Upton's deer poaching escapades, they provide an antecedent to a later disagreement between the owners of Samways and of Cranborne Chase. As will be explained in detail later, almost all the Chase is in Dorset, but the outer bounds creep into Witshire in Berwick St. John and the neighbouring western edge of the parish of Alvediston, especially around Trow Down, part of the Norrington estate.

John Samwaye and the Building of Samways, c. 1530

UPTONS MAY HAVE succeeded Parhams but both sources agree that the next owner was John Samways or Samwaye, and both quote records at Wilton, (the 'First Pembroke Survey' noted in the *V.C.H.*) In 1986, P.M. Slocombe, wrote in the Wiltshire Buildings Record,

> The present name of the house derives from John Samwaye who in the reign of Henry VIII held certain lands freely in the manor of Alvediston paying 12d. rent at Michaelmas. He is said to have rebuilt part of the house in 1530.

John Samways or Samwaye is recorded in 1558 and '67, the early years of Elizabeth's reign and Robert in 1595, when troubles were brewing for the Gawen family at Norrington. It is ironic that the family with the least surviving material has its name immortalised in the property.

The Gould Family, 1610 – 91, Extension of Samways

THEN THE GOULD family appears, but only for less than a century, and probably for four generations each headed by a William. The first is mentioned in Edward VI's commission in 1553 and may be the one who died in 1603. He may or may not have lived in Samways. but his son, whose marriage to Eleanor Chadwell of Ebbesbourne Wake in c.1610 is recorded on the small stone in the church, definitely did, and they brought up a large family there: eight children had been baptised by 1630: Anne, Mary, Averill, Eleanor, William, John, Lucia and Edmund. The father died in 1638 and the mother in 1646; both are recorded as being buried at St. Mary's. William Young, an archaeologist and local historian from Ebbesbourne Wake whose surmises about the claim of the Gould family to Samways become a little out of hand, quotes a document published by the Wiltshire Archaeological Society in 1901 in support of the claim. This document, an 'Inquisition Post Mortem', was a type of survey carried out on the death of anyone holding land belonging to the king, i.e. a 'tenant in chief'. (The layers of ownership are described in the chapter on 'Features of Alvediston'.) From 1219 to 1645, a careful enquiry including a survey of the land was made after the death of a leaseholder to ascertain whether the heir was under age, (in which case the king became guardian until his or her majority) and under what terms the land was held. The importance of these enquiries is illustrated by the fact that they were examined by a jury, and that the earlier ones were kept in the Tower of London. By Bowles' time, those recorded after Richard III, (late 15th century), were kept at the rolls court in Chancery Lane. They provide a remarkably detailed record of properties and those holding them, something along the lines of modern probate, but including details of 'whether the tenant was attainted of treason, or was an alien, as in either of these cases, the lands were immediately seized into the king's hands,' (Bowles). The Inquisition Post Mortem in question does not include any details incriminating of William Gould, but does illustrate the complicated tenancy arrangements. He was a sub-tenant of Thomas Gawen; (son of the one whose burial caused such a furore in 1603. Gawen was enjoying a brief respite at Norrington before the Commonwealth finally ousted the family from their ancient home), and he was also a tenant of the Pembrokes, who owned the manor. The inquisition was taken at Devizes in 1640, two years after the death of William Gould II. Only five years later, this system of 'Inquisition Post Mortem' was abolished.

The 'Inquisition', (Inq. P.m. 15 Charles I, pt 29, No. 18) refers to a survey made in 1609, probably when William Gould II was about to be married and to move into Samways. The word 'messuage' was still used for house, outbuildings and land, comprising: '200 acres of land, 20 acres of meadow, 400 acres of pasture, and 4 acres of wood in Alvedeston.' The 'parcel of said farm situate on the south part of the highway leading from Alvedeston to the town of Barwicke St. John', (note, Berwick was a 'town'!) was two pastures called 'Greate Sandes and the Little Sandes'. Other arable, meadow and pasture fields to the north were: 'Shap Closes, Sheates Meades, Long Meade, Coome Close, Greate Gaston, Little Gaston, Broadlease and Northfield,' in addition to 'depasturation' or land for cattle to graze. Samways was valued as 'worth per annum clear' sixty shillings and the annual rent owed to Thomas Gawen was ten shillings. William Gould's widow, Eleanor, who had moved to 'Newe Sarum' (Salisbury), was provided for, but their eldest son and next heir was only '15 years, 5 months and 20 days' old on his father's death. The other children, (those who survived,) could have ranged from twenty-seven to eight years. Presumably some stayed at Samways and others went to Salisbury with their mother. As for Eleanor, Bowles records a Chadwell of Beveridge or Bowridge House in Cranborne parish who rented out West End Farm in 1620. Perhaps her Ebbesbourne relatives had all moved away.

Although William Young produced the above as evidence of Josiah Gould's claim to Samways two hundred years later, it is still not clear why he became convinced that Samways had been taken from the Gould family illegally, but the conviction seems to have been fuelled by the untrammelled enthusiasm of the church restorers in

1866, three years after the death of the maligned 'wicked Tom King', of whom more later. Perhaps also, the complicated tenancy and sub-tenancy arrangements confused the issue.

In his book about the Wilton Estate 1520-1650, *Arcadia*, Adam Nicolson has an interesting story about a William Gould. He was a leader of the Wiltshire Clubmen, with Thomas Bennett of Broad Chalke, (some of whose descendents are buried in the three coffin-shaped tombs to the west of St. Mary's church). This would have been the young William III, born in 1623. From 1642, during the Civil War, the Wiltshire gentry petitioned the king and then joined others from Somerset and Gloucestershire to petition both king and parliament for peace, and they wore a white ribbon as a sign of peace. Women took an unusual initiative in this movement. The rural economy was being devastated by the depredations of both sides: insatiable garrisons, battles fought on their land, taxes and an erosion of ancient laws and property rights which had been enshrined in the manorial system. Their aims were to maintain both the 'true Reformed Protestant religion' and the ancient 'custom of the manor', with its organic organisation providing mutual support for both lord and tenant. However, this was by then an Arcadian ideal, which was being threatened by modern technology and the autocratic court. Desperation goaded them on, and they took up arms, but were summarily dealt with by Cromwell's Model Army in August 1645, at Hambledon Hill, not far into Dorset. Few of the two thousand Clubmen were killed but many were wounded and three hundred taken prisoner. Overnight they were penned into the church at the foot of the hill, in the village of Shroton or Iwerne Courtney. Now the body of this church had recently been rebuilt by Sir Thomas Freke, the local landowner whose family appears in the story of Samways less than fifty years later, (see below.) It is not clear what the outcome was for William Gould. He seems to have survived, but, with Thomas Gawen struggling to hang on to Norrington, and the fourth Earl of Pembroke agonising over the implications of his decision to support Parliament against the King, Alvediston must have been painfully aware of what the Clubmen described as 'the Miseries of this unnatural intestine War', and Nicolson as: 'The meeting of a retrospective idealism with the overwhelming facts of power.' Landowners had been threatened by the growth of the power of the Crown, but were equally threatened by Cromwell as he assumed power.

In spite of all this turmoil, the Goulds must have been responsible for the extension of the house to the north, creating more formal accommodation.

The Frekes and Pitts, 1691 – 1780

WILLIAM GOULD IV, William and Eleanor's grandson, inherited Samways in about 1670. He sold it to Thomas Freke in c. 1691, so the son of the Clubman William Gould sold to a descendent, perhaps son, of the Sir Thomas Freke who had rebuilt the church where the Clubmen were imprisoned, and who was presumably in cahoots with Cromwell. It is intriguing to speculate how Gould felt about this, but such convoluted relationships must have been common in the turbulent aftermath of the Civil War. The Freke family had become very powerful in the Cranborne Chase area under the Tudors, ranking with the Pembrokes, the Arundells and the Ashleys, all of them outmanoeuvred by Robert Cecil, later Lord Salisbury. Sir Thomas Freke's 1654 memorial in Shroton church, is a sight to behold, while the family also had substantial properties in Hinton St. Mary and Hannington. Freke bought a much reduced Cranborne Chase in 1692, (*V.C.H.*) or 1695 (Desmond Hawkins) of which the Lords Salisbury and Shaftesbury had retained various areas to suit their needs. Rushmore Lodge in the parish of Berwick St. John, although only occasionally inhabited by its owner became the administrative centre for the Chase, and its importance grew accordingly. Thomas Freke left both Rushmore and Samways to a relation, Thomas Pile, whose daughter, Elizabeth, married another Thomas Freke and inherited jointly with her father. Both properties passed to a nephew, George Pitt, of the famous political family, when Elizabeth died in 1714 or '15. Three George Pitts followed, during which time Samways was probably leased to the Foot family of Berwick St. John, and the third George Pitt sold to the first of four Thomas Kings. The habit of passing a Christian name down the generations has its attractions but does make it hard to distinguish the various owners, and, when one rightly or wrongly gains a bad reputation, all those sharing his name tend to get tarred with the same brush.

The King Family, 1780 – 1850s ~ Earlier History

THE KING FAMILY was eminent in Alvediston for a hundred and fifty years. While they do not seem to have changed the house much, one of the Thomas Kings scratched his name on a window of the dining room, at the front of the building. The family was also well-known in a wider local sphere. It should be remembered that both Norrington and the Manor were owned by absentee landlords, (the Wyndhams and Pembrokes respectively) for centuries, so the owner-occupier of the other large property in the village had more direct influence, even if he was not so wealthy. Fortunately, descendants still live locally, so it is possible to discover more about the family and to try to deduce why certain stories arose.

The earliest mention of this King family seems to come with a Thomas who originated in Suffolk. He died in 1558 and his grandson, also Thomas, apparently lived in Compton and also Alvediston. The family line actually comes through Thomas' younger brother, John, whose grandson, Joseph, was granted arms in 1649 for distinguished service on Cromwell's side during the Civil War. This branch lived in the Southampton area but had moved to Sutton Mandeville, a few miles north of Alvediston, by 1723. Joseph's great-grandson was the first Thomas King to live at Samways, also renting the land of Norrington from the Wyndhams and possibly some of the Manor land as well. He was born in 1705, bought Samways in about 1780, and died in 1787, being succeeded by his son, Thomas,(1743-1811), described by Sir Richard Colt Hoare as 'much respected'.

'The Chase Case', 1816

THOMAS KING II married Alice, daughter of Henry and Mary Rooke of Breamore. Their eldest son, Thomas, (1773-1825), is still remembered as 'the village Hampden, who with dauntless breast, the little tyrant of his field withstood', quoted as such by Bowles. (This refers to John Hampden, a cousin of Oliver Cromwell, who resisted the demand of Charles I for 'ship-money', a tax previously imposed intermittently to pay for the defence of coastal towns, and which only became inflammatory when Charles levied it far more frequently and throughout the kingdom. Hampden, from land-locked Buckinghamshire, refused to pay on principle, so a test case was brought against him. When the judge found for the king, Hampden ended up in prison and the justification of 'Rex is Lex', the King is the Law, raised both hackles and questions about regal abuse of power with huge implications for the nation.) Perhaps the parallel was a little overdrawn, but King's fame certainly arose through his challenge of a local abuse of power.

Some seventy years later, the Rev. Canon J.E. Jackson F.S.A. researched the history of Cranborne Chase and provides a useful, measured background to the hotly disputed subject of chase law. Early records indicate that there was a Cranborne manor with lands and a forest. A 'forest' in this case was not necessarily wooded. It included the land, parks and woods which actually belonged to independent landowners, but the whole area was under the protection of severe 'forest laws' which stipulated that the Crown owned all the game on the land and had the sole right to hunt it. If the Crown granted the forest to a subject all these privileges went with it, but it became known as a 'chase'. The original Cranborne Forest consisted of a narrow strip of woodland and pasture stretching for about ten miles along and within the northern boundary of Dorset from near Melbury to Cobley Lodge. However, Saxon and Norman kings loved hunting, so they gradually enlarged the forest to cover an area twenty to twenty-five miles east to west and fifteen to twenty miles north to south. Starting at Child Oakford near Shaftesbury, the boundary ran along a stream to the Stour, followed that river past Blandford Forum to Wimborne, then turned north to Cranborne, south-east to Ringwood, north up the Avon to Salisbury and along the Nadder valley back to Shaftesbury, taking in a generous portion of south-west Wiltshire with seventy-two parishes, part of Salisbury and all of Shaftesbury, Blandford, Wimborne, Ringwood, Fordingbridge and Downton, (see the Harding map, originally drawn in 1618, page 17.)

William Rufus, renowned for his passion for hunting and for his death from a fatal arrow shot in the New Forest, gave the Honour of Gloucester, which included Cranborne Manor and Chase, to a nephew and it remained with various earls of Gloucester until the time of Edward IV, (mid-fifteenth century). John, an early Gloucester who became a most unpopular king and is immortalised in the name of the pub in Tollard Royal, made what was called a 'perambulation' to settle the boundary because discontent was already growing. The perambulation did nothing to pacify local people and the current Abbess of Wilton took particular exception to hunting rights being exercised and to the toll called 'cheminage', (from the French word 'chemin' or road) being demanded at Old Harnham Bridge during 'Fence Month', the fawning season. This toll remained in force until the nineteenth century and incensed the campaigning Thomas King. A stag's head or pair of antlers was erected on the bridge for fifteen days before and fifteen days after midsummer's day to remind people to pay 4d. per wagon and 1d. per packhorse to the waiting chase steward. Although the boundaries set by John were confirmed by a royal grant, complaints rained in fruitlessly, and were dealt with by special courts at Cranborne, which were duly resented, especially as miscreants had to make their way there from all over the chase, and were almost certain to be fined. John of Upton, (believed to have been an early owner of Samways) was one of these. His use of 'deer-hunting as an amusement' amounted to many years of extensive poaching, but his punishment was not capital, as it would have been a few centuries later, only a fine sufficiently severe to put him behind bars for some months while he raised the sum of forty marks (£26 3s. 4d.). It was at this time, the mid-fourteenth century, that the then owner of the chase, Elizabeth de Burgh, managed to get Edward I's Quo Warranto, a registration of the chase boundaries, 'exemplified in Chancery under the Great Seal.' These boundaries remained in place until Thomas King's successful assault five hundred years later.

The chase reverted to the Crown for a hundred and forty years from the 1470s, during which time things got more lax and even legal judgments ratified smaller, 'inner' bounds, but in 1612 James I presented it to Robert Cecil, Earl of Salisbury, who set about tightening things up to the dismay of landowners. At this time the maps by Aldwell and Harding were drawn up on behalf of the opposing sides. Lord Salisbury was beaten by Lord Arundell over land in Tollard Royal but the last Thomas Gawen of Norrington fought for eight days in the Court of Exchequer and lost, which must have been a considerable financial blow. The chase was divided into eight 'walks', some of which were later sold off, e.g. Fernditch Walk went to Lord Ashley, later Lord Shaftesbury. In 1692, he sold it to Mr. Freke, (who had bought Samways a year earlier,) but just kept Berwick St. John. Like Samways, it passed through several inheritances to George Pitt, later Lord Rivers, in 1714 and remained with that family until the abolition of chase laws in 1828. Thus we come back to the third Thomas King of Samways. Lord Shaftesbury had confined his activities to the smaller boundaries except to recover deer which had strayed. He even let landowners kill deer, while Mr. Freke rewarded those who did not kill with gifts of venison. It was a later Lord Rivers' decision to reassert the ancient law of the chase throughout the area of his walk covered by King John's perambulation which precipitated the battles with Thomas King. Landowners were required to remove any fences which were high enough to keep deer off their property and were forbidden to plough downland, which made them furious. Bowles reported the escalating provocation with his customary energetic indignation:

It was boldly advanced in argument by those to whom his lordship listened with too much attention on this subject, that *Cranborne Chace*, though called a *chace*, was in truth a *forest*, and that it had all the *rights* which could belong to a *forest* attached to it . . . In the neighbourhood of Chalke . . . notices were given to persons not to plough up any of their down land; and one who had the courage to do so, was immediately served with a law process for his alleged breach of the chace and forest law; and in an instance when a deer had escaped into Wardour Park, the sanctity of the retreat was broken into, and a pack of blood hounds, headed by more ferocious animals in human shape, was unceremoniously turned into the park, started the game they were in pursuit of, and killed it on the spot, not condescending to ask Lord Arundell for permission for such conduct, or apologising in any manner for this rude and ungentlemanly outrage on his property; nor was this all ~ to such a pitch had the keepers arrived in audacity, that one of them, in exercise, as he said, of his *lawful* authority, in cool blood, *shot one of Mr. King's greyhounds whilst walking quietly behind his master,* because, forsooth, the dog was walking, as the keeper said, within the bounds of Cranborne Chace, within which bounds he alleged that no dog had any right *to use his legs, without the previous consent of the owner of the chace,* which owner, they asserted, was *personated by these keepers.*

Today Charles Bowles might be prevailed upon to share his opinion on the hunting debate.

Naturally, there are several versions of events on 12th. January, 1814. During the trial, held two and a half years later as a result of an incident of deliberate provocation of Lord Rivers by the furious Thomas King, the Salisbury Gazette recorded a very different version from Bowles'. John Durnford, a gamekeeper,

> stated that . . . he was at Trow Down, about one o'clock in the afternoon, and White and another keeper with him. He saw William Bradley [one of the defendants] in Goscombe field with 2 greyhounds; some deer were there; Bradley with the dogs went towards them; and as soon as the dogs saw the deer they drove them into Goscombe coppice, through the coppice and out upon Trow Down, and back again into the coppice. A man stood under a bush on the down, holding a rough dog, which dog he let slip; witness believes it was the defendant Want. Mr. King, the other defendant, walked round the cover with a gun. A deer was heard to cry in the wood, and White made down to the cover, Want following; King hallooed them to take the dogs off; he heard a gun go off; a deer came out into Goscombe field, a dog standing there seized it and threw it down and gnawed it; witness made towards the dog to shoot him, when King said 'Don't shoot the dog, 'tis mine;' witness said he would shoot him if *he was the Devil's dog*; and immediately shot at the dog. Then King, Bradley,

Want, White and the witness met, and King asked Want who shot the dog? Want replied, White and Durnford, and that White had threatened to prosecute him for letting the dog slip; King said 'never mind I'll see you out of it,' and ordered Want to go and see if the dog in the wood was dead. King then said, they cannot say 'tis not a fair action, and they did not know to whom the dogs belonged.

A convoluted report, rivalling Bowles' in intemperate indignation.

This led to King sending some of his greyhounds to drive feeding deer off Trow Down, which he rented from William Wyndham, and he was duly prosecuted. Rulings from virtually every reign were adduced by the opposing sides in wranglings which entertained and exasperated landowners for miles around for over two years, and the case finally came to court in Salisbury in July 1816. William Wyndham supported him in the fight, and Charlotte Grove of Ferne noted in her diary in February, 1816, 'Mr. Wyndham called. He is very earnest about his chace cause against Lord Rivers.' The concern continued for the next six months.

> 2nd. March . . . Mr. King breakfasted with us. The Chace cause is put off.
> 10th. July . . . My father and brothers went into the Chace to meet Mr. Wyndham. The latter is very anxious about his Chace cause.
> 31st. July . . . Charles [her brother] went to Salisbury to hear Mr. Wyndham's Chace cause.

Lord Rivers' case was heard first. His counsel attempted to deflect interest in the fairness of chase law and to concentrate on the historical evidence for the outer bounds being the rightful boundary, even claiming that: 'If my Lord Rivers looked to this magnificent right for profit he would be deceived; he pays more than he receives; it is a mere feather,' or so Simpsons Salisbury Gazette reported. The next day this was seized upon by the defence and embellished by the press. The Salisbury Gazette chortled: 'If he was stuffed all over with such feathers, however beautiful, he would look like a bird of ill omen', while the Salisbury and Winchester Journal crowed that the counsel 'was confident that that feather would now be plucked from the wing of Lord Rivers.' The 'feather' was featured in the Gazette as something far more burdensome to local landowners: 'The effect, Gentlemen, of · the right claimed is this: Owners of lands within the outer boundary will be liable to have their sheep impounded in their own woods; they cannot plough their land, without the consent of the lord of the chace; within all this district no man can cut his own woods without consent; from all quarters the woods must be preserved for the deer and the Foresters are first to consider how far pasturage can be spared; the preservation of the game must be paramount to the wants of man.' No wonder that, at a time of growing agricultural hardship, these anomalies rankled. 'This is the subject of the complaint,' continued the report, '~ that an English farmer and freeholder cannot kill the deer when they come to eat his crops.' By describing the disputed territory as '*Goscomb Turnip FIELD*' the counsel managed to make the whole thing sound even more ridiculous.

One of those called as a witness for the defence was Henry King, of Chilmark, Thomas' brother and father of the last Thomas King of Samways. He said;

> I have known Alvedeston (sic) 30 years. The deer on the north side of the road, [the Oxdrove, marking the line between the inner and outer bounds] were always driven back or killed; never saw one feed there in quiet; know Durnford; never killed one in his presence; *I killed one in Trough close, adjoining Goscomb Field, and sent for Durnford to come and cut it up; he came, dressed it, and cut it up; and for so doing I gave him the skin.* Within the inner bounds of the chace the vert [i.e. the green growth in a wood, making cover for deer, or the right

to cut trees or shrubs] is kept for the deer; there are ridings in all the coppices; and leaps and creeps for the deer in the bounds; and stands are made in the trees for shooting them. I never saw any of these things on the north side of the road; some of Trough down have (sic) been ploughed up; I know the out bounds; *and that 100 acres of furze have been cut in different parishes.*

His evidence illustrates how amicable local relationships had become soured, and highlights the marked distinction between the north and south of the Ox Drove.

Eventually, Lord Rivers' rights of forest within the inner bounds were confirmed, but beyond them, he only had the right of 'per-cursus' or 'running through'. As Jackson remarked,

For some little time, the learned counsel on both sides, and even the still more learned judge on the bench, were puzzled to know what this *per-cursus* or 'running-through' exactly meant: because trespassers may have various objects in entering a park, some, perhaps, not very beneficial to the owner.

However, it was eventually agreed that Lord Rivers had the right to follow deer in the outer bounds only in order to drive them back into the inner bounds, when they had strayed. This verdict 'gave the death-blow to any revival of obsolete forest right, and in fact, was the knell of Cranborne Chase', (Jackson). However, technically, the ruling only applied to Trow Down. It was only because the Rivers family 'acted discreetly' that further litigation was averted. Jackson argued that it was their readiness to accept compromise that led to the final abolition of chase rights in 1828. Benefits were felt all round: 'to . . . the population and labouring class' because

the temptation to lawlessness had been ruinous to them morally. The

Chase was a nursery of idleness and vice: and a source of positive misery to their families in many instances. Among the upper classes also an unwholesome spirit of jealousy had long been fostered by perpetual squabbles and serious litigation, producing discontent and ill-will, instead of friendly and neighbourly feeling. So that there really were none left to mourn over the disenfranchisement, except some few who had been used to unlimited venison and currant jelly, but thenceforth had to learn how to dine without them.

Tenant farmer William Hiscock's reaction was typical, if somewhat utopian:

I have been contemplating the happiness of seeing the dere (sic) destroyed and of an agreement for a general inclosure, which will remove all stubborn disputes and promote peace and prosperity to the inhabitants of Ashmore.

Meanwhile, Charlotte Grove chronicled the suspense of the trial:

1st. August . . . Charles returned from Salisbury. The Chace cause is not finished. He gave us a very good account of it, [and the triumph:]
2nd. August . . . Mr. Wyndham has gained his Chace cause against Lord Rivers, I am <u>delighted</u> about it, [then the censure:]
4th. August . . . We went to Berwick church. Mr. Boys' [the rector] 'did not <u>rejoice so much</u> as he <u>ought</u> upon the Chace cause being gained.

Somehow, as time went on, the cause seems to have been transferred to Mr. Wyndham and the glory with it, at least in Charlotte Grove's eyes, but the entry for 21st. September, 1825, reads: 'Mr. King of Alvediston is dead, an <u>irreparable loss</u> to the poor', so this cannot have been out of any ill-will. The rector's lukewarm response may have arisen out of a reluctance to use the pulpit for political purposes, in which case he would have had a few run-ins with the gentry. Whatever the case, the cause was won and the reverberations felt well beyond the locality. Bowles devotes many pages to a complicated and detailed account of the proceedings, ending with:

> The learned judge in a luminous manner now summed up the evidence, observing on the points on each side most worthy of the consideration of the jury, when these gentlemen, after retiring from the court for a short time, pronounced *a verdict in favour of the defendant*, to the no small satisfaction of a most crowded court, and the infinite joy of the neighbourhood. By this verdict a death blow was given to the intended revival of the obsolete forest laws, and a way opened up to the doing away with altogether *of the rights of the chace*, since so happily effected.

One can only surmise his fury had the verdict gone the other way. In Charles Evans' notes on his King antecedents, we read:

> Family tradition says that the bells of Salisbury, including the Cathedral bell, (the campanile was still standing then) were rung in celebration from morning to night to celebrate the occasion.

Finally, a word or two from the other side, by William Chafin, the 'hunting parson' of Chettle and possibly a friend of the Rev. Mr. Boys of Berwick St. John, whose lukewarm reaction to the outcome of the case distressed Charlotte Grove; Chafin wrote his anecdotes in 1811. He gave them to Lord Rivers' nephew and heir, Horace Beckford, intending that they should be handed to Horace's father, but somehow this did not happen. Indeed, Horace seems to have been a disappointment all round. Anticipating his inheritance, he ran up such monstrous debts that Lord Rivers probably felt constrained to co-operate with a committee of landowners rather than risk more expensive litigation. Horace duly inherited in 1828, the year of the Act of Parliament that led to the final abolition of chase rights, but his inheritance was short-lived; he was found drowned in the Serpentine three years later. Initially, Lord Rivers had hoped to use these 'anecdotes' as evidence in a retrial, but, seeing the possibility receding, agreed to their publication in 1816.

Chafin reminds us that support for Thomas King's crusade was not universal:

> The Eastern boundary of Lord Rivers's Chase, which seems to have been the bone for the late contention, extends no farther than the parishes of Berwick, Alveston, Ebbesbourn, Fifield and the Chalkes; and the rivulet which runs through those villages hath been the boundary line for time immemorial; consequently the Down, and small woods belonging to the said parishes, are within the limits of Lord Rivers's Chase. [Note that, whereas he claims that the boundary is the Ebble, Henry King was adamant that it was the Ox Drove.]
>
> The writer of this hath been conversant with all matters relating to this Chase more than seventy years and can prove, that all that time Lord Rivers and keepers exercised their rights.
>
> Some silly surmises and vague reports having been circulated, that Lord Rivers hath no rights of Chase in Wiltshire, the writer vouchsafes to make a trifling observation of such an unfounded assertion. There is a horse-path, called *The Shire-rack*, which divides [Wiltshire and Dorset through woods in the centre of three walks, Rushmore, Staplefoot and Cobley.] Now if a deer on the Dorset side of the path, should take a freak to skip across this path into Wilts. the property ceases, and the state of the animal is changed also, it becomes a *fera naturae*, and may be killed with impunity by the first person lucky enough to get hold of it. [This,] though true, is so self-evidently absurd and ridiculous, that no more need be said.

Somehow, from this distance, it seems no more 'absurd and ridiculous' than that landowners could not farm their land in case they disturbed Lord Rivers' deer.

He tells a story about Ebbesbourne Wake. Lord Castlehaven of Groveley House was having dinner at the house of Mr., later Sir William Hanham. (As the Castlehaven earldom expired in 1777 with the death of the eighth earl, this dinner was hardly a recent event.) William Chafin and his brother were among the guests. At the end of the meal, news of a deer in a cornfield was brought to the diners, who all rose from table and set off to kill the deer, which they brought back to Mr. Hanham's house. However, a keeper had observed the whole incident and duly turned up to inform them that the deer belonged to Mr. Pitt. His superior, Mr. Jones of Rushmore Lodge, was fetched to back him up and all the miscreants admitted their guilt, upon which an amicable accommodation was reached. From this, Chafin argued that everyone recognised Pitt's control of the deer.

Another story concerns Mr. John Lawes, son of the 'eminent woolstapler of Alveston'. At one time the Lawes family rented the manor and a Katherine Laws who died in 1758 is commemorated on a plaque in the north transept of the church. John Lawes killed a buck in his father's wheat field, took it to Frome 'concealed under some packages of wool' and gave it to some wool dealers. However, he was discovered and had to pay a fine of £30, thus managing to avoid Fisherton gaol.

These stories may seem to be told against local gentlemen, but were adduced to emphasise the easy relationship which he believed existed between them and Lord Rivers. Chafin continued, in slightly sanctimonious tone: 'The writer of these anecdotes hath no other end or view whatever, but to prevent gentlemen from throwing away their money in useless contests, and to promote harmony, friendship, and good neighbourhood. This is the sole end of his labour; and he most sincerely hopes he shall never again have occasion to take his pen in hand on the present subject; and does most solemnly declare that he has asserted nothing but what he believes to be true.'

However, Thomas King's ideas about the promotion of good neighbourhood had rather more to do with contest than harmony, whatever the cost. He also took Lord Rivers to task over the imposition of the toll called 'cheminage' at Harnham Bridge during the 'fence month' of fifteen days either side of midsummer's day. He dealt with this by sending a strong carter and a pair of heavy horses to the bridge with the deliberate design of causing a confrontation over the toll. On being refused entry without payment, the carter simply pulled the barrier away. It was felt politic to leave the way clear thereafter. King descendants remember paintings of this episode, together with one of the shooting of the greyhound and another of dogs pulling down a deer in Cranborne Chase hanging in the family home until the 1930s. According to family history and to Charles Bowles, (but not to a recent history of Broad Chalke,) this Thomas King bought Mount Sorrel Farm with about one hundred acres shortly before his death in 1825, and it passed to his brother, Henry. Both Bowles and the History of Broad Chalke agree that William Woodcock owned it by 1833. He married Henry King's daughter, and they let it to Henry Randall, (or Randoll). In the sixteenth and seventeenth centuries, this had belonged to the Gawen family of Norrington. Whatever the precise chronological ownership, this farm seems to have had a number of links with families also connected with Alvediston: Goulds and Lushes are also mentioned, showing the overlap between the villages.

It was this Thomas King, the third, who left money for the poor in his will. This became known as 'The King Charity'. A board on the south wall of the church tower records:

By the will of the late Thomas King Esq. the interest of 500 pounds 3 pr. ct. Cons's [£500. 3% consols] is bequeathed to be distributed by the minister and church wardens of the parish of Alvediston annually upon the 21 day of December among such of the labouring poor of the said parish as have not directly or indirectly received the relief from the Poor Rates within the year preceding.

This fund, dispersed on St. Thomas's Day, has proved to be useful to many in succeeding generations.

Henry King and Chilmark Descendents

W E NOW COME to a controversial figure in the annals of Alvediston, the fourth Thomas King of Samways, who inherited from his uncle, and it seems only fair to try to put this Thomas in family context, both before and after his time. This is made easier (and more entertaining) by the extensive records kept and generously shared by his descendants today. Family history notes give a striking picture of his father, Henry (1774-1844), which may be relevant to the son. He is described as a 'considerable character; even by the standards of those days'. In 1794, he married Mary Warne, daughter of the squire of Chilmark and rented Chilmark Manor Farm, (1,500 acres in 1837) from the Wilton Estate while living at the manor. Mary must have died very soon because he married Sarah Pinchard from Shapwick, Dorset, in 1796, and she was the mother of his children. He rented many more acres in various parishes, had 6,500 Southdown sheep, and bought 1,400 acres of the Fonthill Abbey estate in 1826. (The breakup of the Fonthill estate was very complicated. King's friend, John Benett of Pythouse, bought 2,450 acres, the Abbey ruins and gardens.) According to the family, the inn at Fonthill Bishop was named 'The Kings' Arms' after the family rather than any monarch. Henry King made no secret of the source of his considerable wealth, which was the steep rise in the price of wheat during the Napoleonic wars. Indeed, a story is recounted in *Family Quartette* by Cosmo Rawlins about the Rev. H.W. Rawlins, who officiated at the wedding of Henry King's son, Frederick, to Mary Pyne in 1833:

> Henry King was a staunch unbending Tory. The Rev. Rawlins was accordingly surprised at his host's choice of portraits; on one side of the dining room fireplace, as a pair to a most appropriate portrait of Wellington, was one of Napoleon. The Emperor was, of course, the symbol of the Revolution and admired only by the most extreme Whigs, such as the youthful Lord John Russell who had visited Napoleon at Elba. A portrait of Napoleon in the house of an extreme Tory was as unexpected as had been one of Hitler in the house of Lord Vansittart. Thinking to obtain an explanation from his host, Rawlins asked him if the portrait was a good likeness of Napoleon. Mr. King replied readily, 'Yes Sir, and I keep him there because he was the best friend I ever had.' 'Oh, indeed', exclaimed Rawlins, 'and in what way did he befriend you?' 'By keeping up the price of wheat Sir' was the prompt rejoinder.

Much had changed since the Goulds' time, with the end of the 'custom of the manor'. Instead of the relative security of the copyhold system, land was held leasehold and by rack-rent, 'the deepest possible transformation of the social fabric of England', (Nicolson). Unable to afford the spiralling rents, tenants became agricultural labourers, at the mercy of farmers and exploitative trends in farming, far from the mutually supportive ideals of the 'custom of the manor'. The practice of enclosure of common land removed grazing rights crucial to the balance of the farming community. By the beginning of the nineteenth century, the 'integrated copyhold community' was replaced by 'a monopolistic landlord and a gang of rightless, dependent, impoverished tenants', with paupers trying to survive around the edges of large farms. Bad harvests, added to the ban on imported wheat, (the acrimonious Corn Laws), led to vicious price rises. As the price of wheat rose from ten to twelve shillings a bushel and that of a loaf of bread from ten to twelve pence while farm labourers' wages remained fixed at a few shillings a week, one effect of the Napoleonic wars was increasing hardship for the poor in this country, exacerbated first by the absence of many men in the war, then by the return of a number incapacitated by their exploits. Many more ex-soldiers and sailors required work just as agricultural developments were responding to rising demand due to industrialisation and the growth of cities. All this led to massive changes in work practices. William Cobbett, in one of his rural rides through the nearby Avon valley in 1826, reckoned that £62.10.0. was the minimum annual wage required for the basics of bread, beer and bacon, but the average was £23.8.0. Poaching and stealing were rife, and a vital necessity. He was first overwhelmed by the beauty and productivity of the downs and valleys, and by the prosperity of the farms, then incensed by the rampant inequalities which ensured that those who worked to produce this abundance were so meanly recompensed. He felt 'deep shame, as an Englishman . . . Dogs and hogs and horses are treated with more civility; and as to food and lodging, how gladly would the labourers change with them!' He foresaw that a 'dreadful' end could not be far off, and welcomed the labourers' growing perception of their grievances.

The battle of Waterloo, heralding the end of the Napoleonic Wars, had been a cause for great celebration and hope generally, as Charlotte Grove recorded in her diary, five days after the event: 23rd. June, 1815 . . . 'The glorious news that Wellington and Blucher have beat Buonaparte. Harriet and I walked to Knoyle to buy a cheese.'

An extraordinary *non sequitur*, but most people today would consider walking from Ferne to Knoyle for household shopping worthy of note. By 1829, she was married to the Rev. Downes, rector of Berwick St. John, where they worked closely with Mr. Foot, the Guardian of the Poor, and with other local people to care for those in need, for the deprivations of the Napoleonic wars were far from over. They themselves paid for coal for those in need.

To add to their troubles in 1833, smallpox had struck. Charlotte Grove of Berwick again: 'They are so long in setting about vaccination in this village that I am fearful the smallpox now at Alvediston will arrive first. Certainly the cowpox does not entirely answer.'

The following year, the 'new' Poor Law came into effect, aiming to coerce the unemployed back into work. 'The need to make life in the workhouse less attractive than employment in field and factory was the principle on which the Commissioners worked, and as they could not in that era raise the attractiveness of employment by enforcing a minimum wage, they felt obliged to lower the standard of happiness of the workhouse. Moreover, in their preoccupation with the problem of the adult workman, the Commissioners overlooked the justice and expediency of treating old people, children and invalids with the tenderness that was in every way their due,' (English Social History, G.M. Trevelyan.) Charles Dickens' 'Oliver Twist', of course, exemplifies this exactly. 'Boards of Guardians of the Poor' who were elected locally, acted under Government Commissioners. In 1836, Charlotte noted that the local poor houses were due to be sold, and that her husband hoped that Mr. Foot would buy a particular one: so much depended on the attitude of the guardian.

January 1836: Mr. Foot 'took great care about' the children of a poor woman, Elinor Cull, who had just married a William Herring.

28th. 'The relieving officer did not bring any bread for the little Culls as their mother's husband, Wm. Herring is to support them ~ and he has no work, being idle and worthless. We gave the children supper.'

29th. 'We called on Mr. Foot. He has taken care, as Guardian, about the little Culls.'

14th. February: 'Tom, [Grove, her brother,] is in hopes with my father to do something about the little Culls.'

During an influenza epidemic a year later:

'We went to see some of our parishioners. The new poor law acts badly with labourers in sickness. They have no wages nor any remedy in lieu of it.'

Ten months later:

'I called on Mr. and Mrs. Shere. We talked a great deal about the present Poor Laws. They agree with me that the winter and sickness is very trying to the poor people and private charity is very much wanted.' In Alvediston, the King Charity, set up by the will of the popular third Thomas King, assisted the poor.

21st. December, 1837: 'St. Thomas's Day. I gave the school children a holiday that they might collect pence at the houses,' a custom which persisted in Alvediston much longer than the school teachers wished.

Henry King does not appear to have been too troubled by Charlotte Groves' scruples over the plight of the poor. He enjoyed the company of the aristocracy and is immortalised in a sketch drawn by Lord Pembroke's secretary in 1803, playing chess with Count Woronzow, the Russian ambassador, at Wilton House. (The count's daughter, Catherine, later married the 11th. Earl of Pembroke, and the east window in Alvediston church was erected in memory of their son, Sidney, Lord Herbert of Lea.)

While Henry's brother Thomas was taking on the might of Lord Rivers in the courts and was recognised as a champion of the poor, Henry was very energetic in Colonel Wyndham's company of Wiltshire Yeomanry, trying to quell the rural unrest due to poverty and the introduction of unpopular farm machinery. The Pythouse riots of 1830 were some of the most notorious, both for the violence of the mob and for its ruthless suppression by the yeomanry and courts.

Men from Bowerchalke were among those transported to Tasmania. Perhaps the justification for Henry's actions in the terms of his class and his day are best encapsulated in the inscription on a jug presented to him by John Benett of Pythouse:

> This is to record the gallant and persevering conduct of Henry King Esq., of Chilmark, who, in the years 1818 and 1819 rode for 25 days at the head of more than 100 brave and independent horsemen to support at the Hustings the Freedom of Election, by defending the candidate of his and their choice from the personal violence of a misguided party.
>
> Their efforts secured the Election of John Benett Esq., on the 4th. day of August 1819 and the names of King and the Wiltshire Cossacks will live for ages in the hearts of all who may value the Independence of the County of Wilts and be more imperishable than the metal on which this is inscribed.
>
> John Benett Esq. to his much esteemed friend, Henry King. A.D. 1819.

John Benett, far from being 'a staunch unbending Tory', was a vociferous independent, whose election slogan 'BENETT AND INDEPENDENCE' is still visible on the street wall of the Boot Inn in Tisbury. It was in his role as landowner and agricultural reformer that he allied himself with his more traditional neighbours.

Henry's younger son, Frederick, built Chilmark House, and the family influence remained strong in that area. Chilmark being only a few miles north of Alvediston, gossip could, and probably did, travel easily both ways, and may have contributed to stories about the last Thomas King of Samways which seem extreme and fantastical today.

'Wicked Tom King' (?) 1825 – 1850s

WHEN IT COMES to the final Thomas King of Samways, the task of unravelling fact from fiction is daunting, often entertaining and ultimately impossible. To start with relatively reliable evidence: he was Henry King's elder son, born in 1806, a year before his brother Frederick, so he was only nineteen when his uncle died. However, the 1841 census describes him as a thirty-year old banker. Despite the fact that he recorded the census details, there continues to be some discrepancy over his age in succeeding records. His wife, Elizabeth Grace Anson, was born in London, and they had one child, Thomas Anson King, who was born and died in 1834, soon after Thomas and Elizabeth took up residence in Samways. He called Samways 'Aston Farm' in 1841 and 'Alvediston House' ten years later, when a lady's maid, three female and two male house servants are listed as living in. He gave up renting Norrington Farm in 1835, but still had five hundred acres and was employing twenty men at Samways in 1849/51. His father was St. Mary's church warden from 1825 until Thomas IV took over in 1833, so it appears that he had made a life for himself, and married, in London before taking over Samways. His notes in the Church Log Book are the most cursory of all. Bread and wine for four 'sacraments', services of Holy Communion, and a few other accounts are recorded. In 1848, Mr. Rogers of the Manor examined the accounts, and Messrs. King, Rogers and Parham were listed as 'persons qualified to serve as church wardens for the year following.' King remained on the list until 1855, but he never served again. The money from the bequest by Thomas King for the poor was not disbursed from 1848 – 51. Sometime in the early 1850s, he sold Samways to William Day, and is thought to have moved to the Old Parsonage in Ebbesbourne Wake, but this is not clear. In the north aisle of the church are two large King memorials. The first two Thomas Kings fill one and the third is remembered at the top of the other. Beneath is gaping emptiness, and there is no record of his death in the church.

It is not clear whether his lifestyle and actions really merited the ire meted out in his memory by William E.V. Young, the archaeologist in Ebbesbourne Wake, who recorded local history notes a century later. Bearing the foregoing in mind, William Young's notes on the Gould Family and the fourth Thomas King are quoted in full. Peter Meers points out that Young became a Roman Catholic in 1913, aged 23. While the Kings seem to have been accepted as the natural church wardens of St. Mary's, Alvediston, throughout their time at Samways, the Goulds in the nineteenth and twentieth centuries were prominent non-conformists, leading the Congregationalists, who met at Bunting's in Ebbesbourne Wake until their chapel was built. Although from opposite ends of the scale, both Young and the Goulds may have been construed as a threat to the established church, and thus drawn together in sympathy.

One day during the summer of 1933 a small white marble tablet, about one foot by nine inches, was picked up in Ebbesbourne Churchyard by a lady who happened to be staying at the Vicarage with Rev. C.N. and Mrs. Arnold at the time.

Carved on the tablet is a shield, bearing the arms of Gould empaling West de la War! [Actually, Gould and Chadwell, the idea of West de la War having gained general credence courtesy of Charles Bowles.] It is a complete mystery how this shield came to be lying in Ebbesbourne Wake Churchyard. The relic is definitely ancient, yet in a good state of preservation ~ perfectly clean and unweathered ~ and it is clearly obvious that it could not have been exposed out of doors for any length of time ~ while for that matter it is difficult to account for its having escaped the notice of anyone acquainted with the history of the Goulds in our parish!

There are several graves of that family in our churchyard. I can

just remember John Gould, who died in 1907 at the age of 82 years
~ a noble looking old gentleman with a magnificent head of white
curls. He was a stonemason by trade, but he was perhaps more widely
known throughout the southern and eastern counties for his expert
art in the construction of dewponds ~ his work in that direction
taking him about a good deal in distant parts of the country.

He left four daughters and one son, who went to Australia
several years ago, and died there on August the 8th. 1932. The old
home at West End, Ebbesbourne Wake, was broken up [i.e. contents
dispersed] at Mr. Gould's death in 1907, his wife having pre-deceased
him in 1902, and the two remaining Miss Goulds left the village.
As far as I know there are two sons of Harry Gould still living in
Australia.

John Gould always maintained that his family were the direct
descendents of the Goulds of Alvediston, the original owners of
'Samways', an estate in that parish, now in chancery, and the fact that
when John's elder brother, Josiah, went to law and made a claim to
the property some years ago 'someone' went to the trouble to chisel
off the Goulds' inscription from their monuments and gravestones in
Alvediston Church and churchyard ~ it certainly looks as if there was
some claim!! [There are no discernable gravestones to Goulds in the
churchyard, although some are indecipherable, whether due to age or
interference.]

There are still people living who can remember this case, and
one incident in connection with it is worth recording, if only to
portray the difficulties that were put in the claimants' way in order
to hinder their cause. The lawyers instructed Josiah Gould to go and
take possession of the Samways estate by felling a tree, whereupon
Thomas King, the leaseholder of the property at that time, placed
his groom, Henry Randall, on guard with a gun, and gave him strict
orders to shoot him if he made such an attempt! [In the 1841 census,
Henry Randall is recorded as a 20 year-old groom and Josiah Gould

as a 28 year-old mason.]

Another stumbling block was the fact that whenever they went to examine the Alvediston Registers, the pages containing the Goulds' entries were found to have been cut out, yet after Josiah's death, and on the day that the Rev. Baynham left the incumbency, [in January 1903], this vicar, who seemed to have sympathised with their side of the case, went to John Gould and told him that the registers were now complete ~ and intact!, and that if he went at once and examined them he would find the missing records. It is evident that the claimant still had enemies left, for at least on this occasion the pages had once again disappeared. [It appears that the claim was still rumbling on forty years after Thomas King's death, in 1863, and through several changes of ownership. This claim about the defacement of the registers can be easily refuted. Registers of births, deaths and marriages were logged in a bound book. Any removal and reinstatement of pages would be impossible to disguise. There is no sign of tampering. Equally, there is no indication in the church log book of the Rev. Baynham or any other vicar having concerns on this score.]

The above mentioned Thomas King was one of several generations of a family who bore the same Christian name, but this particular member had the reputation of being a very evil-living man, and is spoken of to this day as the 'wicked' Tom King. It is said that when he was on his death bed he was so troubled with the thoughts of eternal punishment for his evil life, especially with regard to the wrongs committed to his poorer neighbours, that he sent for a parson, who advised him to leave a sum of money in trust for the poor, in expiation of those offences. [This 'saying', however satisfactory, is patently untrue, as the fund was set up by his uncle in 1825. However, from 1848-51 it was not distributed, for which in the absence of a vicar, Thomas King, as church warden, was probably responsible.]

This he did in the form of the King Charity, which is dispensed every year on the 21st. of December by the Vicar and Churchwardens, amongst those parishioners entitled to receive it.

In Squire King's day there was no resident vicar in Alvediston, the only services in the church, on Sunday afternoons, being taken by a curate who walked over from Bowerchalke for the purpose; hence it appears that the squire wielded sole authority ~ not only over things temporal ~ but also over spiritual matters in the parish, for whenever he felt so disposed he would lock up the church when he saw the parson coming up the footpath through the field, and take himself off with the key!!! [With the paucity of church records during the fifteen years of his apparently undisputed authority, King may well have acted intemperately. It is not hard to imagine the hapless curate dreading his tramp over muddy fields and lanes to St. Mary's, Alvediston, and being intimidated by the church warden, nor hard to imagine how this could escalate in gossip, even if not in fact to the above abuse.]

Here is one of his mis-deeds, the truth of which is vouched for by several old people of my acquaintance, who knew the facts, and whose statements are above suspicion:-

An old widow named Betty Want used to live in the cottage next to the Methodist Chapel at Alvediston (Elm Tree Cottage, now occupied by Mrs. G. Mullins); [since demolished. Mr Want, it will be remembered, was one of the defendants in the 'Chase Case']. It was her own freehold lot, of which she possessed the title deeds ~ until one evil day Tom King came riding by on his favourite 'white' mule, and asked her if there were any writings belonging to the house. 'Oh, yes Sir' replied Betty with a curtsy. 'Well, let me have a look at them' said the squire. Betty went indoors and fetched them, then promptly handed them to him ~ not dreaming for a moment that he would rob her of the precious documents. He simply placed them in his pocket and rode away ~ then, under threats, forced her to pay rent for it!

It seems hard to believe in these days that such injustice could, and did, happen, but it is idle to deny that tyrants of his stamp wielded then such absolute power that it was impossible for the unfortunate poor to obtain redress for wrongs of this kind that they may have been subjected to. I could go on telling stories, which have been handed down, of this man's crimes, but it will suffice to say that parents trembled for their daughters' honour when he was about, while the very mention of his name struck terror into people's hearts. [Although there must have been cause for this level of grievance, inaccuracies make the account questionable.]

Small wonder then that the soul of that man could not get rest after departing from this sphere, for since then has not his 'ghost' haunted the lanes in the vicinity of Samways, and the room in which he died? [This could not have been at Samways, since he had sold it before his death in 1863 and is believed by his descendants to have moved to the Old Parsonage at Ebbesbourne Wake. If this was so, it is surprising that William Young, of an old Ebbesbourne family, did not realise it. However,]

An old man named Samuel Penny, who lived at Ebbesbourne several years ago, often declared to me that he had met Tom King at night ~ riding his white mule ~ not long after his death!

It may seem unfair to recount all these charges against one no longer living, but my reason for doing so will become apparent at the end of this story, and one can only hope and trust that he has, ere now, gained remission and peace from the merciful Judge of Mankind.'

William Young then returns to the story of the Goulds' claim to Samways, describing how he believed that the plaque was removed from the north transept, and quoting Bowles' description of the family in the seventeenth century. He goes on:

The church was restored in 1866, which was about the time, or soon after, Josiah made his memorable claim, [and after both King's sale of Samways and his death!] It was during this 'restoration' that the

Goulds' monument was turned out and, except for the shield lately discovered in Ebbesbourne Wake Churchyard, apparently destroyed ~ for there is no doubt that it is the very shield mentioned by Bowles in 1830.

The mystery to be unravelled now is how the shield came to be in Ebbesbourne Churchyard?

After the restoration of the Alvediston Church in 1866, it is said that some of the materials discarded there was [sic] brought down and used in the restoration of Ebbesbourne Church, ten years later, and the general opinion is that the shield must have been amongst this material. If this were so then it almost amounts to a miracle that it should have survived all these years without being noticed before!

My own opinion is that it must have been placed in the churchyard by 'someone' shortly before its discovery last summer ~ and further, that this person was not only aware of whose arms it bore but also possessed some knowledge of the Goulds' history.

The last generation of the Goulds were staunch Nonconformists. I have often heard it said that one of the family, during the early days of Nonconformity, was a preacher who was several times up against the authorities over the Five Mile Act! [designed to prevent preachers from travelling too far afield to spread their version of the gospel].

The motive which prompted me to write these notes is simply to place on record facts which otherwise might become lost or forgotten ~ since the chance of doing so has now presented itself ~ no less to pay a tribute of respect to the memory of a highly esteemed family ~ the Goulds of Ebbesbourne.

[Young points out that the family tree of the Goulds of Alvediston in the seventeenth century shown by Bowles in the History of the Hundred of Chalke and another of the Goulds of Ebbesbourne from the eighteenth to the twentieth centuries, (while there is a gap between them,) contain many of the same Christian names, strengthening the suggestion that they are the same family.]

'It only remains to add that it is still firmly believed by many of the old families the destruction of the Goulds' monuments, that the erasing of the inscriptions, and the mutilation of the registers, was wilfully carried out by the already mentioned Thomas King, to prevent the Ebbesbourne Goulds from taking further interest in their ancestry ~ a not unlikely state of events!

W.E.V. Young, Gawens, Ebbesbourne Wake, Jan. 29th. 1934.

Note:-

Since writing the above yesterday, we have been favoured with a visit from Miss Rose Gould, John Gould's youngest daughter, who came and had lunch with the Rev. C.N. Arnold today. Miss Gould states that she has no knowledge whatever of the shield found in our churchyard ~ but remembers her father bringing down to their home at West End, some years ago, a larger slab of marble, also bearing the arms of Gould, which he had found thrown out in Alvediston Churchyard!!! She adds that she does not know what became of it and declares that it is not the same one!

If it is another piece altogether it may yet be found ~ very likely built up in a wall somewhere in their old home at West End.'

The chapter on St. Mary's church, Alvediston, includes a memo to the vicar from Lt. Col. J. Benett-Stanford of Pythouse, who was consulted about the shield, and an extract from an unknown journal or paper was appended, without comment, to William Young's account, describing the discovery and restoration of the shield in undramatic terms. Evidently, every effort was made to involve the Gould family in a public act of restitution. Could it be that the surprise appearance of the shield just when Miss Gould visited arose because someone, whose antecedent had 'found' it discarded by the church restorers and whose family had 'kept it safe' for nearly seventy years, felt a prick of conscience which compelled them to leave it where Miss Gould could not fail to find it? If anyone else knew, there seems to have been a conspiracy of silence which even the vicar could not, or did not choose to, probe.

William Young felt that village life was under attack from incomers whose roots lay elsewhere, and 'the march of so-called civilisation'. He watched in dismay as local crafts such as his family's blacksmithing declined and long-standing village families died out or had to move elsewhere. He regretted the passing of those who could identify each field by name and who passed down oral history in tales told 'by grandfather ... in his chimney corner', and feared that local history would be lost as village traditions were forgotten. Many of these anxieties pertain today, when 'so-called civilisation' has marched much further. One only has to catch snatches of village news today to realise that 'village history ~ or gossip if you wish ~ ... handed down by word of mouth' undergoes extraordinary changes en route. Perhaps William Young allowed his reverence for the past and some personal prejudices to cloud his judgment a little. His records of his own family history and his memories of life in Ebbesbourne over a hundred years ago are a very valuable resource. It is to be hoped that he would be encouraged by the resurgence of interest in the past, evidenced by the numbers of local history books published, even if the researchers do not always have the advantages of long local roots.

The fourth Thomas King's tenure of Samways, ending only a hundred and sixty years ago, remains swathed in myth and mystery, and will probably continue to be all the more intriguing for it. Supporting the belief that he moved into the Old Parsonage in Ebbesbourne Wake, Bowles notes that 'in 1824, the rectory lands and tithes came into the hands of the Rev. George Ingram Fisher, the then and now succentor, or subchantor of Salisbury; and he has since granted out the rectory or parsonage, with its appurtenances, to the late Mr. King, for three lives, in whose family it still continues.' This, written in 1830, would imply that the last Thomas King would have it available for his use on leaving Samways. However, if he was wicked, perhaps some justice will be seen in the fact that there are numerous Gould gravestones in Ebbesbourne churchyard, while the massive gap on the second King memorial in Alvediston church is eloquent in its silence about Thomas, his wife and his baby son.

William Day, 185? – c. 1875 ~ the Stud, the Clock Tower and Victorian Changes to the House

A NEW ERA BEGAN. During the 1850s, Samways was bought by William Day, whom *Country Life* described in an article in 1963 as 'owner, trainer, breeder, and author of that remarkable book, *The Horse and How to Breed and Rear Him*', (published in 1888.) This was one of several books which he wrote, and in it he claims: 'In 1873, I was perhaps the largest breeder of thoroughbred stock in England'. In his introduction, he explained the current need for a comprehensive work on the subject in a wider agricultural context:

> The question of improving the breed of our horses, or perhaps I should say of making the most of our already existing advantages in blood and breeding, is an important one, apart from its interest to the breeder of thoroughbred stock. Indeed, I apprehend it is a vital one to the agriculturalist generally. It has for some time been clear that only in unusually favourable circumstances can farming be made to pay by growing grain. Stock-raising is gradually taking the place of arable farming. The extent of pasture is increasing yearly; we have here, therefore, the area for increasing the number of our horses,

whilst that the demand for sound animals is a never-failing one is an incontestable fact.

The strain of 'agricultural diversification', so familiar today, is not entirely new, but the dependence on the horse in farming , transport and military spheres would remain unquestioned for decades to come.

William Day came from a horse-training background and, in 1849, had moved to Woodyates where he leased downland from Lord Shaftesbury and rented a redundant inn and stables, doing so well that he could expand into farming and into breeding horses at Samways. In 1861 Day, flushed with the success of his horse, Dulceabella, in the Cesarewitch race, embarked on a project which gave Alvediston a new landmark and means of telling the time, (especially vital during the years when the school manager, the vicar, resolutely refused to provide a school clock), the estate a new, albeit temporary, name and himself a financial headache. He built the clock tower over the impressive arch into the stable yard. In his book he has this advice for the unwary builder:

'The great object in selecting material [for building] must be to avoid excessive expenditure.' He shared his experience that 'the carriage of heavy material for any considerable distance will prove more costly than many would be apt to believe; and that therefore it is desirable to select that sort of stuff which is nearest to hand.' Unfortunately, the cost of transporting and preparing the stone was twice the value of the edifice itself. Perhaps the fact that Samways became known as 'the Tower', 'Tower House' or 'Tower Farm' reflected local amusement rather than awe. However, it remains impressive, visible for miles from the surrounding hills as well as from the road, causing passing drivers to slow down and stare, regardless of the dangerous bend by the gates, and providing a familiar and comforting ringing of the hours, although sadly, the brass sculpture of Dulceabella on the weather vane proved to be too heavy to be effective, and had to be discarded, another example of Day's exuberance getting the better of him.

The *Country Life* article goes on to describe the 'avenue of centuries-old limes in a small paddock, covered with rich-looking grass', which is known as 'the Park'. However, Day found this to be unsuitable for grazing brood mares for, he explained, 'Mares are sometimes kept in enclosures where noxious herbs and trees abound, the leaves of which, when eaten, will produce abortion.' One autumn, he put brood mares out in the Park during the day. 'The soil was rich, the herbage rank, and strange to say, nearly if not the whole of them slipped or were barren;' adding: 'There were no yew trees in or near the place, but a splendid avenue of limes, which, like other deciduous trees, such as the elm and ash, were scattering their leaves in all directions, covering the ground,' and he believed that the mares aborted after eating the leaves. Incidentally, Archie Miles in his book, *Silva*, recounts another story about horses and lime trees:

> In Greek mythology, Cronos was in love with Philyra, the daughter of Oceanus, and on the island of Philyra was caught lovemaking by his wife Rhea. To escape he changed himself into a stallion and galloped off. Philyra gave birth to his son, called him Cheiron, the learned centaur, half man and half horse. Philyra was so ashamed of herself that she begged the gods to change her into a tree. She became the lime tree, and Philyra is still the Greek word for this tree.'

Although Alvediston cannot produce such an exotic story, even allowing for the myths and embellishments that abound, the limes are still there and the smell of the flowers in July is exquisite and very powerful.

William Day's stud was on an impressive scale, and must have provided welcome employment. In 1873, there were three stallions, fifty-three mares, many with foals, and thirty-three yearlings, and the stud 'was described', according to *Country Life*, 'by Lord Ribblesdale, an acknowledged authority on all matters pertaining to the Turf, as including the best collection of young mares that he had seen in the possession of any one man at the same time.' A local detail to note is that one eleven year-old mare was called Bigly, after the downland farm which was part of the Samways estate at the time.

He also played his part in the local community. In 1863, the first plans to restore the church were mooted, and in March the following year, Mr. Day attended a Vestry Meeting as Minister's church warden. He made the very generous subscription of £100 towards the restoration; (to put this in context, the next highest donations were £50 and £25.) Collections in church services were not yet established, so when Messrs. Day, Rogers and Parham, representing the three main houses in the village, Samways, the Manor and Norrington respectively, 'agreed . . . to pay £4 each towards defraying the expenses of the church' the Rev. Desprez must have breathed a sigh of relief. William Day also owned an establishment in Woodyates. He is not mentioned in the 1881 census, nor is 'The Tower', 'Tower House' or 'Samways', and his foreword to 'The Horse, How to Breed and Rear Him' was written, in 1888, from Salisbury. As well as the work on the stable yard, he was probably responsible for most of the Victorian changes to the house.

Frederick Gray, c.1875 – 1904 ~ Sale Particulars 1904

HOWEVER, BY 1875, Mr. Frederick Gray was minister's church warden, having bought Samways. His main residence was Pippingford Park, in Uckfield, Sussex, so he cannot have been available for much of the time. Most of his time as an Alvediston landowner coincided with a very low period in the history of the church, and of scanty records, but he was also involved with the school, as far as anyone could be under the Rev. Woods' management. As soon as the Rev. Ousby Trew breezed in on the scene, Mr. Gray appears more prominently. He served on the school Committee of Management which Mr. Trew set up on arrival. To celebrate Queen Victoria's Diamond Jubilee in 1897, the Grays hosted a supper in the loft at the 'Tower' for all the parish, which was followed by a bonfire on Middle Down, while the following year they gave such a generous 'meat tea' soon after a long spell of illness in the village that hardly any children could stagger into school the next day, and those who did manage it were promptly given the day off to recover. Mr. and Mrs. Gray also featured among those who contributed to the various funds and good causes set up by the Rev. Charles Ousby Trew during his six year blitz on the village, and, in his statement on leaving the parish, Mr. Trew particularly mentioned how much the financial support of Lord Pembroke and the Grays for the Coal and Clothing Clubs and for the school were appreciated. In 1898, a note in the church logbook reads: 'Some perturbation was caused by the statement that the Tower estate had changed hands.' This must have led to the *Victoria County History*'s vague entry: 'Frederick Gray may have been the owner in 1875 and 1890. The farm was sold, perhaps in 1898, and certainly in 1904.' In fact, Mr. Gray was still contributing a half-yearly tithe of £8.13/11d in January 1899, and the sale particulars of 1904 begin with 'F. Gray, Esq., deceased', which should clarify matters.

These particulars give a detailed account of the estate at that time, printed in a glorious selection of type faces, with a liberal use of capital letters. The sale was to be by auction through the agents, Waters and Rawlence, 'at their Rooms, Canal, Salisbury', on Tuesday, July 12th, 1904, and the solicitor was E.F. Pye-Smith Esq., Salisbury.

A freehold agricultural estate...with the residence, extensive farm buildings, enclosed yards and cottages, and about 389a. [acres] 2r.

[rods] 8p. [perch] sound arable and productive grass lands, including some of the richest pasture land in the valley, and at the two ends of the estate, about 150a. maiden down and down pasture, a considerable portion of which is fenced, and is especially valuable as a run for cattle and sheep, or as exercising ground for horses; now for many years in the occupation of the late owner, and well-known as formerly the racing establishment, breeding stables and paddocks of Mr. William Day, to which will be added 25a. 3r. 37p. lifehold land, now occupied with the farm. The residence, with its surrounding shrubberies, terraces, pleasure grounds, and productive kitchen garden, possessed during the occupation of Mr. William Day considerable attractions, and the house was enlarged by him to render it suitable for a gentleman's family residence.' This last sentence prepares the reader for the next, which is in much smaller print:

But ~ although he took considerable interest in Farming Pursuits, and yearly bred Horn Stock which attracted considerable notice in the sale ring ~ the late Owner's occupation of the Residence was of a very limited character, and confined to the occasional use of a few Rooms only, with the result that an expenditure will be necessary prior to permanent occupation. The surroundings, however, afford attractions of a high order for Residential Purposes, and include in an adjoining Paddock a GRAND AVENUE OF LIMES through which a longer and improved Carriage Approach to the present House could easily be arranged, whilst in the Grass Lands in the Village *sites possessing considerable attractions* could easily be found upon which a Residence of more moderate dimensions could be erected if so desired.' This last might have got a few village hearts fluttering anxiously. Mercifully, this, which would have resulted in the decay or destruction of the old house, did not appeal to the buyer. To return to the sales particulars, omitting capitals and italics:

The farm lands will be found in excellent heart, and the pastures include some of the richest land in the valley......The home farm buildings are unusual in their extent and structure, and are approached through a massive stone archway surmounted by a clock tower. Considerable additions were, at heavy cost, made by Mr. William Day in connection with his racing establishment, and although they are of a more extensive character than would, in the usual course, be provided for the farm lands now attached to the estate the loose boxes, enclosed breeding yards, and well-arranged buildings surrounding them are invaluable for horn stock, and have for years been used by the late owner in connection with his dairy; whilst on one side of the upper yard a fine range of piggeries affords every facility for the breeding of pigs.

The down farm buildings known as 'Bigley buildings' are substantial, and include a double cottage, now and for some time used for stores, but easily restored to the purpose for which it was originally erected.

The residence is constructed chiefly of stone, with slated roof, and possesses carriage approaches from the road on the south and east.' The house particulars detail the division between the entrance hall, garden lobby and main reception rooms, (drawing room, dining room and west library,) and the 'new hall' at the end of a passage and behind a studded oak door. This hall opened onto a warren of rooms, vital to service the household's needs: a housekeeper's room, a pantry, a larder, a kitchen, several wine and beer cellars, a game larder or dairy, a servants' hall, a coal house, a brew house and a woodhouse, with a w.c. indoors and 'a brick and tiled Privy, with pebbled pathway from the Garden Lobby on the ground Floor, ...in the garden near the House.

One big difference upstairs one hundred years ago was, of course, the dearth of bathrooms. There were about ten bedrooms of varying size and aspect, a dressing room and a 'centre wardrobe and hanging cupboard' in a passage, but not a single bathroom.

The pleasure grounds and garden 'have not been cultivated for some years, and the erections therein of lean-to vinery and conservatory … with fuel houses at back of same, a pheasantry in three divisions, a summer house or oratory … with arched roof, coloured glass window and tiled floor, are all more or less in a state of dilapidation.' (Was the 'oratory' on the site of the original oratory or chapel believed by Bowles to have been built by John of Upton in 1343, or was it just a Victorian conceit?) The kitchen garden, having been cultivated by the caretaker, was less bedraggled, while the farmyard and buildings, approached through the 'massive stone archway, surmounted by a clock tower erected in 1861, which forms a covered way into the farmyard' were clearly in good order and use. They comprised: a coach house, a pump house, stables, loose boxes, store rooms, a slated fowl house, a tiled barn, a dairy house, a carpenter's shop, a slated barn, an open cart and wagon shed, a smithy, an iron house, a blacksmith's shop and lofts. Beyond these was a 'range of farm buildings with enclosed yard … of a very substantial character, and admirably adapted for a dairy and piggery, as now occupied. They all communicate internally, and possess brick floors, with open drain, and consist of a bull's house … cow house to tie eight cows' (and two others to tie eight and five more respectively;) 'mixing house with chaff house in the tower over same; . . . [and] the piggeries with root house and meal house.' There were two further 'enclosed yards with buildings … for entire horses or other breeding purposes', (now converted into a house and garden) and a slated granary on staddle stones nearby. Two more ranges of summer loose boxes were, in 1904, used in connection with the dairy, while there were two more 'stone-built and tiled' loose boxes in Sands Meadow on the other side of the road from the rest of the buildings.

In the Street were 'two detached cottages, brick and stone-built and tiled, with good gardens, … well placed in the village … and each contains kitchen, pantry, wash-house, and three bedrooms,

Post Office in the Street, before 1910. (Peter Daniels)

with woodhouse.' Charlie May's photographs of about this time illustrate these perfectly, and many other cottages around the village would have been similar. The lower, or northern one was used as a Post Office at this time. They are now known as Street Cottage and Quince Tree Cottage and were joined up in 2010. Finally, up on the Ox Drove, 'the down farm buildings, known as Bigley Buildings … are substantially constructed of brick and flint, with slated roofs, and comprise a pump-house with pump to tank and root-house; … enclosed cow shed; … manure house; … open shed; … open cart shed … with loft over same; … a barn; … stable for horses … with loft over same; and a double cottage, … now and for some time used as stores, but easily restored to the purpose for which it was originally erected.' Quite recently, these buildings which had fallen into disrepair and were used to house stock, have been converted into a farmhouse, with farm buildings built or restored around it, and the land around used for sheep, although formerly for dairy cattle.

These details have been quoted so fully, although without all the measurements, to illustrate the complexity and activity associated with Samways a hundred years ago. Almost all the staff required would have lived locally, but the owner, like that of Norrington and the Manor, did not. Also, Bigley, or Bigly, is now a separate farmstead, and is occupied and worked by its owners. In Frederick Gray's time, the farm bailiff was Josiah Sims, whose family remained in Alvediston and was increasingly influential among the farming fraternity until the middle of the twentieth century. Josiah's mother was a Benjafield.

Frederick Benjafield, 1904 – 11 ~ Local Family Links

IT IS INTERESTING that nowhere in the particulars is the estate named. However, the Kelly's Directory of 1907 refers to Tower House, citing Frederick Benjafield as owner, described as 'farmer and landowner.' George Benjafield appears as an Ebbesbourne Wake farmer in the 1855 Kelly's Directory; the 1871 census notes that he had 860 acres, employing twenty-two men and nine boys, with a growing family, a servant and a nurse, replaced in the next census by a governess. By 1901, of his six children (all of whom seem to have survived into adulthood), George Herbert, the eldest son, was farming Prescombe and living at the Old Rectory, now Glebe Farmhouse, and Percy, the youngest, had taken over at Manor Farm in Ebbesbourne. Frederick was a year older than Percy and he migrated west to Tower House, Alvediston. There seem to have been numerous Benjafield relations who appear as visitors in the censuses. Josiah Sims' mother was a Benjafield. Thus, this prolific family was well known in local farming circles, but Frederick moved on in 1911, after only seven years. Tragedy struck the Benjafield family in 1928. George Herbert had moved to Stoke Verdon, (now Stoke Farthing) Farm on the eastern side of Broad Chalke, in 1922. From church burial records it appears that he had a daughter, Emily Joan, who was killed in a flying accident near Wallingford in Surrey in June 1928, aged only eighteen. She was buried on 16th. July and her mother, forty years her senior, was buried only twelve days later. George Herbert gave up Stoke Verdon Farm in 1932.

The Hoole Family, 1911 – 86

AT SOME STAGE the new owner, yet another Frederick, Mr. Hoole, reverted to the name 'Samways'. The Hooles' fortune came from their foundry in Sheffield, but Frederick's background was in farming and stud management, while Mrs. Hoole's family had a lucrative business making buckram for bookbinding in the Midlands. Diana Farrow relates that, when she was tidying the house seventy-five years later, after the death of their daughter, Olga, (known as 'Mick'), she 'came across a picture postcard of Samways from Mick's father Fred Hoole to her mother, then Beatrice Cherry, saying on the back, "Would this make a nice beehive?" (Beatrice was usually called Bea.) They bought it and it was done up by a friend of Fred's who was a leading light in a big London store, I think Whiteleys.' This 'doing up' was extensive but it was not a regular indulgence: indeed, nothing more was done to the interior during their or Mick's lifetime. Mrs. Hoole told Diana Farrow that when the newly married couple left for their honeymoon the railway track was lined with guests – rather like the Whitsun Weddings. A wagon of coal was dispatched from her family in the Midlands every year.

The Stable Yard and Clock Tower, Samways. (Country Life)

Her sister's daughter Helen married the actor, Trevor Howard. As Diana recalls, 'Mick's Uncle Norman Hoole lived with them when I knew them: I never worked out how he fitted in. He waged constant war on thistles and plantain, and also enjoyed bonfires.' Fred Hoole was rather vigorous in his woodcraft, so he and Norman made a good partnership. Unfortunately, Tommy Chubb lost a limb in the cause: he was trying to cut the top out of a tree when it fell; he landed under it and squashed his arm. Living with severe disability was not uncommon among those who had faced the First World War and frequent agricultural accidents. There was Joe Collis the entertaining vicarage gardener whose leg had been amputated after a football accident. Another was Dick Haynes, (photographed with Bill and Stuart Marks outside Doug Compton's house in West End, where he lived.) He managed to shoot with only one arm. In those pre-myxomatosis days there were plenty of rabbits to shoot for sale, but they were also the days when one simply had to find ways around misfortune with the aid of friends, family, sympathetic landowners and ingenuity, or risk the Workhouse in Tisbury.

In Fred Hoole's time the covered yard was the latest in overwintering cattle, with mangers that could be lifted as the muck increased. Diana Farrow writes: 'Stable lads lived in the attic, all the windows in what is now the kitchen were frosted glass so the men couldn't see the kitchen staff. There are some great photographs of people mowing the bank with staff holding a rope to prevent the mower descending down the bank.'

Frederick W. Hoole, 'with his elder brother,' (perhaps 'Uncle Norman'), 'operated the famous Wisdom Stud, near Wetherby, Yorkshire, for a number of years before the first world war,' according to the Country Life Annual, 1963, and he set about developing the stud at Samways, although 'as he was not a wealthy man . . . [he] was limited in his choice when he felt it necessary to infuse fresh blood into the stud.' However, in 1917 he bought Love Oil for thirty-five guineas, selling her a few years later, after successfully breeding from her, for seven thousand one hundred. 'Another judicious purchase' eventually produced Vestal Girl, who was the dam of four winners including Henry the Seventh, 'considered by many to be the best middle-distance racehorse in England today' (1963) and Henry's Choice. By then, Mr. Hoole had died and his daughter was running the stud. To quote the *Country Life Annual* again: 'The two 'Henrys,' who have put Miss Hoole's stud at Alvediston high up on the list of successful breeding establishments in the country, provide an illustration of the good luck that is a necessary adjunct to skill, knowledge and intuition in this particular occupation; for when Miss Hoole's father bought their grand-dam, Vestalia, at the December sales in 1928, he did so under the impression that she was a winner. And so she was, in a manner of speaking, but it transpired that her only victory had

Charlie Roberts with a winner, when stud groom for Mr Hoole, Samways. (Pat Scrivens)

consisted of a walk-over in a modest event, and it is doubtful, had he been aware of this fact, whether he would have acquired her.'

Other horses still remembered locally were 'Make and Break', which may be the one photographed in the stable yard with Charlie Roberts, and 'Legatee', which sold for £3,000 or £4,000 in the 'thirties. Another memory is of George Day, a mason working for the builder Foyle who, when working at 'The Tower', would run over daily from Bowerchalke along footpaths, which may have helped to alleviate the effects of his notorious drinking habits.

Miss Hoole's hard work and dedication were commended in the article which continued:

'Since 1951, when Miss Hoole inherited Samways from her father, she has run the stud with the help of one man only, and when her groom and old family friend, Vic Watts, died suddenly in 1960, she engaged George Lodge, who had worked on the farm for eight years and who had a natural aptitude for handling animals, but no experience with bloodstock, and set about teaching him, instead of advertising for an experienced groom, as most people in her circumstances would have done. The two of them run the entire establishment, mares, yearlings and foals, unaided, and they continue to find time to keep the precincts of the house and stable yard in immaculate order. Indeed, when I visited Samways Miss Hoole had just finished clipping a high laurel hedge at least 100 yards long that protects the house from the road. And since it is not feasible to cut laurel with a mechanical clipper, as the leaves have to be removed individually at the stalk, the job had been done entirely with secateurs.'

Diana Farrow, who had first met 'Mick' in 1959, also remembers her phenomenal knowledge of bloodstock and how she 'enjoyed her trips to Newmarket to see her foals sold, except in the later years when they didn't sell and she felt strongly that people were paying over the

George Lodge, with a yearling by Matador out of Vestal Girl. (Country Life)

odds for fashionable horses, and hadn't paid enough attention to breeding... . . . Mick was born in the house and although she went away to school, spent most of her life there. When she was young she had been to dances; (lots of little programmes with pencils for booking partners)' were kept at Samways to the end of her life, 'and hunt balls and racing events. There was also some good embroidery and drawings of plants so who

Olga 'Mick' Hoole. (Country Life)

knows how domestic she would have been had she married. She also told me she used to help her father take the horses over the hill to Tisbury to put them on the train and I imagine when he died she just felt she had to keep the place going.' In 1963 the widowed Mrs. Hoole was described as continuing to deal with all household matters ~ in her own style, however, for Diana Farrow writes of her early visits: 'I vividly remember staying in what is now the Red Room (to the left of the front door) which was distempered in peeling pale green, all hung about with cobwebs. Hair mattresses with hollows in and linen sheets which were so cold they seemed to stick to you . . . [Mick's] mother was not interested in the outside activities and not really even the horses, as far as I could tell. At the end of her life she survived almost entirely on Devonshire toffees and whisky. When she fell and broke her hip she refused to eat in hospital until Mick turned up with the right food, though even so she died in hospital.

'Mick was unique. Outspoken, but never said anything behind your back that she hadn't already said to your face. When I first met her, and for many years after, she smoked Players and usually had one stuck to her lip . . . Mick lived a very structured life. Until we managed to persuade her to give 'house room' to an electric stove, she cooked on the big range in the kitchen about once a week (a joint) and then used an old fashioned paraffin heater to fry her meals. Washing up was done once a day and plates put to drain on a solid teak drainer, where they threatened to slide into the sink and break. She would notice if they did ~ she would know exactly where everything was and even a button out of place would be spotted......After [her mother] died Mick's own horizons gradually shrank, until she stayed mostly in the big end room, sitting on one end of the sofa all day and then pulling out her duvet to sleep the other way round on the same sofa.' Her cats pursued prolific and cannibalistic habits behind furniture in the kitchen.

Claire Farrow, 1986 – 2009

WHEN CLAIRE FARROW, John and Diana's daughter and Mick Hoole's god-daughter, inherited Samways in 1986, it presented a massive challenge. Like her predecessor, Claire, with her husband William Morris, whom she married in 2002, has been directly involved with the work and maintenance of the property. After a few years foaling ceased, but the stables continued to be used for livery and for visiting horses, as the bed and breakfast, self-catering and riding holiday business developed. William also began to renovate shepherd's huts and to breed North Devon Red cattle, while one of the barns was converted for functions and the Stallion Yard into a home for Diana. In 2008, four hundred and fifty years after it became known as Samways, and almost a century after Frederick Hoole's purchase of his 'bee-hive', sale negotiations began and the property changed hands in July 2009. It is now being extensively renovated.

Description of the House in 2009

I N 1986 P.M. Slocombe surveyed the property for the Wiltshire Buildings Record. Her dating is tentative but will be used here.

There have been extensive changes to this Chilmark stone, slated property over the centuries, but the earliest surviving rooms are to the south, i.e. to the left of the property, and are sixteenth century or even earlier. Much of it was probably built by John Samway. There was a separate barn, while the bulk of this house became the service area in Victorian times. At the front, (east), is a huge area with twenty-two inch thick walls to north and south. This was the brewhouse and the long sink, copper and fireplace survive from that time. A pantry is tucked into the gap between the brewhouse and the original outside wall. The oldest rooms at the back, (west), were converted into a scullery/ dairy/ game larder and most recently into the kitchen, with the housekeeper's room in the corner of the original building. The splendid 'Improved Patent Herald Range', which Miss Hoole used to the end of her life, is against the north wall, (sixteenth century or earlier), and the board for the bell system is over the door. William Day probably created the servants' hall, with its tiled floor, wooden staircase and back door within the old building.

Seventeenth century changes were made in the Goulds' time. The barn and main house were joined by a stable, and a room later used as a fuel store was added south of the brewhouse, but the biggest change was the 'L' shaped extension, providing the main rooms of the house. A passage from the servants' hall leads to one room at the front of the house. The deep chimney stack suggests that it may once have been a kitchen, but it later became a dining room and a billiard room, finally a family sitting room. One of the Thomas Kings scratched his name onto a window pane. Opposite, and adjoining the housekeeper's room was a parlour, later the 'west library' or study, when book shelves obscured the original panelling. This has now been uncovered, and the room has been the dining room. The entrance hall has a cellar below. The panelling is seventeenth century, the staircase, early eighteenth. The wall stencilling which extends upstairs to the landing is yellow and green on a red-brown background, and was probably applied straight onto the plaster when the staircase was fitted. It is rare for so much to survive. A small room behind the stairs may have been a buttery, later a garden lobby and a study. Finally, the drawing room had a large bay window added in the nineteenth century, and Mr. Hoole had a marble fireplace with a mirrored overmantle fitted. In his daughter's later years, as cleaning became less and less of a priority, she was so delighted when an owl flew in and imprinted its wingspan in the dust on the mirror that she left it there. When she inherited the property, it fell to her god-daughter to pluck up the courage to clean it off.

The earlier mullioned and transomed windows were replaced with larger sashes, and the front doorway was probably reconstructed in the nineteenth century. In spite of the confusion of change over the centuries there is a sense of continuity in its use as a family home, and now a new era has begun.

Alvediston

Memories

Frank Roberts, born 1922

ONE OF FRANK Roberts' earliest memories, in the early 1930s, is of the rook shooting. There was a rookery near Samways and another in the lime kilns, which used to be halfway up the hill on Elcombe Lane. A twelve bore shot gun was used and, when he was twelve or thirteen years old, Frank used to carry Mr. Hoole's cartridge bag for him. Confusingly, Mr. Hoole called him Tommy. Anyone was free to shoot rooks and to enjoy rook pies. Elcombe Lane is still raucous with the sound of rooks, although they tend to escape the gun, and certainly the plate, now.

Frank's uncles were stud grooms who helped to look after Mr. Hoole's race horses. One day, Charlie Roberts was exercising a horse when he saw a tree fall down and realised, to his horror, that Tommy Chubb had been up the tree. As he could not leave the horse untended, Charlie had to stable it before calling for help. Poor Tommy Chubb lost an arm in this accident, but continued to work for Mr. Hoole, tidying the garden and trimming the hedges, for £1. per week. Mr. Hoole's life revolved around his horses. To avoid disrupting their feeding time he never changed his clocks, so his grooms (including George Dimmer and Bert Young who cycled over from Ebbesbourne wake) had to work from 7 a.m. to 5 p.m. in the winter and from 8 a.m. to 6 p.m. in the summer, for 30 shillings (£1.50) per week at the most. Bill Mullins was the full-time gardener. Charlie Coombs, who worked for Mr. Hoole at one time then went to Tom Sims as carter, is remembered for his loud voice, his 'Waaay' to the horses resounding around the village. According to the 1925 'Kelly's Directory' he lived in what is now Cross Cottage, where his wife ran the Post Office. Frank tells a story of an event which happened before he was old enough to remember, but which was still recounted. The son of the policeman who lived up Elcombe Lane, confided in Charlie Coombs that his 'old man' had spent a night up on Samways land, collecting timber to make a pigsty. The boy was warned not to tell Mr. Hoole 'or he'll have the coat off your Dad's back!'

Frank's childhood home was Buntings in Ebbesbourne Wake, a cottage with an interesting history described in Peter Meers' book, 'Ebbesbourne Wake Through The Ages'. However, his grandmother, universally known as 'Granny Kitchen', had married Jack Kitchen, whose story demonstrates the value of listing those who served, as well as those who died in the First World War, for lives were irrevocably changed. Jack (or John, as he is named on the memorial,) served in the Grenadier Guards, but suffered from shell-shock. On his return, he was sent to work as carter for Mr. Parham, at Norrington, and he named one of the horses 'Warwick' because he originally came from there. He married Laura Watts, the widowed mother of Vic Watts, who also appears on the war memorial. They lived at No.1, Twenty Acres, later moving to Castle Hill, hence Frank's close association with Alvediston on both sides of his family. He recalls that everyone knew not only all the farmers, farm workers and families by name, but even all the local horses too. Other Twenty Acres residents, who all worked at Norrington, were Bert and Frances Goudge, Henry and Annie Lush with their son Douglas, who also served in the war, and Sam and Elsie Moxham with their son Brian. Mr. Parham also had a gardener-handyman named Arnold, who had two sons. They attended Berwick St. John school, presumably because Norrington is on the west side of the village, so nearer to Berwick than Ebbesbourne, where most children went to school. One of the Arnold boys joined the Navy but tragically died of pneumonia, contracted as a result of diving into a pool to cool off after P.T. (physical training). The family subsequently moved out of the area. Jack Parham, who received the Croix de Guerre, served in both World Wars and joined the Army, rising to the rank of Major General. At Dunkirk, he used a motorbike to round up his exhausted men, thus ensuring that they reached a boat for evacuation. The Parhams were great hunters, while their farm at Norrington, rented from the Wyndham family, consisted of a dairy herd, sheep and arable land.

Generally, less land was used for arable purposes than now, and there were many more cows. Mr. Sims had two dairies, one at Long Ground, (now Manor Farm Stud) near the pub and the other to the north, at Church Farm. George Compton, landlord of 'The Crown', also had a small dairy at Bigly, on the southern downs. None of the farmers went in for pigs, although Tom Sims and George Compton each had

Bill Marks with his Hobart motorcycle in Shortsmead Lane. (Roy Marks)

a few, but cottagers kept a pig and a few hens in their gardens. Jack Compton, George's eldest son, did some rabbit catching in his spare time but Billy Marks (Roy's father, William Henry) used to ride around on a 2 ½ horse power B.S.A. motor bike or with a donkey and cart with about 30 rabbits tied to a string and hung around his neck, which was known as 'hardling up the rabbits'. He went up as far as Fifield Bavant and to the farm at Prescombe, which by then was run by the Hulls, relations of the Sims family. Molly, Billy Marks' daughter, drove a Rover with a bundle of rabbit wires up one arm. With a mallet, she would drive the wires into the ground up in Elcombe Copse. Naturally, everyone grew their own fruit and vegetables and there were many more cider orchards then. Strawberry Russets were especially favoured for cider making, and Enos Foyle put up a cider press at the 'Horseshoe' inn in Ebbesbourne. The surplus apples were sent to the West Country; however, wages were lower in the west, so many local families had originally moved into our villages in search of better remuneration.

Frank's father worked for Tom Sims and for Mr. Hoole before moving to Ebbesbourne Wake, where he worked on the Manor Farm. He was still looking after David Fergusson's cows when he was eighty years old. Frank is vaguely related to Sid Roberts, whose father Joseph is mentioned on the Alvediston war memorial, and who lived in the thatched cottage opposite the Manor. This has long since been demolished, but the site remains as a clearing near what is now known as Quince Tree Cottage. Food in a cottage home was simple: there would be an egg in the morning if you were lucky, and bread, cheese and cocoa after school. The International Store at Tisbury delivered groceries and Frank's Mum would sometimes buy a forehock of bacon from them, and a joint of beef from Mr. Fry of Broad Chalke. On his fifth birthday, Frank walked with his elder brother to Bowerchalke to buy boots from the shop there. The roads were full of flints especially in February, after the frosts, so extremely hard to walk on. In the early 1930s Mendip stone was brought over and rolled into the roads, with tarmac on top. Although he grew up in the next village, much of his time was spent in Alvediston, and life was much the same there.

Ellen Budden, (nee Willmott) born

1916

THE WILLMOTT FAMILY moved from Berwick St. John to Alvediston in the 1920s. Ellen's story demonstrates how the village was divided between those who looked west and those who looked east. This was exacerbated by the closure of Alvediston School shortly before the family's arrival.

Ellen's real name was Dorcas, but she was known as Ellen or Nellie. She was the eighth of ten children, the eldest being born in 1904, the youngest in 1926. Two died as young children, one at eight, and one at thirty, but the other six lived to their seventies, eighties and nineties; Ellen is the only one 'still', as she says, 'going strong'!

When they lived in Berwick, 'Dad worked for Mr. Follett and we lived in Water Street, where I think one of the sons now lives. We moved to Trow cottages, but still had to go to Berwick School, because Alvediston School had been closed some time before. Anyone living further down the village went to Ebbesbourne.' In fact, although Ellen lived in Alvediston for some years and has vivid memories of life there, she never ventured as far as Ebbesbourne. This seems extraordinary to a resident today, but is unsurprising to her. Transport was scarce and, although everyone walked miles without a thought, they would not do so without good reason. Energy was conserved for work and survival; any entertainment was local, drawing in large families who knew each other well through shared employment. It has to be said that some residents today probably rarely visit Ebbesbourne or Berwick and vice versa, but they will readily and easily venture further afield.

'Mr. Parham was then Dad's employer. I remember the workmen lining up at the farm window fortnightly for their wages, (when we collected milk.) This same ritual was shown in one of Thomas Hardy's films; I was thrilled to see this. Jill Parham used to ride in the Point-to-point races around here, I saw her several times. Jack was shown on T.V. once when he flew a plane over Norrington. On the occasion of his marriage, all the workers and families had a wonderful party in the big barn.'

The gardener, Mr. Arnold, lived adjoining Norrington Farm. He had four children who also walked to Berwick School. The Carters, a large family, lived at the bottom of Crook Hill in Keeper's Cottage, now Bushy Garson. Ellen remembers the 'Collis, Grace and Sheppard' families at the top of Crook Hill. In the 1925 Salisbury Directory, George Grace is recorded as living at Twenty Acres, but they all worked for Mr. Parham at Norrington. The other family at Crook Hill was actually called Shergold, but Ellen's memory of 'Sheppard' arose because of his job: the farm shepherd. 'Next door to us at Trow were the Moxham family, I think some of the offspring still live in the locality. Bridmore Farm was Hannam's, the cottages near the road housed Kelly and Conway.' As the young Willmotts walked to Berwick School from Trow, they would therefore have been joined by children from these families.

'Going on to Alvediston, were Hoole at The Towers,' (note the plural), 'Comptons at the Crown, I remember the names of Mabel, Dolly, Douglas and Joan. Jack, [the eldest] . . . then had 'The Talbot", the Berwick pub where, 'On the wall which shows many old photographs, there is still one of my older sister with her classmates.' (The Comptons, of course, also had ten children.) Among other names recalled by Ellen are: King, Chubb, Lodge and Marks.

'Mr. Sims had Church Farm, and his brother [actually his father] lived where later on Anthony Eden resided, [the Manor]. He must have made <u>his</u> mark on the village. We went there when he had an Open Day, and he made it his business to chat to everyone individually. Looking around his glasshouses was absolutely superb. I had never before seen oranges and lemons actually growing.'

The thatched building which Ellen remembered as 'the little Post Office' had 'become the gardener's cottage to Eden's house. This said Post Office only sold postal orders and stamps. A postman cycled from somewhere in the valley to his morning round of the parish.' However, in the afternoon, he just delivered to the Post Office and 'the letters, which were but few, were spread out in the window, to be collected by villagers, be it for themselves, or for anyone on their homeward route. This would not be allowed now. Scarcely believable, but letters were fast moving then.'

Mr. Oborn of Ebbesbourne Wake ran a 'market bus' from Berwick to Salisbury on Tuesdays and Saturdays, Salisbury market days. 'It seems that these were only used for necessities, no gallivanting then, too much work to be done, with large families mostly. Whatever the weather, we children were not allowed to use the bus, as it did not get to Berwick before 9.30 or later, and that would have upset all the classes.

'Around Xmas time, the Duke and Duchess of Hamilton', of Ferne, to the west of Berwick, 'gave a grand party to all the school children, and evening entertainment. He put on a "charabanc" for the occasion. My first glimpse of film, albeit silent ones. After Lady Mary died from an accident with her horse, the parties were held in Berwick Reading Room.'

Ellen adds a story about changes in her life after leaving Alvediston: 'When we moved to Wimborne, we had to get used to gas lights and cookers, penny in the slot. When the meter reader called, the pennies were put into piles of 12 on the table, and a rebate was given according to the amount used. The money was then put into his big leather bag and strapped to his cycle. And to think that was mod cons!' She also has an anecdote relating to a Berwick family which shows her lifelong connection with this part of the world, despite her relatively short residence here. 'I have met and talked to 6 generations of Rosa Denton's people. Her great-grandfather, Mr. Stretch, was a Prudential agent, his daughter was Mrs. Emm, her daughter was Linda, who I knew at school, Rosa is the next generation, then I met her son and grandson at Berwick Fair in September, [2010]. Wonder how many folk you will find who will beat that!'

On that same day in September, both Ellen and another former resident visited Alvediston church and left their names in the visitors' book, unfortunately not at the same time, because Ellen would have liked to talk to her. 'She was a cousin of Maud Goudge, whose Dad was dairyman at Norrington. This said Maud was attracted to my brother Albert at one time, and while in the Army he had a tattoo on his arm, 'I LOVE YOU, MAUD', which of course he carried till his death in 1996.'

The Willmott family's time in Alvediston ended in tragedy. 'My father died in the harvest field, at only 44 years old. Being in a tied cottage, we were obliged to move, also my mother had to get some sort of work, so we went to Wimborne to share a rented house.

'Mr. Parham was very understanding in allowing us to stay on for 8 months, probably because Mum then had a small child of a year old and had just lost an eight year-old.' Ellen has a photograph of her mother, Clara, holding baby Clifford outside Trow Cottages in 1926, not many months before the double blow. In the immediate aftermath of these bereavements, the other children had to be fostered out. Ellen went to live with her married sister. Frederick Willmott was buried to the west of the church, in an unmarked grave, (as so many were), in August 1927, next to his young daughter, Kathleen. This little girl was always sickly and had been sent to a hospital in South Hayling Island, which must have made visiting difficult. She was buried just eight months before her father, in January 1927. There is a record of burials in the churchyard, but the plan is missing, so it is especially helpful when surviving relatives can point out burial places and they can be recorded on the new plan, a copy of which is kept in the church. Ellen still visits the graves over eighty years later and, in spite of all the sadness, so simply described, she has written: 'I can only wish for you as much happiness there as we all had.'

Joan Reeves, née Compton, 1918 – 2011

JOAN WAS THE youngest of eleven children born to George and Jane Compton. George's family are thought to have lived in Tollard Royal at one time. His mother, Mrs. Anne Elizabeth Compton, was a widow when she took over the Crown inn from William Mullins sometime between 1881, (when he appears in the census), and 1885, when she is recorded as proprietor in the Kelly's Directory. George was recorded in the 1891 census as a seventeen year old agricultural labourer, born in Berwick St. John. In 1897 he is described in the school book as a 'haulier', who delivered coal to the school and he appears as proprietor of the Crown and shopkeeper from 1899, where he remained for many years and before long, he was recorded as 'licensee and farmer', so he must have been both versatile and hardworking. Joan remembers his horse-drawn carrier's van. The shop was closed during the First World War, when rationing made it impossible to keep it stocked. Jane Compton was born in Donhead. They started their married life at Shortsmead, where their eldest son, Jack, was born. All the others were born at the Crown Inn: a boy who died in infancy, then Annie, Violet, Mabel, Dolly, Vera, Lucy, Frank, Douglas and Joan.

Douglas was born in February 1916. When he was about 18 months old, he had a narrow escape which has gone down in the annals of family and village history. He toddled to the well in front of the pub and somehow managed to fall down the shaft, the well cover not being correctly in place. The well was 40 foot deep with 15 feet of water at the bottom, but Doug was saved by, of all things, his petticoats. In those days little boys wore dresses and somehow the various layers of material got caught between the beam across the well and the side.

Mr. Hennings the postman cycled by on his rounds just as the drama was unfolding. His duties involved making two trips from Broad Chalke by bicycle daily; delivering mail in the morning and collecting from the post office at about 2 in the afternoon. Throwing down his bag and discarding the boater which he wore in the summer instead of his cap, he volunteered to be let down the well on a line by George, since he was the lighter of the two. Baby and postman were hauled up amidst great rejoicing, but extremely wet. Blankets were stripped off beds to dry and warm them, and another dress was found for Doug, while Mr. Hennings was decked out in some of Jack's clothes, (the eldest son being away at the war), upon which he remounted his bicycle and resumed his postal duties. When he reached Norrington, Mr. Parham, surprised to see him in slightly ill-fitting mufti, enquired the cause. He rushed off to the Crown in great concern, arriving only about an hour after the incident, to find little Doug running around apparently unharmed. Mr. Hennings received a National award for his brave actions.

Alvediston School was closed shortly before Joan was old enough to attend. Lucy went to school in Berwick St. John, where she had music lessons, but Vera, Frank, Doug and Joan joined neighbouring children in the walk to and from Ebbesbourne Wake School, a journey which was made more fun by dint of 'playing horses', with string attached to the horse/child as reins. They did not dare to miss school if it was wet, for fear of being dubbed 'Sugar Baby', i.e. someone in danger of dissolving in the rain. Joan remembers taking sugar and cocoa to school in a tin. A kettle was heated on a tortoise stove and at 12 noon the children were allowed to make cocoa, supplemented with milk provided by the teacher. Cloths which had been made by girls in the sewing class were laid on the tables, and afterwards the girls washed up the cups and put them away. Joan passed the entrance examination for South Wilts Grammar School for Girls, but could not take up her place because there were no daily buses and she would have had to lodge somewhere in Salisbury, so she remained at Ebbesbourne School until she finished her education at 14. She does not have any regrets.

At home, the children were never bored, even in wet weather. With the simple materials of paper, cardboard, pencil and ruler they invented and played games at the living-room table, which Joan remembers being scrubbed twice a week. There was also Sunday School. The vicar, on inspecting the registers used to quip: 'I don't know why we've got a lot of Comptons here,' and noted that the girls in the family were 'very regular' in their attendance, while the boys were 'not so regular.'

As in every family at that time, the First World War changed lives and expectations. Against his father's wishes, Jack joined the army, declaring 'If you think I'm staying in Alvediston when the other lads are joining up . . . ' and cycling off to enlist. Annie joined the WAACS, (Women's Army Auxiliary Corps) leaving Vi helping her father on the farm. George Compton had a farm building near the pub which was rented from Mr. Sims and he also rented Bigly, at the top of Elcombe lane, from Mr. Hoole of Samways. Vi met her future husband, Len Frampton, when he was working for Mr. Sims. After their marriage, they moved to Woodyates, where Len worked as a shepherd with his father and brother. They also lived in Zeals among other places before returning to Alvediston. Len used to join Mr. Marks and Mr. Cooper (of Berwick) at sheep shearing time. For a while they lived in the back cottage at Shortsmead, then at Twenty Acres, before coming back to work with George, renting the Old School House close to the Crown. The rent was due on a Saturday afternoon, but, as Vi was busy milking the cows then, she would leave the rent book, with the money, at the

Crown and the vicar would come up to collect it, since the house and schoolroom still belonged to the church. At haymaking time other sisters were expected to lend a hand in response to George's injunction: 'I want you girls up in the field' turning the hay to dry it evenly before it was piled into ricks. The Compton children, like most children in the village at that time, were expected to work hard on the farm before school, which finished later than state schools today.

The Compton family had dairy cattle up at Bigly Farm, but kept two cows in the field behind the pub to produce milk for the family. George would bring milk down the hill from Bigly, for collection by the United Dairies lorry. Some was delivered to a few neighbours. At the Crown, Mrs. Compton would strain this milk into a large basin, then measure it out using pint or half pint mugs from the bar. Before school, Joan would deliver milk to the Pimms at Elcombe House, the Whites and Kings next door, the residents of the Old School House, Mrs. Coombs at the Post Office and Mrs. Mullins at Castle Hill. After having walked home from school, she often had to walk up to Trow Cottages to deliver more milk. As Mrs. Moxham in the further cottage had four or five sons, she needed a good supply daily. Joan carried the milk in two cans, but she felt that she got off lightly in comparison with some of her brothers and sisters who had heavier work to do. Some people came to collect milk from the Crown, where Joan's mother had a selection of jugs for her regular customers. If the family was having tea when someone came to buy milk, one of the children would be dispatched to find the appropriate jug and to transfer the milk into the housewife's jug. For all this they received the sum of two or two and a half old pennies a pint, (about one new pence.) When Lady Glanusk bought the Manor in 1938, she enjoyed local milk so much that she bought a Jersey cow and asked George Compton to milk it for her. She needed six or seven pints a day for her household, so sometimes had to supplement her supply with some from the Comptons. After school, Joan and Vi would be sent up to

Bigly with two cans of tea and two baskets of sandwiches wrapped in napkins for the farm workers. Thirsty herself after the steep climb, she would try to sneak off with a mug to get milk straight from the cooler in the dairy, much to her brother Jack's disgust.

When Frank left school at fourteen, he helped his father on the farm. About ten years later he got first a small lorry and later a bigger one for cattle hauling and for transporting sheep to sheep fairs. Eventually he started his coal round. F. Compton's coal merchants' business remains in the family, being run by Frank's nephew and great-nephew, Tony and Christopher Lodge, with other family members assisting.

The Rev. Mr. Jones is remembered with great affection. In spite of his deafness being exploited by some good humoured mischief, he would always 'take a joke'. He would cycle around the village with his youngest child, David, on the saddle and he wore a distinctive, rather flat-crowned hat. The village children attended Sunday School and services in the church afterwards. Joan helped David Jones follow the words of the hymns. Joan remembers the Vicarage gardener Joe Collis's pranks and mishaps. When he was only thirteen or fourteen, he had broken his leg very badly while practising football and had to have it amputated, but could not have an artificial leg until he had stopped growing. Joan recalls Mr. Jones requesting that Joe attach a shoe to his wooden leg to 'save all those holes in the lawn' as he limped around the garden. Joe's bicycle brake-mending deficiencies nearly ended in disaster for the vicar. During the process of replacing the brake blocks he left the bike for a few minutes, during which Mr. Jones decided to cycle off on a visit. In Joan's version of the story, Mr. Jones swerved violently at the last minute to avoid the gate while in Dave Collis's, he landed 'smack into the gate'. Either way he survived to cycle about the village on his round of visits and the story was enjoyed by all. (Incidentally, the practice of visiting by the clergy, generally appreciated, and much lamented since its decline, was made infinitely easier in the halcyon days of at least one member of the clergy resident in each parish and of most villages, however small, enjoying the status of parish in their own right. The chapter on St. Mary's Church highlights how rarely, during its long history, this was the case in Alvediston.) The older Jones children were away at boarding school, Harry at Bluecoats and Christine at one time in Bristol, while David, being the youngest, was still at school in Salisbury when the family lived here. The village mourned with the family when the other brother, Trevor, was killed in an air raid on Romsey during the Second World War.

A few years earlier there were two other untimely deaths. Annie Compton, who had been in the WAACs in the First World War, met a soldier, William Churcher, and married him. After the war his army service took them abroad for six years and their second child, a daughter, was born in Bangalore (when her 'Aunt' Joan was only seven.) Annie died at Christmas, 1935. Only about a month afterwards, Doris Sims, a contemporary of Annie's, returned to the Manor from New Zealand, where she was a music teacher. She needed to have a tooth extracted and decided to have it done at home, where she prepared her room for the operation, as was possible in those pre – N.H.S. days. Unfortunately, in spite of a doctor being in attendance, there were complications during the operation and she died for lack of oxygen. The shock of this made a great impact on the village and is still remembered by those who were around at the time.

After she left school, Joan went into service at a vicarage in Alderbury. When she was only about 15, she had influenza sufficiently badly for a doctor to be called. It was decided that she should go home to recover, so the vicar borrowed the nurse's car and drove her to Salisbury to catch the bus home. She developed pleurisy and was bedridden for a month, after which she was sent to Salisbury for more tests. She was still sufficiently unwell to be sent on to a sanatorium at Winsley, between Bath and Bradford on Avon, where she remained

Joan Compton in uniform. (Pat Scrivens)

among T.B. patients for four months. However, she was still conscripted into the army in the Second World War. She was concerned about leaving her parents, who were elderly by that time. At the Crown, they had to contend with an influx of soldiers from the searchlight field on Mr. Hoole's land.

The Rev. Mr. Courteen, who preceeded Mr. Jones, presided at the marriages of all five of Joan's sisters: Annie, Violet and Mabel during his incumbency (1918-28), returning to marry Dolly and Lucy after he had left for West Moors. The war memorial, with its list of all who had served as well as those who died, was a focal point in the village and was maintained with pride. Joan's father hauled it from Tisbury to its place in the village. Lucy and Joan made a laurel wreath for it on Armistice Day and Mrs. Hoole of Samways gave them some poppies to twine into it. They also helped to keep the grass tidied with shears. During the Second World War their niece, June, was born on an unforgettable day, just after bombs were dropped on a hill near Norrington.

Finally, Joan remembers that two precious photographs, now in her possession, hung in frames on either side of the living room window at the Crown. In the one reproduced here the entire Compton family is gathered for Annie's wedding to William Churcher on 3rd.

Wedding of Annie Compton and William Churcher, 3 April 1920. The photograph was taken in the school garden. For names see Appendix. (Pat Scrivens)

April, 1920, together with Jack's and Vi's fiancés and four of Annie's sisters as bridesmaids. Joan is sitting on her mother's lap on the front row. The picture is taken in the garden of the Old School Hall, a popular venue for wedding receptions, with the bank behind rising to the garden at the Crown inn. The Compton family stopped running the Crown after the death of Mrs. Compton, in December 1952, and it was sold a few months later.

Roy Marks, 1926 – 2011, and Bella Marks

ROY WAS BORN and brought up at Shortsmead, Alvediston. His family came from Chard in Somerset. In the 'Kelly's Directory' of 1925, his father, is recorded as a keeper of Shorts

Meadow. William Henry Marks, known as Bill, bought the rights of
rabbit catching on all the farms from Mr. Sims' in Alvediston all the
way through to Fifield Bavant. He would catch about 200 rabbits a day
and sent them to Smithfields in London, to a Miss Smith in Salisbury
and to Portsmouth among other outlets. Sometimes there could be
a thousand rabbits strung up in the kitchen at Shortsmead, ready
for sale. Ernest Oborn of Ebbesbourne Wake ran a bus between
Salisbury and Shaftesbury on Tuesdays and Saturdays (Salisbury
market days). Being a family friend, he obligingly transported
rabbits under the seats, making a detour from the Cross down to
the bottom of Shortsmead drive to collect them. As there would
be twenty rabbits strung on a stick and one stick under each seat,
a good number could be transported this way. Of course, this was
in the days before myxomatosis, when thousands of rabbits could
be seen grazing the fields and downs. Bill also did thatching for Mr.
Sims at Manor Farm.

Roy got involved in agriculture at a young age. George Grant
owned Glebe Farm at Fifield Bavant at that time, and lived there with
his aunt, Miss Lucas, (whom Roy remembers as being very strict).
Bill Marks rented all the fields except one behind the house, where
the owners kept a large number of hens. From the age of eight, Roy
would help to milk his father's cows before school and again in the
afternoon, once school had finished, and Bill's cousin, Cyril Marks,
also joined them. Of course, Roy attended Ebbesbourne Wake school,
the one in Alvediston having closed. He also started driving when he
was only eight, a Morris Cowley van converted by dint of 'cutting off'
the back and replacing it with a lorry trailer. They used this to haul
hen food up the hill for Miss Lucas's chickens.

More ingenious work was undertaken on a car which Miss
Hoole of Samways loaned them. Designed for gentler pursuits this was
a Studebaker, with velvet upholstery and pipes connecting the back
seats to the front ones so that passengers could communicate with the

Haymaking time, Church Farm, with Miss Hoole's converted Studebaker: Tom Sims and Bill Marks (back row); Keith Sims, Faith Sims, Roy Marks (front row) (Roy Marks)

driver. Nevertheless Miss Hoole was quite happy for a hay sweep with tines to be attached to the front, for the Sims' and Marks' haymaking. Unfortunately, when hay was piled up on this it stopped the air getting in to the engine but the resultant overheating was overcome by the removal of the car's bonnet. As time went on, the Marks family owned tractors: a Standard Fordson and an Allis Chalmers B, but they still undertook their own maintenance and adaptations.

Bill Marks bought Bigly and Elcombe farms from Mr. Sims in the 1940s, a total of 300 acres for £6,000. Twenty years later he sold Bigly farm alone to Johnny Wort also for £6,000, thus 'making straight', to his great relief. As Roy says, 'People worried about debt in those days.' Bigly Farm should not be confused with Bigly Buildings, the site of the old coaching inn on the Ox Drove which, with a hundred acres, still belonged to the Comptons. The farm had a big stone and thatch barn, where they stored corn, situated opposite the junction of Elcombe Lane and the Ox Drove. When Roy and Bella (nee Parsons) married on a damp midsummer day in 1950, they rented Trow Cottage from Miss Parham but, on the sale of Norrington to Mr. Sykes, they had a bungalow called Shortlands built, and moved there in 1956, remaining there ever since, while Roy's parents continued living in Shortsmead nearby until their deaths. At the roadside of their plot was a ruined building called 'The White House', which had belonged to the Hooles of Samways. Roy recycled the stone in their drive. 'The Hut' by the war memorial, formerly the village hall, became obsolete when the old school hall was used as a church hall, (but effectively a village hall). Roy's brother, Bernard, bought it as his first home when he married Margaret and moved it to the field where Shortlands was built some years later. They lived there for some years and their son Trevor was born there, but then the family moved into half of Shortsmead, while the hut still stands in Shortlands garden. Some ingenuity was clearly required from first-time buyers fifty or sixty years ago, but there were fewer planning and health and safety regulations to deal with.

When Roy was growing up, life was much more dependent on the land, the seasons and the neighbours. Haymaking and harvesting were communal activities, and most people would keep a pig in the garden. October was pig-killing time and families would help each other with the messy business of slaughter and butchering. As Roy points out, there were no humane killers then; one person had to hold the pig while another slit its throat and the noise of the frightened pig was terrible. However people realised that this had to be done to provide meat for the winter and got on with it as quickly and efficiently as possible. Before long a ham and other joints would be hanging to 'cure' in an alcove under the stairs. After hanging, Roy's father would lift the meat down and put it in a 'silt' which he had made out of an old, upturned kitchen table with the legs cut off and kept in the 'backhouse'. There the meat remained while it was salted. The only other cool place for food storage was a 'safe', a cupboard with doors and sometimes sides made of fine, flyproof mesh, hung outside, on a north-facing wall.

In Roy's childhood, Shortsmead housed seven or eight Marks at one end and ten Haywards in the other. The Knapp, now two cottages, was even more populated. It was divided into four, and twenty-two people lived there: the Chancellors, the Percy Weedons, the Topps and the Reg Weedons. He remembers the Post Office moving from Cross Cottage to Street Cottage, (modern names), where the Watts family ran it. There were cottages near the chapel. Joe Roberts lived in the field opposite, later moving to the cottage opposite the manor, and then to one in Foyle's Field; all of them have now disappeared. The Brachers had a tiny, one-room shop, selling cigarettes and a few sweets in a cottage in the field opposite the forge but Roy does not remember the forge in action: by then every one went to Ebbesbourne for ironwork, where the Young family held sway.

The church played an important part in social life. The residents of Twenty Acres would walk across the fields to meet others coming down the street and past the Knapp (opposite the stream) in time for a chat at the roadside before all going up the path to the church. Molly, Roy's sister who later married Frank Compton, played the organ, which was an older model than the one currently in the church. It was in the north vestry, also known as the 'choir' or 'organ vestry'. Roy was in the choir and also took turns at pumping the organ. However his other, unofficial, duty was to keep an eye out for the Rev'd. Mr. Jones emerging from the Vicarage, and to alert Molly, who was seizing the moment to play popular tunes at full volume, egged on by Keith Sims and Roy. Given the acoustics in the church and the proximity of the north vestry to the Vicarage it is hard to imagine that Mr. Jones was completely unaware of the choice of voluntary, but he was less strict than his wife and also conveniently deaf. Molly worked for the vicarage family and Mrs. Jones would find extra jobs to keep her busy in the house if she discovered that Molly had plans to go out for the evening. Their elder sister, Pearl, worked as a housemaid for the Parhams at Norrington at one time, where their cousin, Reg, had his first job.

Agriculture was incredibly labour-intensive. Roy remembers growing mangolds and kale for the cattle and also cow cabbages which could grow to the size of a dining table and could only be carted one at a time. One year most local farmers lost their cow cabbages in a drought, but Bernard and Roy, who had planted 11,000, watered them all with a bucket and a tin, and saved their crop. Sacks weighed 2 ¼ cwt. (hundredweight, i.e. 380lb. or about 175 kilos, to give the full range of weights used in a lifetime!) The Marks family kept seventy dairy cattle and forty 'followers', (steers and heifers) while Bella looked after twelve breeding sows, walking up to Elcombe Farm and back to Shortlands every morning and evening.

Changes inevitably came in the Second World War. Bernard met and married Margaret, who came down from Manchester as a land girl. She stayed at Donhead House and helped with the threshing on local farms. Jack Parham rose to Major. Wood was commandeered and Mr. Hoole sold many trees. Several older residents remember his obsession with burning out the stumps, and his somewhat unorthodox methods. Roy recollects him attaching a bellows to a pipe so that he could fan the fire from a suitable distance. Mr. Hoole had an uncanny way of reading minds and Roy remembers once ploughing a field for him at great speed because he wanted to go out, only to see Mr. Hoole's face appearing over the hedge to shout instructions for another job. A 'Home and Beacon' searchlight was fixed, first at Crockerton, near the Herepath, and then in what became known as Searchlight Field, nearer Samways, to light aircraft on their way back to Boscombe Down after raids on Germany. This naturally made a huge impact on the village; when in operation, the whole of

Alvediston would be illuminated, (an extraordinary prospect even now, as we do not have any street-lights and enjoy unpolluted night skies), and when the seventy-odd soldiers manning it congregated at the pub, it is easy to imagine the flutter of excitement among the younger residents whose lives, dedicated to producing food at home, must have seemed at times a little unglamorous in comparison with those of their friends and relations serving abroad, whatever danger and tedium reality incurred. The men working on the farms had guns but never used them, even when a German plane crashed into the hill on the south side of the village. Roy spotted the plane but first had to change into his khaki cadet uniform before he could inspect it.

There were no survivors although all the parachutes were open. One of the dead was assumed to be a woman because Roy noticed hands with nail-polished fingers, and the reality of war struck home in an unforgettable way. The bodies were all taken to Salisbury for burial. However, Mark Dineley, from Berwick St. John, came over from the pub shortly after the crash and characteristically seized the opportunity to increase his munitions collection. He challenged Roy: 'Come on Marks, we want one of those guns!' and got it mounted on his Rolls Royce in no time. Such planes carried both rifles and machine guns, and Alvediston had another narrow escape when a Blenheim bomber flew twice over the village and then disappeared towards Dinton railway, where it was shot down. On another occasion, the famous night-fighter 'Catseyes Cunningham' picked up a plane near Gillingham, followed it south-east and shot it down over Norrington Farm.

Seventy years later, these events are distant memories, but in spite of all the threats to agriculture, the Marks family have continued to farm their land in Alvediston, and with Christina joining her great-uncle Roy and her parents Trevor and Sue, they have notched up four generations. In 2011, Elcombe Farm was put up for sale, but the Marks family will still rent grazing in Alvediston. Roy died in July 2011.

Reg Marks, 1916 – 2004

Reg's grandfather came up from Somerset and lived at Badger's Glory in West End, Ebbesbourne Wake. Reg was born next door, at Brooklands. His family moved to Alvediston, first to Twenty Acres, then to the Knapp. When he was seven, they moved again, to Pound Cottage, Ebbesbourne Wake, when his father went to work at Prescombe Farm, (this would have been when Alfred Hull left Alvediston Manor and bought Prescombe.) Later, Reg lived in No. 4 Pound Street, Ebbesbourne, and his last move was to No. 3, where he lived until his death.

His parents moved back to Alvediston, to The Knapp and then to Gardener's Cottage, (now Cross Cottage.) He married Nellie in 1941, and they spent their honeymoon at Gardener's Cottage.

Reg started school at Alvediston in 1920, just two years before it closed, and he features in the photograph that year, the smallest and youngest pupil, next to his sister, another Nellie, whose one hundredth birthday was celebrated in March 2011. He remembered, on his first day, being given a little book of squares, which he had to pencil over to get a picture. After the closure of the school, the children had to go to Ebbesbourne or Berwick for schooling, and the Alvediston school was used as a village hall, then sold.

Mrs. Marks worked at Alvediston Vicarage, and Reg's brother worked as a gardener there. At 14, Reg started work at Norrington, in indoor service. It was a lonely life as all the other servants were elderly. Wages were 6/- per week and no clothing was provided. He had half a day off each week, from 2 until 9 or 10 p.m., with no other time off except alternate Sunday afternoons, so he was isolated from his family and friends, although still geographically close. His day began at 6 a.m. when he had to light the kitchen fire ready for Mr. Bernard Parham, who would come in at 7, after seeing his men off to work on the farm. Reg remembers Mr. Parham as a 'gentleman' who treated his staff well, but has less complimentary memories of his wife. He could finally retire to bed in the attic at 9 or 10 p.m., having washed up the dinner. There was only one flush W.C. in the house, and servants were not allowed to use it: there was one outside for them.

After a year or two of this, Reg joined his mother at the Vicarage, but he was still a 'live-in' servant on 6/- per week. One day, he packed his bag and complained of toothache because he was so desperate to get away. The vicar, the Rev. Jones, escorted the 'patient' home and he never returned.

Finally, Reg joined the building firm of Burge and worked with Percy Hare. He became an expert painter and decorator and reckoned that he had 'seen the inside of most houses in the village.'

Reg's father worked as a gardener at the Manor when Lady Glanusk lived there. She had bought it from Mr. Sims in 1938 and gutted it, using a London firm, Turner and Cooper. Reg remembered staircases being delivered from London. His father planted every hedge and shrub and laid every turf by hand. In 1939, he planted the rose which was still growing over the wall sixty years later. Reg himself worked on the house until he joined the Army. He built the wall by the roadside. Lady Glanusk later divorced and remarried, a Mr. Frere. She moved to Ansty and built a wing onto the farmhouse there almost identical to Alvediston Manor. A very sad memory from the time previous to lady Glanusk's was of the tragic death of one of Mr. Sims' daughters, aged about thirty. She had complained if toothache, so a dentist was called to the manor, but she died under the anaesthetic.

At that time, there was a big pond adjacent to the Manor field, near Shortsmead. Water went under the bridge by the first gates, through a drain under the road and field and on to the pond, then continued behind where Shortlands now stands and on into the Ebble. It was filled in by the Masons after it had dried up one summer. Mrs. Frere sold the Manor to Mr. Mason (of Mason sauce fame); he sold it to the Beckinghams and they to Anthony Eden, Lord Avon. Lord Congleton then bought Manor Farm.

The street was variously known as 'Church Street', 'High Street' or simply, as now, 'The Street'. People would 'go down Church Street' from the cross. Opposite the Manor's lower set of gates there was a stone and thatched cottage. Other buildings which are now derelict or have disappeared completely include the little building by the chapel which was a blacksmith's, a cottage beyond the chapel and another opposite the blacksmith's, all of which were of stone and thatch. Up Shortsmead Lane, on the left, there was a derelict slate-built house, [the White House.] There was also a cottage in Foyle's Field, below Castle Hill, but Reg could not remember the cottages which once stood in Elcombe Lane. The Council Houses were built in the 1930s and '40s, the left two being earlier. The pub was run by George Compton, Dolly Lodge's father and Tony Lodge's grandfather. Elcombe Farm was bought by Bill Marks, Roy's father, from the Sims family. The field between the chapel and Roy's bungalow [Shortlands] is called Shortsmead.

Samways was then known as 'The Tower House'. Mr. Hoole was 'mad on burning tree stumps' and could be found at midnight, pouring tar into stumps, ready to burn them. He used to buy a 5/- rocket for November 5th. and, as 5/- was then a day's farm pay, this was a splendid sight. Reg remembered Mrs. Hoole as 'a lovely person'. Mr. Chubb, who had only one arm, worked for Mr. Hoole. He kept the hedge from the Cross to the Tower trimmed to a point and weeded below, using hand shears and a hoe.

Elcombe House was known as the Police House, as P.C. Pimm lived there with his three daughters, who went to school with Reg. In those days it had a studded entrance door. Little Elcombe [3 Elcombe Lane], was used by Mr. Sims to house a bull. The porch had a stable door and Reg remembered seeing a bull leaning his head over it. Its stable was the current sitting room, which Reg had to clean out and decorate when Mr. Sims sold it. In the Avons' time, Mr. Fishlock, an ex-naval man who worked for them, lived there.

Other details recalled included:

The Village Hall: after the old school was sold, a tin and wooden hut, 12 yards by 6 yards, was put up by the war memorial and used for recreation. The young men played darts in it.

The Post office was in the Gardener's Cottage in the 1920s and earlier. Mail came from Tisbury; the postman used a pushbike. Later it came from Broad Chalke.

Shopping and Deliveries:

Bakers ~ Wyatts (Ludwell) and Bailey (Broad Chalke)

Butcher ~ Fry (Broad Chalke) ~ as now

Milk ~ from farmers locally

Grocer ~ Co-op delivered once a week from Tisbury: a man with a huge basket cycled over the hill!

Local Shop ~ Ebbesbourne Wake: people usually went there on Saturday night because they were paid that day

Boots and Clothes ~ Broad Chalke

Drapers ~ Tisbury, probably the Charles Alfred Walsh & Son mentioned in Kelly's Directory), who sold clothes. One suit would be bought at Easter to last the year, and would be paid for in instalments.

Bus ~ Mr. Ernie Oborn from Ebbesbourne. His bus went to Salisbury on Tuesday and Saturday (market days). Its wheels had solid tyres. He would fetch things from e.g. the chemist.

Carrier ~ George Compton went to Salisbury with a pony and trap to collect things for people every Tuesday.

Roadmen ~ Jack Mullins for Alvediston and Walter Lush for Ebbesbourne.

Further information from *Kelly's Directory*, 1923: Tisbury
Rural District Council covered Alvediston; it met at the Poor Law
Institution, i.e. the workhouse, as did the Board of Guardians of the
Tisbury Union. The Magistrates; Court, Inland Revenue, 'Labour
Employment Exchange' and Registrar were also based in Tisbury.

George and Mary Kellow (arrived in Alvediston on 26th September, 1957)

GEORGE STARTED WORKING for the Sykes family at
Tytherington in 1944, but moved to Alvediston when
Mr.Frank Sykes bought Norrington. The isolation of Twenty
Acres was rather a shock to Mary after the village life to which she had
become accustomed at Tytherington. Each morning she would walk
the children up the muddy track to the bus stop in their wellington
boots, where they would all change into shoes ready for the school
transport and then she would meet them with their wellies on their
return. She was very much in two minds whether to stay, but she
remained there for almost fifty years. Mary died in 2007, and is buried
in the churchyard.

In 1957, almost everyone in the village worked on the farms,
and George was foreman at Norrington. There was a great deal to be
done as the farm had been neglected for some time. Miles of fencing
were needed and the yard at Trow was in such a state that there were
complaints from the local police about the mud strewn over the road
as farm vehicles went to and fro. The Parhams ran a dairy but this

was not continued under the Sykes family. They had a large poultry business with units at Tytherington and Norrington, hatching about half million chicks a week. (I remember, in the 1950s, the excitement of the arrival of boxes of day-old chicks, carefully transported to my father's farm on the Isle of Wight, where they were reared under lamps until they could run free-range in the fields.) George also remembers that Norrington manor was very dilapidated and held a few surprises such as calf bones stored in cupboards for Miss Parham's beloved greyhounds. Two grand pianos were sold for £2. at the house sale, and Mark Dinely took one up to Bigly, where it was blown up in the cause of art ~ a film.

For some time, George was a churchwarden. He helped on the churchyard-clearing team. At one time, he and his sons cut the grass by hand, using scythes and shears, and reversing a tractor and trailer up to the wall to cart it off. One of his most memorable duties was to heat the church. This involved walking over to light the boiler on a Saturday afternoon, returning at 10 p.m. to make it up with more coke, and then opening up the grates on a Sunday morning, a total of six trips along a muddy footpath and across fields. However, this method of heating was reasonably effective until the bitter winter of 1962-3, when the pipes froze and the whole system collapsed.

When they first arrived, church attendance was high and they remember the church being so full for Harvest Thanksgiving in 1957 that extra chairs had to be brought down from the Village Hall. (It is interesting that it was known as the 'Village Hall', the original intention of the villagers, in spite of the stipulation by Salisbury Diocese that the old school hall could only be sold if it was known as the 'Parish Room'.) Until 2003, the year of their diamond wedding anniversary, George and Mary continued to clean the church and arrange flowers with the help of their daughter-in-law, Pat Scrivens née Lodge, and could always be relied upon to do it especially thoroughly.

The Kellow family enjoyed activities in the Village Hall,

especially the Children's Evenings on Thursdays, run alternately by George and Tony Lodge. The Samways Rookery still featured in village life, with Miss Hoole's annual evening rook-shoot. There was a saying that 'If you don't shoot a rookery, it will die out', a prophecy which, in our experience, may take some time to be fulfilled.

✳ Alvediston ✳

11 November, 2008, 11 a.m.

TUESDAY, NOVEMBER 11, 2008 was a peerless autumn day in Alvediston, after Monday's violent winds and flash floods. As three last survivors of the First World War, Harry Patch, (108), William Stone, (110) and Henry Allingham, (112 years old) were wheeled to the Cenotaph to lay their wreaths, I was walking up Elcombe Lane to the Ox Drove, a track taken daily by members of the Compton family from their home at the 'Crown' to Bigly, where George kept a dairy herd. On 11th. November, 1918, his wife Jane gave birth to their eleventh and last child, a girl called Joan, who was celebrating her ninetieth birthday as I made my way uphill. Of their ten surviving children, the two eldest were away, Jack in the army and Annie in the Woman's Army Auxiliary Corps; only Joan remains, and she has contributed her memories to this book.

At 11 a.m. I paused half-way up the hill, at a point where one can see for miles east along the Ebble valley to Salisbury Cathedral spire, illumined from the south by a hazy sun but giving no indication of the city below, with more misty folds beyond. David Walsh, the local artist, immortalised this view in pastels, a small picture which hangs in our sitting-room. Apart from development at Cleeves Farm on the first hill, and a truck trundling past it, there was little sign of buildings or transport. In 1918, although the fields immediately below were being sold by the Wilton Estate they were still farmed by the Sims /Hull partnership. The Marks family, who now own the land, were relative newcomers and lived at Shortsmead. In the past nearly thirty years that I have known them, these fields have supported dairy cattle, arable crops, beef cattle and now sheep, with a couple of teepees in the summer.

The leaves, swirled by the stiff breeze, pattered to the ground like yellowing poppy petals. Those trees not yet denuded ~ field maple, beech, hazel ~ stood translucent in the soft sunlight among khaki trunks and branches, as conspicuous as officers in the trenches. Most of the ash leaves had fallen, some had bunches of keys hanging like rags on barbed wire. Skeletal elms reared up, bereft of twigs and hopeful buds. Unappetising remnants of blackberries mingled with purple leaves; in 1917 the schoolchildren foraged on Gallows Hill for blackberries as part of the war effort. Muddied crimson bryony beads straggled over old man's beard. All three veterans at the cenotaph were clean-shaven, not even a military moustache among them. Old man's beard or 'traveller's joy': those old men's travels brought them memories too painful to share, yet some soldiers experienced moments of exquisite joy even in the trenches, from a sunset, a flower, a letter, a kindness in the brutality. Today joy is often sought in travel; television advertisements make extravagant promises or suggest to viewers that they should choose the most luxurious travel company 'because you deserve it.' It would be obscene to suggest that the young lads of Alvediston who enlisted so exuberantly, expecting goodness knows what in exchange for the plodding reality of their rural lives 'deserved' what they endured on their travels. Jack Compton was twice wounded, and twice returned to the fracas at the Front. Polished red drops of rosehips startled from the hedgerows. Tucked away in the valet case which Captain Tommy Agar-Robartes, Liberal M.P. for South–East Cornwall and heir to the great estate of Lanhydrock took with him to the trenches was a tiny pot of the rouge which he applied to hide the pallor of his fear from the men whom he led into battle, some of whom he was rescuing when he was fatally wounded in 1915. Did the young Jack Parham, who lived to fight in another great war and to pursue an illustrious career in the army, resort to such a ruse? Spindleberries, with their crazy defiance of colour brought to mind the frenzied efforts of the twenties to put the pain aside, before the Depression and the next huge conflict proved that the last was not the 'war to end all wars'. The hill where a German aeroplane crashed in the 1940s was out of sight, but how many more landed in apparent rural idylls like this, in Britain and France, but also in Germany? If my father, a navigator in the R.A.F. had met such a fate, one obvious result would be that I would not be here to spend precious moments of peace, surveying one of the loveliest landscapes in the area.

Surprisingly for this time of year, the air was not rent with the sound of shooting. Perhaps the guns stayed silent out of respect, but the uncanny quiet was not unbroken. Somewhere in the distance a helicopter was whirring military reminders to the world below. No other traffic disturbed the peace, but buzzards, whose numbers have recovered in recent years, wheeled and squealed, occasionally a rook, quieter at this time of year, cawed, and a raven flew over from Samways, crying eerily. Every so often a pheasant tumbled out of hiding in raucous celebration of safety. The wind rustled leaves and tormented twigs, once giving rise to an ominous crack as a branch was bent for the last time. Later, as I passed the spot on my return from Bigly (where a tiny baby boy now lives), I was diverted by a flock of long-tailed tits chattering excitedly in the trees, as if gossiping good news. Yet, the Armistice merited no mention in the school log book. When did the news seep through to a village demoralised by the lack, not just of comforts, but of necessities: coal for the belching schoolroom stove, workmen to mend anything that had broken, farm-labourers to tend land and animals, carriers to deliver essential supplies . . . hope . . . not to mention the trials of leaking roofs, damp walls, blocked chimneys, influenza, brutal dentistry, snow, floods, rotten harvests, nits . . . cold . . . ? Those who made it home did not return to a rosy, chocolate-box retreat, but they did come home to a chance to rebuild their lives, loves and emotional equilibrium slowly, often silently and stoically, remembering those who did not have that chance.

Biddy Trahair

Appendix
Names on Photographs

Alvediston School Photograph, c. 1907 (see page 44)

Back Row (names from left): (4) Cecil Moxham
Second Row: (3) Gwen Sims, later Gillam; (8) Annie Compton
Third Row: (1) Violet Compton
Front Row: (3) Ivy Andrews; (9) Mabel Compton; (13) Percy Moxham

Alvediston Football Team, 1910 (see page 48)

Top Row (left to right): (2) Ernest Oborn (Ebbesbourne); (5) Bill Mullins; (6) Jack Compton
Front Row: (3) Bill Marks (Captain); (5) Bill Moxham

Alvediston School Photograph, c. 1920 (see page 144)

Back Row: Miss Cooper; Vera Compton; Queenie Roberts; Margaret (Peggy) Hull; Lucy Compton; Flora Roberts; Beryl Andrews, Dorothy Alford
Second Row: Pearl Marks; Ivy Collis; Frank Compton; Cyril and Clifford Marks; Joe Carter; Fred Hacket; Percy Dalton; Jack Moxham; Nellie King; Winny Carter
Third Row: Myrtle Marks; Alfred John (Jack) Hull; Gwen King; Joe Collis; Edmund Roberts; Eddie Dalton; Stewart Marks; Nellie and Reg Marks
Sitting: Dorothy; Edith Carter; Phyllis Watts; Florence Hacker

(Note: Jack Hull went on to Oxford and obtained a first-class honours degree in Mathematics.)

Wedding of Annie Compton and William Churcher, 3 April 1920 (see page 336)

(Photograph taken in school garden)

Back Row (left to right): Charlie Roberts; ? ; four uncles (mother's brothers); Uncle Harry Compton (father's eldest brother); Len Frampton (Vi's fiancé); Mr Mullins; ? ; Jack Compton
Middle Row: Mrs Mullins; twin cousins (Harry's daughters); Mrs Frank Isgar; Alfred Churcher (bridegroom's brother); Dolly Compton; Revd. Courteen; Mabel Compton; Vi Compton; Auntie Maud Isgar; Mrs Ernest Isgar; Jack Compton's fiancée ; Mrs Gillam (Mr Sims's daughter); Mrs Charlie Roberts
Front Row: Auntie Edie (Mrs Walters); Auntie Flo (mother's youngest sister, Mrs Mountie); between them is Will Mountie and on Mrs Mountie's lap is Eva; Frank Compton; Mum (Mrs Jane Compton) with Joan on her lap; Vera Compton; William Churcher (bridegroom); Annie Compton (bride); Lucy Compton; Dad (George Compton); Mrs Courteen; Ruth Walters; Douglas Compton; Leonard Walters

Appendix
The Family of the
Rev. William Aron Woods

RECENTLY, Paul Sinclair Woods, great-grandson of the Rev. W.A. Woods, made contact through the church visitors' book. He was able to shed some light on the lives of the 'Master Wilfrid Wentworth Woods and Master Percy Sinclair Woods' who made such a stir in 1884, when they began to attend Alvediston School, albeit probably only briefly. When they were eleven they went to school in Shoreham, Kent, which may account for their absence from the 1891 census. Wilfrid went to Oxford and served in the Navy, in submarines, throughout the First World War. He remained in the Navy and rose to become an admiral. He later moved to a large farm in Ringwood, Hants. Percy's career was not quite so illustrious. He was a school teacher in Newcastle for about a year before his marriage to Florence Emily, a marriage which was delayed until after his father's death in 1904, as Florence, a Roman Catholic, did not meet with parental approval. While in Newcastle he and Florence met a Japanese torpedo instructor, an experience which was presumably more useful to Wilfrid than his brother. Percy and Florence went abroad after marriage, and were in the Gold Coast of Africa until the end of the

First World War. When they finally returned to England, they bought the White Horse Hotel in Romsey, Hants, where their history is recorded in a book. He sold the hotel to Trust House Forte in 1920, but by 1929 he had lost all his money and ended up living in a tenement in London, a far cry from his brother's life.

Percy and Florence had three boys, the eldest, Denys, like his sister Joan, was probably born in Africa. Paul and Maurice were always very close, and both joined up in the Second World War: Paul in the Air Force and Maurice in the Army, the Tank Force. Paul was shot down and killed in Egypt while Maurice was on his way to meet him, a tragedy from which Maurice never fully recovered. His first wife was a wartime bride, and they had a daughter, Florence, but the marriage did not last. As well as the emotional scars from his bereavement, Maurice was disabled in the war, so did not have a happy or easy life. He eventually remarried and had a son, named Paul after his uncle, and who is twenty years younger than his step-sister. It is this Paul Sinclair Woods who has provided these detials. He was not surprised to hear that the Rev. William Aron Woods was not the easiest of vicars to get on with!

Glossary

Acres, Rods and Perches Measures of areas of land. One acre is a little over 0.4 ha. although customary acres varied in extent. There are 4 rods per acre, and 40 perches per rod.
Demesne Land occupied and farmed on behalf of the landowner, usually the manorial lord, not by his tenants. The demesne farm was therefore the 'home' farm.
Furlong One-eighth of a mile; also a block of arable strips in an open field.
Hide A hide varied between 40 and 160 acres (16-65 hectares), depending on the productivity of the land; the amount of land nominally required to support one extended household.
Knap or Knapp Crest of a hill or rising ground.
League A 'modern' league measures 3 miles, but the Normans used the league of about 1.4 miles.
Mark 13 shillings and 4 pence, (about 66p.); 3 marks = £2.
Messuage A dwelling with outbuildings; a 'capital messuage' was a manor house.
Prebend Part of the revenue of a cathedral or collegiate church granted to a canon or member of the chapter as his stipend; portion of land or tithe from which this stipend is drawn.
Prebendary One who holds a prebend; generally a canon of a cathedral chapter.
Tithe Tax of one tenth in money or kind, used to support the clergy and church.
Tithing Ten householders living near each other and acting as sureties for each other's behaviour.

Tithingman Official responsible for keeping peace locally, equivalent to a parish constable.

TRE *tempore Regis Edwardii*, in the time of King Edward the Confessor, 1042-1066. The abbreviation is used in Domesday Book to denote the value of an estate before the Norman conquest.

Yardland About 30 acres; also known as a virgate, and originally reckoned to be one quarter of a hide.

Bibliography

Wiltshire Family History Society, *Alvediston Baptisms and Burials*. WFHS.

Alvediston Parish Meeting, Minute Book

Bowles, Charles, *Modern Wiltshire: Hundred of Chalke*, 1830

Best, Nicholas, *The Kings and Queens of England*. Weidenfeld and Nicolson, 1995

Breeden, David (ed), *The Wedding of Sir Gawain and Dame Ragnell, Anon. c. 1450.* www.lone-star.net/mail/literature/gawain.htm: (acc-essed 3 August 2011)

Broad Chalke, a History of a South Wiltshire Village, its Land and People over 2000 Years, by the People of the Village. Broad Chalke Millennium Book, 1999

Buxton, Jean, and Wildsmith-Towle, Alan, *Footprints Through a Century, 1880s-1980s*, Plum Publishing, 2008

Chafin, William, *Anecdotes and History of Cranborne Chase*, introduction by Desmond Hawkins. Dovecote Press, 1991

Citizen, Salisbury District Council

Coward, Michael, and others, *The Donheads Past and Present*. Hobnob Press, 2007

Davies, Norman, *The Isles, a History*. Macmillan, 1999

Day, William, *The Horse, How to Breed and Rear Him*. Richard Bentley, 1888

DfEE, *Primary Accommodation Guidelines: Guidelines for Schools*, 2007

Draper, Jo, and Chaplin, Christopher, *Walking Dorset History*. Dovecote Press, 1997

Drury, Jill and Peter, *A Tisbury History*. Element Books, 1980

Elton, G R, *England Under the Tudors*; 3rd ed. Routledge, 1991

Elyard, S John, *Some Old Wiltshire Homes with short notices on their Architecture, History and Associations*. Charles and Clarke, 1894

Emeny, Richard, *A Description of Orchard Wyndham*. Wyndham Estates,1996, and later eds.

Eyre, John, *Pythouse and the Benetts*. Country Houses Assoc, 2002

Fergusson, Barbara, *The Ebble River*. Wake Press, 1997

Fisher, H.A.L. *A History of Europe*, vol. 2. Fontana Classics , 1977

Giffard, Hazel, *The Biography of a Country Church, Berwick St. John*. Winkelbury Publications, 1999

Green, Martin, *A Landscape Revealed 10,000 Years on a Chalkland Farm*. Tempus, 2000

Harte, Jeremy, *The Green Man*. Pitkin, [c.2001]

Haste, Cate (ed), *Clarissa Eden, a Memoir from Churchill to Eden*. Weidenfeld and Nicolson, 2007

Hawkins, Desmond, *Cranborne Chase*. Dovecote Press, 1998

Hawkins, Desmond (ed), *The Grove Diaries, the Rise and Fall of an English Family, 1809-1925*, Dovecote Press, 1995

Hutton, Edward, *Highways and Byways in Wiltshire*. Macmillan, 1917

Jackson, J E, 'Cranborne Chase', *Wiltshire Archaeological & Natural History Magazine*, 22, 1885, pp. 148-73

James, Robert Rhodes, *Anthony Eden*. Weidenfeld & Nicolson, 1986

Kelly's Directory of Wiltshire, various years, 1848-1939

Ketton-Cremer, R W, *Felbrigg, the Story of a House*. National Trust Classic, 1986

Meers, Peter, *Ebbesbourne Wake through the Ages*, 2nd ed. Dial Cottage Press, 2003 [and subsequent notes]

Miles, Archie, *Silva, British Trees*. Ebury Press, 1999

Morshead, Sir Owen, *Dorset Churches*. Dorset Historic Churches Trust, 1975

Nicolson, Adam, *Arcadia: the Dream of Perfection in Renaissance England*. Harper Perennial, 2009

Nightingale, J E, *The Church Plate of the County of Wilts*. 1891

Olivier, Edith, *Wiltshire*. Robert Hale, 1951 (County Books)

Papers of W.E.V. Young. MBE, (1890-1971), from the Goodfellow family

Parham, Jack, *Flying for fun: an affair with an aeroplane*. Belinda Parham, [c.1983]

Phillips, Roger, *Wild Flowers of Britain*. Ward Lock, 1977

Philipps House, formerly Dinton House, Wiltshire. National Trust, 1998

Phipps, Howard, *Ebble Valley*. Whittington Press, 2007

Sawyer, Rex, *Nadder:, tales of a Wiltshire Valley*. Hobnob Press, 2006

Slocombe, P M, *Wiltshire Buildings Record*, 1986

Snyder, Christopher, *Exploring the World of King Arthur*. Thames & Hudson, 2000

Southern, R W, *The Making of the Middle Ages*. Pimlico, 1993

Strong, Roy, *A Little History of the English Country Church*. Vintage, 2008

Stokes, Ethel (ed), *Abstracts of Wiltshire Inquisitiones Post Mortem, Edward III 1327-77*. British Record Society, 1914

Thompson, Flora, *Lark Rise to Candleford*. Penguin, 2008

Thompson, Paul, *The Edwardians, the Remaking of British Society*; 2nd ed. Routledge, 1992

Thorn, Caroline and Frank (ed), *Domesday Book: Wiltshire*. Phillimore, 1979

Thorpe, D R, *Eden, The Life and Times of Anthony Eden, First Earl of Avon, 1897-1977*. Pimlico, 2004

Trevelyan, G M, *English Social History*. Pelican, 1967

Twinch, Carol, *Tithe War 1918-1939, The Countryside in Revolt*. Media Associates, 2001

Wigan, Dare, 'Triumph for a Small Stud', *Country Life Annual*, 1963

Wilcockson, Helen, 'College to Council House', *Sarum Chronicle*, 7, 2007, 19-30

Wilton House Guide Book. various eds.

Wood, Margaret, *The English Medieval House*. Bracken Books 1983

W(iltshire &) S(windon) A(rchives) 1052/20: Alvediston Church Book, 1799-1943

WSA 1052/55: Inventory of Alvediston church Goods

WSA 1052/58: PCC Minutes, 1934-70

WSA 1699/106: Report of Wiltshire Monthly Meeting, Quakers, Trust Property Group,

WSA F8/500/5/1/1-2: Alvediston C.E. School, Oct.1874-1895, 1895-1922

Wyndham, H A, *A Family History 1688-1837: the Wyndhams of Somerset, Sussex & Wiltshire*. Oxford UP, 1950

Wyndham, K, and Haslam, R, 'Orchard Wyndham, Somerset, parts I and II', *Country Life*, 21 and 28 March 1985

Thanks

Many, many people have contributed to this book, among them those listed below. If I have forgotten anyone during the past eleven years, please remind me.

I am hugely indebted to Dr. John Chandler for his help and for publishing this book.

Carla Allen
Henry Ashwell
Elizabeth Anstee
Keith Attenborough
Clarissa, Countess of Avon
Rosalyn Barnes
Nicholas du Quesne Bird
Amanda Bristow
Ellen Budden
John Buckland
Sylvana Chandler
Jim Collins
Fritz Curzon
Peter Daniels
Francis and Libby Dineley
Perin and Sonya Dineley

Ben Elliott
Russell Emm
The late Charles and Mrs. Evans
Diana Farrow
Alastair and the late Judith Fergusson
Robin and Astrid Garran
The late Dennis Gates
Keith Gawen
Pay and Jo Grant
James Grasby
Nick Griffiths
Jean Heaney
Rodney Heath
George and the late Mary Kellow
Tony and Christopher Lodge
Mike and Elaine Longstaffe

* Thanks *

The late Reg Marks
The late Roy Marks and Bella Marks
Trevor Marks
The late Peter Meers
Puffin Moore
William and Claire Morris
Kathleen Mould
Jill Painter
Chris Ralph
Mildred Reed
The late Joan Reeves
The late Christine Richardson
Frank Roberts
Olive Rogerson

Robbin Rouse
Rex Sawyer
Pat Scrivens
Dennis Sewell and Gail Harrison
Robert Stallard
The late Tristram Sykes and Sheila Sykes
Jonathan and Liliana Sykes
Alexander and Rachel Sykes
Richard Trahair
Valerie Trew
Andrew Wardall
Alan Wildsmith-Towle
Phil Wilson
Paul Sinclair Woods

Also the staff at Salisbury and Gillingham libraries, the former Wiltshire Record Office, Trowbridge and the Wiltshire & Swindon History Centre, Chippenham.

Index

Vincent, Herbie, 47, 50
Vitalis, 13

Wallingford, Prior of, 195
Walsh, David, 351
Want, Betty, 296
Want, ('Chase Case'), 277-8, 296
War Memorial, 43, 45ff
Wardall, Andrew & Rachel, 153, 188
Wardner, Thomas, 244
Wardour Castle, 110
Wareham/Warom family, 233
Waterloo, battle of, 190, 288
Watts family, 340
Watts, A., 43
Watts, Laura (Granny 'Kitchen'), 49, 322
Watts, Phyllis, 49
Watts, Vic, 47, 49, 315, 322
Weedon family, 340
West & de la Warre families, 72, 266
West End, 15, 20, 28
Whaten, J., 91
White Sheet Hill, 17ff
White/Whit family, 77, 233, 332
White, ('Chase Case'), 277-8
White, Henry, 40
White, Richard, 264
White House, 42, 45, 339, 345
William I, the Conqueror, 11f, 154, 195
William of Orange & Mary, 66
Williams, Rev. John, 184
Williams, Rev. Rowland, 61
Wilmott family, 325-9
Wilmott, Ellen, see Budden
Wilton Abbey, 11, 62-4, 67, 151, 154, 195, 261, 264, 275
Wilton Estate, 37, 42, 117, 154, 156, 167, 173, 270, 286, 351
Wilton hare warren, 22
Wiltshire Clubmen, 270
Wiltshire County Council, 121, 123, 137
Windmill Hill, 34
Windmills, 33, 203
Win Green, 30
Winklebury Hill, Berwick St. John, 26

Wisdom Stud, Yorkshire, 313
Withies, The, 27
Women's Social & political Union, 119
Women's Union, 119
Wood, Margaret, 257-9
Woods family, 105f, 110, 356-7
Woods, Mrs., 103, 105, 108f
Woods, Paul Sinclair, 356-7
Woods, Wilfrid Wentworth & Percy Sinclair, 102, 356-7
Woods, Rev. William Aron, 76, 96, 100-10, 305, 356-7
Woods, W. K., 96, 105, 107, 109
Workhouse, Tisbury; 39, 76, 313, 347
Wort, J.M., 152, 175, 338
Wright, John, 35
Wyatt, James, 74-5, 248
Wyatt/Wyatville, Sir Jeffry, 248
Wyatt, Thomas Henry, 54, 74, 248
Wyndham family, 50, 193, 223-43, 248, 254-5, 263, 272
Wyndham, Anne, 155f, 241-2
Wyndham, Lady Barbara, 230-2, 234
Wyndham, Sir Edmund, 225
Wyndham, Florence, (Wadham), 227-8
Wyndham, George, 255
Wyndham, Hon. H.A., 238
Wyndham, Henrietta, 239
Wyndham, John I of Felbrigg, 223-7, 240-41
Wyndham, Sir John of Felbrigg, 224
Wyndham, John & Elizabeth, (Sydenham) of Orchard Wyndham, 225
Wyndham, Sir John & Joan, (Portman) of Orchard Wyndham, 226
Wyndham, John I & Alicia/Alice, (Fownes) of Norrington, 58, 219, 235-6
Wyndham, John II & Anne, (Barber) of Norrington, 236, 239
Wyndham, monuments, 54, 58f, 186, 231, 236-7
Wyndham, Thomas, Lord Finglass, 58-9, 226, 236-8, 241
Wyndham, Wadham, M.P., 225
Wyndham, Sir Wadham, 27, 197, 200-1,